The Effects of Political Institutions on Varieties of Capitalism

Matthew P. Arsenault

The Effects of Political Institutions on Varieties of Capitalism

palgrave
macmillan

Matthew P. Arsenault
Mount Aloysius College
Cresson, Pennsylvania, USA

ISBN 978-3-319-50891-7 ISBN 978-3-319-50892-4 (eBook)
DOI 10.1007/978-3-319-50892-4

Library of Congress Control Number: 2017931361

Cover image INTERFOTO / Alamy

Printed on acid-free paper

This Palgrave Macmillan imprint is published by Springer Nature
The registered company is Springer International Publishing AG
The registered company address is: Gewerbestrasse 11, 6330 Cham, Switzerland

To Jessica and Tom.

Contents

List of Figures

List of Tables

CHAPTER 1

Political Institutions and Varieties of Capitalism

A strong correlation exists between political regime and the liberal market economy (LME) and coordinated market economy (CME) dichotomy posed by the varieties of capitalism (VOC) framework (Gourevitch, 2003). However, debate continues regarding the connection between political institutions and VOC. The purpose of this book is to open the proverbial "black box" and identify the causal mechanisms linking political institutions and variation in capitalist systems.

Capitalism

Adam Smith's *The Wealth of Nations* is perhaps the most widely cited study of capitalism to be published in the past 240 years (1991 [1776]). Smith's conception of capitalism is characterized by privately held property and the unrestricted accumulation of additional wealth. Human beings, driven by self-interest, are motivated to maximize personal profit through the productive use of accumulated property (Sargent, 1999, p. 80). The inborn desire to pursue and maximize individual interest is the driving force of the capitalist system.

For Smith, competition is structured within a system of free markets in which buyers and sellers enter commercial transactions free from coercion and government interference. The system of competition regulates the types and quantities of goods produced and the prices at which they are sold. The quantities of goods and services are then efficiently produced

M.P. Arsenault, *The Effects of Political Institutions on Varieties of Capitalism*, DOI 10.1007/978-3-319-50892-4_1

with accompanying competitive prices established by the laws of supply and demand. As such, the market serves as a self-regulating mechanism whereby individual profit motive is transformed into socially and economically efficient outcomes (Heilbroner, 1986, p. 57). In brief, the logic of Smithian laissez-faire capitalism posits that under a system characterized by freedom of exchange and unrestrained competition, economic efficiency and optimal resource allocation occur, and subsequently, the "wealth of nations" grows.

Although influencing political and economic thought for the past 240 years, the question becomes, how relevant are Smith's ideas of capitalism to the study of political economy today? A major advancement in the field of comparative political economy is the general consensus that there is no one form of capitalist economy (Howell, 2003). Rather, capitalist systems vary. The "cowboy capitalism" of the United States remains distinctly different from the social democratic and christican democratic systems of continental Europe (Gersemann, 2005).

Diversity in Capitalist Systems

Smith's conception of individual rationality, the "invisible hand," and his confidence in the autonomy of market forces serve as one ideal type along a continuum of modern capitalist systems (Crouch, 2005). At one pole lie the LMEs of Anglo-Saxon countries.[1] Such systems are based largely on the neoliberal principles of minimal state involvement in business and social policies, deregulated labor markets, weak unions, strong competition between political and economic actors, and "free market solutions to economic problems" (Campbell & Pedersen, 2001, p. 5).

At the other pole lie the social democratic and corporatist arrangements of continental Europe. Such CMEs are characterized by compromise and coordination between business, labor, and government; higher levels of social welfare expenditures; and a greater degree of government involvement in nonmarket coordination mechanisms (Hall & Soskice, 2001; Katzenstein, 1985; Streeck & Yamamura, 2001).

Explanations of Capitalist Diversity

Although there is a general consensus regarding the existence of capitalist variation, a pressing issue for comparative political economists "has been how to explain the absence of convergence upon a common form of industrial policy, and the continued distinctiveness of national capitalisms" (Howell, 2007, p. 241).

In the mid-1960s, Shonfield's *Modern Capitalism* served as one of the earliest systematic comparative studies of capitalist political economies. Specifically, Shonfield differentiates between the *etatist* French economy, the laissez-faire British model, and the corporatist German system (1965). For Shonfield, a major factor leading to the various types of capitalism was the degree of state intervention in the economy (Howell, 2007; Schmidt, 2009; Shonfield, 1965).

In the 1970s, advanced political economies were essentially divided between neocorporatist and neoliberal systems. The neocorporatist conceptions of capitalism tended to focus on the strength of labor, and the role of unions in shaping economic and social policy (Schmidt, 2007). In systems where labor and business interests were organized into "singular, noncompetitive, hierarchically ordered representative 'corporations'" a system of consensus and cooperation would emerge between the competing interests and would prove conducive to a more coordinated capitalist economy (Schmitter, 1979). On the other hand, the Anglo-Saxon states, characterized by weak labor organizations, a multitude of interest group organizations, and a "hands-off" state, created an environment of "competitive interaction" between various actors and a more liberal market economy emerged.

In the 1980s, neocorporatist ideas began to decline, and were replaced by a neoliberal ideology which seemed to permeate the international economy. The rise of neoliberalism was in part due to changes in the global economy—increased globalization, increased international trade, the internationalization of capital, and greater global competition—which led to strong moves toward market liberalization (Coffey & Thornley, 2009; Hooghe & Marks, 1999; Simmons, 1999).

Many of the traditional neocorporatist states, like the Netherlands and Sweden, seemed to be experiencing a breakdown in neocorporatist cooperative arrangements (Schmidt, 2007). It was argued that these changes to the global economy would ultimately lead advanced industrial societies to converge toward a neoliberal model in order to remain competitive in the new economic reality. Others argued that differences in state structures would create variation in responses to global neoliberalism (Katzenstein, 1985; Swank, 2001, 2002). Ultimately, convergence around neoliberal ideals did not occur, and even with advancement in regional integration, a significant degree of capitalist variation remained (Thelen, 2001; Wood, 2001).

The early 2000s ushered in the ascendance of the firm in studies of comparative political economy (Schmidt, 2007, p. 2). The VOC framework is perhaps the most notable firm-centered approach. The VOC framework contends that capitalist production regimes can be classified into two forms: coordinated market economies (CMEs) and liberal market economies (LMEs). According to the VOC approach, variation in production regimes stems from institutional structures which either promote or impede cooperation and competition between industry-specific firms (Soskice, 1999, p. 109). The VOC approach tends to view the state and state institutions as playing a minimal role. Schmidt writes that VOC theorists assume "that the state has little role to play beyond that of creating a positive regulatory environment in a global economy dominated by firms" (2009, p. 519).

Although an increasingly popular explanation of variation in capitalist economies, the VOC framework is not without its limitations. The following sections examine in greater depth the benefits of the VOC approach, and draw special attention to some of its limitations.

Benefits and Limitations of the VOC Framework

The VOC literature has brought a number of advancements to the study of comparative political economy (Deeg & Jackson, 2007; Howell, 2003). First, the VOC framework has brought greater attention to the behavior of firms and how the strategic behavior of firms affects the variation of capitalist systems. Instead of focusing on the ways that institutions allocate power and govern behavior, the VOC framework focuses on the ways that institutions, "facilitate the flow or deliberation of information among actors, permit 'decentralized cooperation,' and solve familiar collective action problems" (Howell, 2003, pp. 105–106). That is, firms must interact with many different actors—banks, other firms, customers, labor, stakeholders, shareholders, and others—in order to optimize productivity. Such interactions largely occur within five arenas: industrial relations, vocational training and education, corporate governance, inter-firm relations, and employee–labor relations (Hall & Soskice, 2001). Actors operating within these arenas often face various coordination problems. Firms then develop institutions to limit uncertainty and address coordination problems in order to ensure greater efficiency. "The relationships firms develop to resolve these problems condition their own competencies and the characteristics of an economy's production regimes" (Hall & Soskice, 2001, p. 7).

Secondly, the VOC framework has illustrated the ways that institutional complementarities and, subsequently, comparative institutional advantage lead to variation in capitalist economies. The idea of institutional complementarities implies that an increase in the efficiency of one institution will lead to an increase of efficiency in other, complimentary institutions (Hall & Soskice, 2001, p. 17). Institutional complementarities then form comparative institutional advantages for some firms and sectors, while disincentivizing others.

In short, the concept of institutional complementarity, and subsequently comparative institutional advantage, illustrates that

> Economic 'models' should not be considered just as a collection of more or less random institutional forms, but also a set of complimentary relations between these institutions, which form the basis of coherence between the specific institutional forms of each model. (Amable, 2003, p. 6)

By identifying the "institutional forms of each model," states can then be "clustered" into specific capitalism types (Howell, 2003).

For all its intellectual contributions, the VOC approach faces a number of criticisms. In Hancké's review of the VOC literature, critiques are grouped around three broad themes: those who question capitalist variation itself, those who recognize variation between capitalist systems but are critical of the "constituent elements" of the approach, and lastly, those who recognize capitalist diversity, but call for "conceptually richer, approaches to capitalist diversity" (Hancké, 2009, p. 6).

The first cluster of critiques rejects the basic premise of capitalist divergence. Such scholars contend that capitalism continues along a historical path of convergence toward liberal market institutions. Scholars often cite changes in the international economy—specifically globalization, increased competition from newly industrialized countries, and European integration—that led to a retrenchment of "institutions that had previously made workers less dependent on markets" and subsequently strengthened the bargaining position of capital holders (Hancké, 2009, p. 6; Pierson, 2001; Simmons, 1999).

The second cluster recognizes capitalist diversity, but questions the duality of liberal market and coordinated market economies posed by the

VOC framework. Scholars here view the dichotomy of CMEs and LMEs as overly simplified. For example, Shonfield (1965) identifies three types of capitalism, Amable (2003) identifies five institutionally similar capitalism models, while Crouch (2005) contends that nearly any number of capitalist models are theoretically possible.

The third cluster recognizes variation in capitalist economies but remains skeptical of the underpinnings of causal logic. Whereas the VOC approach focuses largely on the strategic behavior of the firm, scholars operating within this camp "look for the sources of diversity elsewhere—in politics, history, or culture rather than in the micro-structure of markets" (Hancké, 2009, p. 8). Wood falls squarely in this camp in arguing that "Governments may face strong pressure to deliver policies that are congruent with production regimes and company strategies, but they are also prone to a variety of other pressures—ideological, political, and electoral—that compete for attention" (2001, p. 248).

This book falls within the third group of critics. Although recognizing the dichotomy of liberal market and coordinated market economies, I question the lack of emphasis on institutional genesis and, most importantly, the failure to fully explore the function of politics and political institutions on variation in capitalist systems. Such weaknesses are only recently being addressed in the comparative political economy literature. As such this book builds on an emerging and rapidly developing research program (Amable, 2003; Amable & Palombarini, 2009; Deeg & Jackson, 2007; Schmidt, 2009; Wood, 2001).

The absence of an emphasis on political variables is largely the result of the VOC framework's overemphasis on the strategic behavior and coordination problems of firms. The strategic behavior of firms does not occur in a political or social vacuum. Rather, I contend that the behaviors of political and economic actors are shaped and constrained by the political institutional environment within which they occur. As Wood points out, "Economic activity is not only situated within distinctive constitutional and political contexts, but depends upon the legislative and regulatory activities of governments for its viability" (2001, p. 247).

As such, greater emphasis on the role of politics and political institutions is imperative to explaining variation between capitalist systems. As North illustrates, the state and those controlling the state apparatus play a central role in structuring the "rules of the game" in a political economy (1981, 1990). North contends that institutions specify "the fundamental rules of competition and cooperation which will provide a structure of property rights" and subsequently the structure of the economic system (1981, p. 24).

This book expands on the current VOC literature by lending greater emphasis to competing interests and the formal political institutions that shape and structure cooperation and competition between interests.

A New Theoretical Approach

In proposing a theory explaining capitalist variation, I begin with the assumption that the political economy of advanced industrial societies is largely divided between two competing groups: capital holders and labor. The assumption proves useful in that the proposed labor-capital cleavage is a characteristic of all developed economies (Lijphart, 1984; Manow, 2009).

I argue that power asymmetries between these rival groups lead to institutional configurations designed to overcome collective action problems and maximize the utility of the dominant group (Knight, 1992; Olson, 1965). In part, power asymmetries take the form of competing configurations of political institutions. As such, this book follows on the recent investigations of Cusack, Iverson, and Soskice (2007) and Martin and Swank (2008) who explore the formation of political institutions as the result of competing interests between capital and labor.

Political institutions in turn shape the bargaining power of rival groups. The political institutions under investigation fall under the majoritarian/consensus dichotomy as proposed by Lijphart (1994). Specifically, I examine electoral and party systems, the number and type of constitutional constraints, coalition structures, and partisan control of government and policy legacies.

Majoritarian political regimes create an environment of intense competition between political and economic actors and subsequent policy instability throughout the political economy. This in turn makes credible commitment to nonmarket coordination mechanisms difficult. This, coupled by the propensity of majoritarian systems to be governed by the center-right (Iversen & Soskice, 2006), lead majoritarian systems to support the LME model.

Consensus systems, on the other hand, create a political environment conducive to cooperation between political and economic actors. Due to the high numbers of political and economic actors with access to the political and policy process—and the resulting institutional checks on the autonomous interest group action—an environment of cooperation and credible commitment to nonmarket coordination mechanisms emerge. This, coupled by the greater power of the center-left in consensus systems, can lead to a more coordinated market economy.

Broadly, this study seeks to explain the relationship between political institutions and economic structures of CMEs and LMEs. Within the CME/LME systems, the economic institutions to be explained (the dependent variables) include corporate governance, industrial relations, inter-firm relations, education and training systems, and employee structures. These economic institutions compose the core structures of production regime as illustrated by the VOC framework (Hall & Soskice, 2001). The emergent complementarity configuration between political regimes and economic institutions supports a specific variety of capitalism, either a CME or an LME.

The logic of the proposed causal model draws heavily on comparative political economy studies exploring the relationship between VOC and the welfare state (Estevez-Abe, Iversen, & Soskice, 2001; Huber & Stephens, 2001; Iversen & Stevens, 2008; Mares, 2001, 2003; Soskice, 2007). Whereas much of the scholarship on the welfare state uses government expenditures, social security transfers, government employment, or pension spending as dependent variables in order to capture variation in welfare states, a similar model can be applied where industrial relations, inter-firm relations, skill system, and corporate governance serve as ***dependent variables*** which will capture variation in production regime.

Conclusion

In conclusion, the role of political institutional configurations in shaping variation in the political economies of advanced industrial societies should not be understated. The correlations between political regime and VOC are strong. However, correlation does not explain causation. Still, the strength of the relationship allows us to disregard the argument that political institutions and capitalist variation are in fact independent of one another (Gourevitch, 2003; Roe, 2003).

Although a relationship between political and economic institutions exists, theories regarding causal mechanisms—processes that link causal relationships between independent and dependent variables—remain abstract at best and contradictory at worst. The purpose of this book is to open the proverbial "black box" and identify the causal mechanisms linking political institutions and capitalist variation.

This book adds to the comparative political economy literature in that it will lend greater insight into the role of politics on variation in the capitalist economies of advanced industrial societies. As such this book contributes to a substantial and current academic debate (Amable, 2003; Amable & Palombarini, 2009; Berman, 2006; Schmidt, 2007, 2009).

Chapter 2 will consist of a comprehensive review of the literature relevant to the VOC debate. First, I chronologically review and critically analyze the academic lineage of the VOC framework. I begin with a discussion of neocorporatist theories of capitalism and the limitations of the neocorporatist approach. I then discuss the rise of neoliberalism in the 1980s, and the subsequent convergence and divergence theories of the 1990s. The review ends with the rise of the VOC framework and the ways by which an emphasis on the firm has shaped recent conceptions of capitalism variation.

Next, I identify common critiques of the VOC paradigm. I discuss the paradigm's failure to adequately explain the causes of capitalist divergence, and the framework's overly functionalist nature. Next, I address questions of an oversimplified dichotomous typology. Specifically, I defend the coordinated and liberal market dichotomy in the face of pressures to develop an increasingly complex, and differentiated system of categorization of capitalist types. Lastly, I focus on the VOC's lack of emphasis on the role of politics and role of political institutions as possible causal variables on capitalist variants.

Third, I review and critically analyze the emerging research program attempting to create a more systematic understanding of the role politics and political institutions play on capitalist divergence. I begin by focusing on the identified correlation between capitalist systems and political regime, and examine the causal logic proposed to explain such correlation. Next, I explore the relationships between the component institutions of majoritarian and consensus political regimes and the ways such component parts affect the structure of capitalist economies. I ground my proposed relationships between political institutions—particularly those associated with the majoritarian and consensus dichotomy—and the economic arenas proposed by the VOC framework within the broader comparative political institutions literature.

Chapter 3 will discuss the methodology to be employed in this book, as well as explain and defend the mixed-method approach. I cover major research questions, relevant variables, hypotheses, and predicted outcomes. I draw attention to other studies applying similar techniques, specifically those using panel-corrected standard errors (PCSE) analysis supplemented by process-tracing case studies. Lastly, I discuss the delimitations of the book and defend the time frame and case selection.

Chapter 4 will provide quantitative analyses exploring the relationship between political institutions and capitalist variation for 18 OECD countries, spanning the years 1960–2006. Data will be drawn from two sources: the Comparative Welfare State (CWS) Dataset (Huber, Ragin, Stephens, Brady, & Beckfield, 2004) and the Comparative Political Data Set I 1960–2006 (CPDSI) (Armingeon, Gerber, Leimgruber, & Beyeler, 2008). Analyses will apply both cross-sectional and time-series techniques.

The analyses begin with a series of ordinary least squares (OLS), cross-sectional investigations of the relationship between political regimes and VOC. This section of the study will establish the strength and direction of the relationship between political regime and capitalist type. Additionally, this section will identify what political institutions are related to variation in capitalist systems, "distinguish between the systematic component from the nonsystematic component of the phenomena we study," and assist in identifying the crucial variables to be explored further in the study (G. King, Keohane, & Verba, 1994, p. 86).

I then apply a time-series cross-sectional (TSCS) OLS regression with PCSE. This technique is selected to correct for issues of serial and spatial correlation and heteroskedasticity which characterize panel data (N. Beck & Katz, 1995). A similar strategy is common in studies of comparative political economy as illustrated by Manow (2009), and Huber and Stephens (2000, 2001), in their work on partisan governance and the welfare state.

This section will establish which political institutions serve as the strongest indicator of capitalist variation, assist in estimating causal effects, and lend further support to the proposed causal theory. Lastly, the analysis will explain the relationships between specific political institutions and the economic institutions—corporate governance, internal firm structure, industrial relations and training systems, and inter-firm relations—which compose the coordinated market and liberal market dichotomy. By examining the effects of various configurations of political institutions on the disaggregated arenas of LMEs and CMEs, it is hoped that multiple causal processes, if evident, will be revealed.

The quantitative analyses will be supplemented by three case studies (Chaps. 5 and 6). The case studies seek to build upon, and are in part guided by, the quantitative findings of Chap. 4. Inherently, statistical models possess degrees of uncertainty, have difficulty in identifying "equifinality," and lack an emphasis on "sequential interactions between individual agents" (George & Bennett, 2005, pp. 12–13). As such, the case studies are designed to add validity and reliability to the quantitative assumptions by examining the proposed mechanisms linking proposed cause and effect.

Through process-tracing methods, the case studies will largely serve as a "test" of the quantitative results and either confirm or call into question the proposed hypotheses (Lijphart, 1971). As such, the qualitative chapters seek to answer three broad questions. First, do the proposed causal relationships between political and economic institutions identified in the quantitative analysis exist in real-world cases? Second, how do the political institutions affect economic structures? Third, what alternative or intervening variables become apparent through the qualitative research?

Using "purposive modes of sampling" as suggested by Seawright and Gerring (2008), I examine the cases of Britain and Germany in greater detail. A general consensus exists, and purposive sampling confirms, that Britain represents an ideal LME, while Germany represents CMEs (Ahlquist, 2010; Hall & Soskice, 2001; Howell, 2007; Schmidt, 2009; Wood, 2001).

Chapter 5 will focus on the behavior of relevant political and economic actors in the United Kingdom and Germany during the 1980s in the face of major global pressures to adopt more neoliberal economic policies (Katzenstein, 1985; Kitschelt, Lange, Marks, & Stephens, 1999; Schmidt, 2007, 2009). Although both countries faced similar and significant pressures, the outcomes differed. Britain made drastic moves toward greater market deregulation, a severe weakening of labor, and other neoliberal reforms (Hall, 1986). While facing similar pressures, Germany ultimately made much less far-reaching adjustments (Schmidt, 2007).

As such, the question posed and addressed by the quantitative chapters is why a convergence toward neoliberal policies failed to occur. As my causal process suggests, I contend the variation in political institutions between Britain and Germany served as a constraint on the relevant political and economic actors, and subsequently constrained or furthered reform.

In addition to the British and German cases, Chap. 6 will examine the effects of institutional change on the economic structures of New Zealand. New Zealand, having undertaken a rare change from a first-past-the-post (FPP) electoral system to a mixed-member proportional (MMP) system, will prove a useful "natural experiment" to test the hypotheses suggesting that political institutions shape the political economy of advanced industrial democracies.

In the 1980s, under FPP, New Zealand underwent the most drastic neoliberal reforms of any OECD country with the exception of England (Castles, Gerritsen, & Vowles, 1996a). I contend that the reason that the New Zealand government was able to pass such sweeping reforms was due to the majoritarian nature of the New Zealand political system (Castles, Gerritsen, & Vowles, 1996b; Huber & Stephens, 2001; Palmer & Palmer, 1997). In 1996, New Zealand held its first election under MMP rules. Implementation of MMP saw an increase in the number of political parties represented in legislature, more consensually focused coalition structures, and increased numbers of constitutional veto points. My causal argument and the hypotheses to be tested suggest that the institutional changes which occurred in New Zealand should be accompanied by movement away from, or the retrenchment of, the neoliberal policies adopted in the 1980s.

Chapter 7 will synthesize the findings of the quantitative and qualitative analyses. Here, I reiterate the insights gleaned from the quantitative analyses, and illustrate the ways by which the case studies either support or call into question the proposed causal relationships. Furthermore, I discuss the degree of certainty with which the findings can be accepted, the generalizability of the results to advanced industrial societies, and lastly suggest avenues for further research.

Note

1. The Anglo-Saxon differentiation is drawn from Crouch (2005, p. 45) and includes the United Kingdom, Ireland, the United States, Canada, Australia, and New Zealand.

References

Ahlquist, J. (2010). Building strategic capacity: The political underpinnings of coordinated wage bargaining. *American Political Science Review, 104*(1), 171–188.

Amable, B. (2003). *The diversity of modern capitalism*. Oxford and New York: Oxford University Press.

Amable, B., & Palombarini, S. (2009). A neorealist approach to institutional change and the diversity of capitalism. *Socioeconomic Review, 7*(1), 123–143.

Armingeon, K., Gerber, M., Leimgruber, P., & Beyeler, M. (2008). *Comparative political data set 1960–2006*. Institute of Political Science, University of Berne. Retrieved from http://www.ipw.unibe.ch/content/team/klaus_armingeon/comparative_political_data_sets/index_ger.html

Beck, N., & Katz, J. (1995). What to do (and not to do) with time-series cross-section data. *American Political Science Review, 89*, 634–647.

Berman, S. (2006). *The primacy of politics: Social democracy and the making of Europe's twentieth century*. New York: Cambridge University Press.

Campbell, J. L., & Pedersen, O. K. (Eds.). (2001). *The rise of neoliberalism and institutional analysis*. Princeton: Princeton University Press.

Castles, F., Gerritsen, R., & Vowles, J. (1996a). Conclusion: The great experiment in perspective. In F. Castles, R. Gerritsen, & J. Vowles (Eds.), *The great experiment: Labour parties and public policy transformation in Australia and New Zealand*. St. Leonards, Australia: Allen and Unwin.

Castles, F., Gerritsen, R., & Vowles, J. (Eds.). (1996b). *The great experiment: Labour parties and public policy transformations in Australia and New Zealand*. St. Leonards, Australia: Allen and Unwin.

Coffey, D., & Thornley, C. (2009). *Globalization and varieties of capitalism: New labour, economic policy and the abject state*. Hampshire: Palgrave Macmillan.

Crouch, C. (2005). *Capitalist diversity and change: Recombinant governance and institutional entrepreneurs*. New York: Oxford University Press.

Cusack, T. R., Iverson, T., & Soskice, D. (2007). Economic interests and the origin of electoral systems. *American Political Science Review, 101*(3), 373–391.

Deeg, R., & Jackson, G. (2007). Towards a more dynamic theory of capitalist variety. *Socioeconomic Review, 5*(1), 149–179.

Estevez-Abe, M., Iversen, T., & Soskice, D. (2001). Social protection and the formation of skills: A reinterpretation of the welfare state. In P. A. Hall & D. Soskice (Eds.), *Varieties of capitalism: The institutional foundations of comparative advantage*. Oxford: University of Oxford Press.

George, A., & Bennett, A. (2005). *Case studies and theory development in the social sciences*. Cambridge, MA: The MIT Press.

Gersemann, O. (2005). *Cowboy capitalism: European myths, American reality*. Washington, DC: Cato Institute.

Gourevitch, P. A. (2003). Review: The politics of corporate governance regulation. *The Yale Law Journal, 112*(7), 1829–1880.

Hall, P. A. (1986). *Governing the economy: The politics of state intervention in Britain and France*. New York: Oxford University Press.

Hall, P. A., & Soskice, D. W. (2001). *Varieties of capitalism: The institutional foundations of comparative advantage.* Oxford, England and New York: Oxford University Press.

Hancké, B. (2009). Introducing the debate. In B. Hancké (Ed.), *Debating varieties of capitalism.* Oxford: Oxford University Press.

Heilbroner, R. L. (1986). *The worldly philosophers: The lives, times and ideas of the great economic thinkers* (6th ed.). New York: Simon & Schuster, Inc.

Hooghe, L., & Marks, G. (1999). The making of a polity: The struggle over European integration. In H. Kitschelt, P. Lange, G. Marks, & J. Stephens (Eds.), *Continuity and change in contemporary capitalism.* New York: Cambridge University Press.

Howell, C. (2003). Varieties of capitalism: And then there was one? *Comparative Politics, 36*(1), 103–124.

Howell, C. (2007). The British variety of capitalism: Institutional change, industrial relations and British politics. *British Politics, 2,* 239–263.

Huber, E., Ragin, C., Stephens, J., Brady, D., & Beckfield, J. (2004). *Comparative Welfare Data Set.* http://www.nsd.uib.no/macrodataguide/set.html?id=8&sub=1

Huber, E., & Stephens, J. (2000). Partisan governance, women's employment, and the Social democratic service state. *American Sociological Review, 65,* 323–342.

Huber, E., & Stephens, J. (2001). *Development and crisis of the welfare state: Parties and policies in global markets.* Chicago: University of Chicago Press.

Iversen, T., & Soskice, D. (2006). Electoral institutions and the politics of coalitions: Why some democracies redistribute more than others. *American Political Science Review, 100*(2), 165–181.

Iversen, T., & Stevens, J. (2008). Partisan politics, the welfare state, and three worlds of human capital formation. *Comparative Political Studies, 41*(4–5), 600–637.

Katzenstein, P. J. (1985). *Small states in world markets: Industrial policy in Europe.* Ithaca, NY: Cornell University Press.

King, G., Keohane, R. O., & Verba, S. (1994). *Designing social inquiry: Scientific inference in qualitative research.* Princeton: Princeton University Press.

Kitschelt, H., Lange, P., Marks, G., & Stephens, J. D. (Eds.). (1999). *Continuity and change in contemporary capitalism.* New York: Cambridge University Press.

Knight, J. (1992). *Institutions and social conflict.* Cambridge: Cambridge University Press.

Lijphart, A. (1971). Comparative politics and the comparative method. *The American Political Science Review, 65*(3), 682–693.

Lijphart, A. (1984). *Democracies: Patterns of majoritarian and consensus democracies in twenty-one countries.* New Haven, CT: Yale University Press.

Lijphart, A. (1994). *Electoral systems and party systems: A study of twenty-seven democracies, 1945–1990.* New York: Oxford University Press.

Manow, P. (2009). Electoral rules, class coalitions and welfare state regimes, or how to explain Esping-Andersen with Stein Rokkan. *Socio-Economic Review, 7*, 101–121.

Mares, I. (2001). Firms in the welfare state: When, why, and how does social policy matter to employers? In T. Iversen & D. Soskice (Eds.), *Varieties of capitalism: The institutional foundations of comparative advantage*. New York: Oxford University Press.

Mares, I. (2003). *The politics of social risk: Business and welfare state development*. New York: Cambridge University Press.

Martin, C. J., & Swank, D. (2008). The political origins of coordinated capitalism: Business organizations, party systems, and state structure in the age of innocence. *American Political Science Review, 102*(2), 181–198.

North, D. C. (1981). *Structure and change in economic history* (1st ed.). New York: Norton.

North, D. C. (1990). *Institutions, institutional change, and economic performance*. Cambridge: Cambridge University Press.

Olson, M. (1965). *The logic of collective action: Public goods and the theory of groups*. Cambridge: Harvard University Press.

Palmer, G., & Palmer, M. (1997). *Bridled power: New Zealand and government under MMP*. Oxford: Oxford University Press.

Pierson, P. (Ed.). (2001). *The new politics of the welfare state*. Oxford: Oxford University Press.

Roe, M. J. (2003). *Political determinants of corporate governance*. Oxford: Oxford University Press.

Sargent, L. T. (1999). *Contemporary political ideologies: A comparative analysis* (11th ed.). New York: Harcourt Brace College Publishers.

Schmidt, V. A. (2007). *Changes in comparative political economy: Taking labor out, bringing the state back in, putting the firm front and center*. Paper presented at the European Studies Association Meeting.

Schmidt, V. A. (2009). Putting the political back into political economy by bringing the state back in yet again. *World Politcs, 61*(3), 516–546.

Schmitter, P. (1979). Still the century of corporatism? In P. Schmitter & G. Lehmbruch (Eds.), *Trends toward corporatist intermediation*. London: Sage Publications.

Seawright, J., & Gerring, J. (2008). Case selection techniques in case study research: A menu of qualitative and quantitative options. *Political Research Quarterly, 61*(2), 294–308.

Shonfield, A. (1965). *Modern capitalism: The changing balance of public and private power*. London and New York: Oxford University Press.

Simmons, B. A. (1999). The internationalization of capital. In H. Kitschelt, P. Lange, G. Marks, & J. Stephens (Eds.), *Continuity and change in contemporary capitalism*. New York: Cambridge University Press.

Smith, A. (1991 [1776]). *The wealth of nations*. New York: Alfred A. Knopf.

Soskice, D. (1999). Divergent production regimes: Coordinated and uncoordinated market economies in the 1980s and 1990s. In H. Kitschelt, P. Lange, G. Marks, & J. D. Stephens (Eds.), *Continuity and change in contemporary captialism* (pp. 101–134). New York: Cambridge University Press.

Soskice, D. (2007). Macroeconomics and varieties of capitalism. In B. Hancké, M. Rhodes, & M. Thatcher (Eds.), *Beyond varieties of capitalism: Conflict, contradictions, and complementarities in the European economy*. New York: Oxford University Press.

Streeck, W., & Yamamura, K. (Eds.). (2001). *The origins of nonliberal capitalism: Germany and Japan in comparison*. Ithaca, NY: Cornell University Press.

Swank, D. (2001). Political institutions and welfare state restructuring: The impact of institutions on social policy change in developed democracies. In P. Pierson (Ed.), *The new politics of the welfare state*. New York: Oxford University Press.

Swank, D. (2002). *Global capital, political instiutions, and policy change in developed welfare states*. New York: Cambridge University Press.

Thelen, K. (2001). Varieties of labor politics in the developed democracies. In P. A. Hall & D. Soskice (Eds.), *The varieties of capitalism: The institutional foundations of comparative advantage*. New York: Oxford University Press.

Wood, S. (2001). Business, government, and patterns of labor market policy in Britain and the Federal Republic of Germany. In P. Hall & D. Soskice (Eds.), *Varieties of capitalism*. New York: Oxford University Press.

CHAPTER 2

A Political Approach to Explaining Variation in Capitalist Systems

Following the collapse of the Soviet Union, democratic capitalism has risen to be the dominant political-economic system of advanced industrial societies (Fukuyama, 2006). However, it would be erroneous to classify all capitalist economies under one overarching typology. It is readily apparent, to even the casual observer, that capitalist economies differ. The continental European states, emphasizing "big employer confederations, big unions, and monopolistic banks," often appear in direct opposition to Anglo-Saxon systems characterized by laissez-faire transactions, competition between firms, and weak labor movements (Phelps, 2006, p. A14).

The study of capitalism has a robust and extensive academic history. However, the study of variation *between* modern democratic capitalist economies has a much younger intellectual tradition.

Academic Lineage

The study of modern comparative capitalism emerged after World War II. The Second World War left much of the globe in political and economic ruin. A return to political and economic stability proved a long and arduous process. It was not until the late 1950s to the early 1960s that a degree of autonomous economic and political stability returned to Europe (Judt, 2005). Over the course of rebuilding, states adopted vary-

M.P. Arsenault, *The Effects of Political Institutions on Varieties of Capitalism*, DOI 10.1007/978-3-319-50892-4_2

ing strategies to cope with emerging challenges (Hall, 2007). One of the earliest systematic studies of the emerging political-economic systems was Shonfield's *Modern Capitalism* (1965).

In 1965, Andrew Shonfield's *Modern Capitalism* attempted to explain the resurgence of capitalist economies from the "cataclysmic failure" of the 1930s and 1940s into the "great engine of prosperity of the postwar Western world" (1965, p. 3). He hypothesized that such a revival was largely the result of a "rebalancing" of public and private power. Such rebalancing ultimately led to greater governmental influence in economic planning and led to an increased growth and prosperity throughout Western economies. However, as Shonfield illustrated, not all states adopted the same postwar strategies.

Shonfield differentiates between the *etatist* French economy, the laissez-faire British model, and the *corporatist* German system. Shonfield contends that ideological control of government largely shaped the variations in economic planning (and capitalism more generally) of different countries (1965, p. 151). That is, Shonfield concentrates on variations in culture and history as shaping, in part, the structure of the economic system. For example, Shonfield explains that strong French governmental intervention largely stems from the historical traditions of centralized political control and a well-entrenched bureaucracy. On the other hand, he explains the British laissez-faire approach as stemming from "the underlying view of the limited role of the state, which was shared in large measure by the Labour and Conservative leadership" (1965, p. 91).

In short, Shonfield explained divergence between capitalist systems largely through the degree to which states—driven by tradition, ideology, and path dependence—intervened in the economy. However, in the 1970s, with the rise of neocorporatism, such an emphasis on the state fell from favor.

Neocorporatism

In the 1970s to the early 1980s, neocorporatism proved the main theoretical avenue for the study of European political economy (Gerber, 1995; Schmidt, 2007). The rise of neocorporatist frameworks found comparative political economists focusing largely on the ways by which interests were mediated, and how such interest mediation shaped economic policymaking (Schmitter & Lehmbruch, 1979). From the neocorporatist perspective, the advanced industrial economies were largely divided between pluralist and corporatist arrangements (Gerber, 1995; Korpi, 1983; Schmitter, 1979a).

Unlike Shonfield (1965), neocorporatist scholars deemphasized the role of the state. Rather, prominence was given to the role of labor and other interests operating between the government and society. In Schmitter's conception of societal corporatism, "the legitimacy and functioning of the state is primarily or exclusively dependent on the activity of singular, noncompetitive, hierarchically ordered representative 'corporations'" (1979b, p. 20). According to neocorporatist accounts, such "corporations" proved to be the major players and catalysts in policymaking, and under such arrangements, the political economy is characterized by a "culture of compromise" in which interest groups enter into cooperative arrangements (Katzenstein, 1985; Lehmbruch, 1979). As Schmidt writes, "in democratically neocorporatist countries, the social partners—with or without the government—would solve the problems of economy cooperatively" (2007, p. 5).

Whereas corporatism is characterized by "organized capitalism," pluralism is characterized by "classical liberal-competitive capitalism" (Lehmbruch, 1979). As Schmitter points out, pluralist systems are composed of much more decentralized bargaining structures between interest groups "in which the constituent units are organized into an unspecified number of multiple, voluntary, competitive, nonhierarchal ordered and self-determined (as to type or scope of interest) categories" (1979b, p. 15). As such, competing interests enter the political and economic arena with only limited institutional structures in place to promote cooperation, and subsequently rely on more neoliberal, market-oriented mechanisms to set policy (Katzenstein, 1985).

"Bringing the State Back In"

By the 1980s, the popularity of neocorporatist ideas began to decline. The focus on the role of labor, specifically labor power, began to fall from favor. A shift in the global economy led to significant moves toward neoliberal ideologies. Scholars argued that such a shift was the result of increased globalization, increased international trade, the internationalization of capital, and increased global competition (Coffey & Thornley, 2009; Hooghe & Marks, 1999; Kitschelt, Lange, Marks, & Stephens, 1999; Simmons, 1999). Such changes, according to corporatist scholars, would ultimately lead to a convergence toward neoliberal policies, and a subsequent weakening of the state in the face of the rising power of capital holders (Hall & Soskice, 2001, p. 56). However, a convergence toward neoliberal models did not occur. Schmidt writes:

> Importantly, governments that in the 1960s and 1970s may have sought to coordinate policymaking with labor and business began in the 1980s to act more autonomously in the face of crisis. But different countries took different paths even as they all sought to loosen labor markets, liberalize financial markets, and deregulate business. (Schmidt, 2007, p. 5)

Paralleling Shonfield (1965), scholars explained the lack of convergence to the degree of state involvement in the economy. That is, "the state came 'back in' as governments began increasingly making decisions on their own, with or without the acquiescence or event participation of labor or business" (Schmidt, 2007, p. 5). Examples of state autonomous decision making include the deregulation policies of Britain under Margaret Thatcher, the move toward a more centralized system of market regulation in Germany, and the move away from governmental interference in labor relations in France (Hall, 1986, 2007; Schmidt, 2009).

The Rise of Global Business

In the 1990s, emphasis on state influence in comparative political economy was once more in decline. Scholars argued that changes in the international economy, especially the increasing liberalization of capital markets, increased the power of global business and weakened the power of the state (Schmidt, 2009; Simmons, 1999). The argument suggests that changes to the international economy, especially the liberalization of capital, altered the strategies of firms.

Under such conditions, it was argued that firms have a strong exit option which then weakens the bargaining position of labor, as well as weakens government influence over business. That is, big firms could invest in liquid assets with a higher short-term payoff instead of long-term investments in increased productivity, which in turn limits government autonomy in regard to shaping policy, thus leading to a more neoliberal policy regime (Boix, 2003; Coffey & Thornley, 2009; Hirschman, 1970).

Ultimately, democratic capitalist systems once again failed to converge on one type of capitalism. Rather, systems still "clustered" around either a neoliberal model or a coordinated model. However, the 1990s did offer an invaluable insight to the study of comparative capitalism, that is, scholars began to focus on the influence and behavior of the firm on capitalist diversity.

Europeanization

Other scholars contend that Europeanization will lead to the convergence toward liberal market economies (LMEs). However, Europeanization should not be viewed as a power capable of superseding domestic institutions. Hooghe and Marks contend that changes in European economies—integration of capital markets, decline of traditional industry, high unemployment, and so on—has led to contentious debate regarding authority structures and decision-making processes in Europe at the national, sub-national, and supra-national levels (1999). These structures have changed from technocratic decision making of various elites [based on mutual agreement] to a much more contentious and politicized process. For example, many more groups—interest groups, labor movements, corporations, public interest groups, regional governments, and so on—have mobilized to pressure political elites to represent the strategic interests of the various groups.

Hooghe and Marks contend that the debate between competing political actors can be divided into two "political designs or 'projects'." The neoliberal projects "seeks to insulate markets from political interferences," and limit an overarching democratic structure allowing the EU to regulate markets, and promote competition between states (1999, p. 75).

On the other hand, the "project for regulated capitalism" seeks greater EU economic cooperation regarding a social democratic approach, increased regulatory powers of the EU over economic policies, and a strengthening of the EU parliament (Hooghe & Marks, 1999). These two projects illustrate two contested dimensions in the EU, supranationalism versus nationalism, and the classic left–right spectrum. The neoliberal project falls closest to nationalism and right government, while the project of regulated capitalism falls closest to left government and supranationalism. As such, when political actors—national, sub-national, and supra-national—come into negotiations, they bring with them their beliefs regarding these dimensions and decisions become hotly contested. Not only is this contention at the EU level, but within nations, and even disaggregated down to parties, and so on.

As such, the political elites making EU decisions are not isolated, but rather face domestic political pressures, not the least of which is reelection. Hooghe and Marks write, "The sheer fact that cross-border transactions are increasing within Europe does not mean that further integration will be the outcome. To understand European integration one must understand its irreducible political character" (1999, p. 97). I contend that the "irreducible political character" is largely constrained by the existing political institutions within a given state.

In part, this logic is based on Swank (2001, 2002) who contends that the variation in domestic political institutions will address globalization or, here, regional integration, in different ways. That is, domestic political institutions can allow for the continued domestic "variety of capitalism" despite international pressures.

Varieties of Capitalism

The varieties of capitalism (VOC) framework contends that capitalist production regimes can be classified into two forms: coordinated market economies (CME) and liberal market economies (LME). The CME production regimes are typified by cooperation, that is, cooperation between industry-specific firms (especially on issues like wage determination), cooperation between the labor force and firms, and cooperation between the companies and capital holders (Soskice, 1999, p. 106). Under the CME production regime, the government serves to collectively negotiate with companies. This allows for the development of a framework within which all companies operate. CME production regimes include long-term firm financing, "cooperative industrial relations" between labor and the firm, specialized skills, and technology transfer and "standard setting" between sector-specific firms (Soskice, 1999, p. 107). Soskice argues that the institutional structure of the CME production regime leads to unique "product market strategies." For example, nations with CME regimes tend to "produce complex products, involving complex production processes and after-sales service with close customer links" (Soskice, 1999, p. 113).

Where the CME production regime is characterized by cooperation, the LME regime is typified by strong competition. Under an LME regime, the economic actors have only a limited ability to coordinate their actions. The actors' "inability to act collectively means that they cannot combine to negotiate discretionary framework solutions with the state" (Soskice, 1999, p. 110). LME production regimes include short-term financial time-frames, "deregulated labor markets," an emphasis on general skills in the workforce, and fierce competition between firms (Soskice, 1999, p. 110). The LME framework leads to a far different "product market strategy" than its CME counterpart. LME production regimes tend to produce "highly innovative products (often in purely intellectual patented form) developed in venture capital start-ups in new high-technology areas"(Soskice, 1999, p. 117).

The VOC literature contends that the key causal difference between production regimes is the "strategic interaction central to the behavior of economic actors," particularly the coordination capacity between firms (Hall & Soskice, 2001, p. 5). Hall and Soskice contend that issues of coordination between economic actors usually occur within five arenas.

The first arena addresses industrial relations which include negotiation between the firm and labor, as well as the firm and other employers. The authors suggest that negotiations usually revolve around coordinated wages, working conditions, and output. The second arena includes vocational training and education, as well as the creation and maintenance of a suitable labor force for companies, including employment security for workers. Corporate governance composes the third sphere and includes a company's access to financial resources and guarantees on investor capital. Fourth, the VOC approach looks at coordination between corporations. This includes issues like competition between firms versus sector-wide cooperation. Lastly, issues of coordination capacity occur between the corporation and employees. Issues include the relations between workers and management regarding corporate structure, as well as negotiations regarding information exchange (Hall & Soskice, 2001).

"The relationships firms develop to resolve these problems condition their own competencies and the character of an economy's production regimes" (Hall & Soskice 2001, p. 7). In other words, firms will pursue production policies shaped by the existing institutional structures: particularly financial, industrial relations, education, and inter-company relations systems. Where interactions within the above arenas are governed by institutions favoring competition and other neoclassical economic principles, we will see an LME production regime emerge. In cases where the above arenas are governed by institutions promoting cooperation, collaboration, exchange of information, sanctions for defection, and so on, we will find the emergence of CME production regimes.

So, institutions, to a greater or lesser extent, shape the behavior of the firm. The strategy of the firm does not shape the institution. The institutions provide the firm with a set of opportunities and the firms then develop product market and innovation strategies that take best advantage of those opportunities. As such, complementarity exists between institutions and the corporate strategies of firms. Complementarity draws on the economists' conception of the production function (Crouch, 2005). That is, the presence of one institution will increase the efficiency of another.

The VOC framework contends that coordination in one arena of the economy will likely lead to the development of complementary institutions in another (Crouch, 2005; Hall & Soskice, 2001). As such:

> institutional practices of various types should not be distributed randomly across nations. Instead, we should see some clustering along the dimensions that divide liberal from coordinated market economies, as nations converge on complementary practices across different spheres [specifically, CME and LME production regimes]. (Hall & Soskice, 2001, p. 18)

Critiques of the Varieties of Capitalism Framework

The VOC approach faces a number of valid criticisms which must be addressed. In Hancké's review of the VOC literature, critiques are grouped around three broad themes: those who question capitalist variation itself, those who recognize variation between capitalist systems but are critical of the "reductionist" CME/LME dichotomy, and those who recognize capitalist diversity, but question the causal logic of the VOC approach and call for "conceptually richer, approaches to capitalist diversity" (Hancké, 2009, p. 6).

The first cluster of critiques rejects the basic premise of capitalist divergence. Drawing heavily on Marxist theory, such scholars contend that capitalism continues along a historical path of convergence toward liberal market institutions. Scholars often cite changes in the international economy—specifically globalization, increased competition from newly industrialized countries, and European integration—that led to a retrenchment of "institutions that had previously made workers less dependent on markets" and subsequently strengthened the bargaining position of capital holders (Hancké, 2009, p. 6; Pierson, 2001; Simmons, 1999).

However, convergence, toward either a liberal market model or a coordinated market model has failed to occur. Rather, globalization, instead of forcing a convergence toward one model, has actually pushed capitalism apart (Hancké, 2009; Katzenstein, 1985). As the VOC framework suggests, various political-economic models offer comparative institutional advantage for states and firms to adopt one production regime over another (Hall & Soskice, 2001; Hancké, 2009). As Hancké writes, comparative institutional advantage:

> refers to the idea that national institutional frameworks impose a relatively narrow set of choices on the competitive strategies of firms in them adopt, and that different countries therefore specialize in particular export activities ... when deciding on where to locate particular activities in the value chain, multinational corporations will arbitrage between different institutional environments. (2009, p. 10)

Questioning a Binary Dichotomy

The second cluster recognizes capitalist diversity, but questions the reduction of capitalist economies into two types: CMEs and LMEs (Crouch, 2005; Molina & Rhodes, 2007; Schmidt, 2009). Here, the dichotomy of CMEs and LMEs is viewed as overly simplified. For example, Shonfield (1965) identifies three types of capitalism, Amable (2003) identifies five institutionally different capitalist models, while Crouch (2005) contends that nearly any number of capitalist models are theoretically possible. Some have argued that a number of advanced industrial economies do not fall cleanly into either camp (Hancké, 2009). Possible additional categories include "mixed market economies" represented by etatist countries like France and Japan (Hall & Gingerich, 2004; Katzenstein, 1985), a Mediterranean model including Italy and Spain (Molina & Rhodes, 2007), and a social democratic Scandinavian model (Crouch, 2005). However:

> One of the problems with such expanding typologies is that ultimately one could claim that every capitalist country has produced its own 'variety,' in which at least one institution or combination of institutions is historically specific, and therefore different from other related types. (Hancké, 2009, p. 15)

Such a debate illustrates a continuous dilemma of social science research. That is, social scientists are faced with the dilemma of balancing parsimony, generality, and accuracy (Przeworski & Tenue, 1970). A problem with expanding the VOC's binary typology to include a third, fourth, or any number of additional type of capitalism stems from "conceptual stretching" and the subsequent possibility of "empirical vaporization" (Sartori, 1970, p. 1043).

For the sake of parsimony, and overall generalizability, this study will retain the CME and LME dichotomy as posed by Hall and Soskice (2001), but recognizes that that these are ideal types. Cases categorized as CME or LME may not have *identical* characteristics. However, the purpose of this concept is to simplify the world around us while allowing for a degree of generalization to the population at large.

As such, the CME and LME dichotomy is a "family resemblance" category. That is, the various cases are similar, but not identical. These cases, however, will still fall under the same "family," CME or LME (Collier & Mahon, 1993). As such, the LME and CME dichotomy falls into Sartori's medium level of categorization (1970).

Questioning the Cause of Capitalist Diversity

The third cluster recognizes variation in capitalist economies but remains skeptical of the underpinnings of the proposed causal logic. Whereas the VOC approach focuses largely on the strategic behavior of the firm, scholars operating within this camp "look for the sources of diversity elsewhere—in politics, history, or culture rather than in the micro-structure of markets" (Hancké, 2009, p. 8).

This book falls squarely within this third group of criticisms. I question the lack of emphasis on the genesis of the economic arenas which structure the LME and CME dichotomy. I contend that a promising avenue lies in a closer examination of political institutions. Greater emphasis on the role of politics and political institutions is imperative to explaining differences between capitalist systems. As North illustrates, the state (and state structures) plays a central role in structuring the "rules of the game" in a political economy (1981, 1990). North contends that institutions specify "the fundamental rules of competition and cooperation which will provide a structure of property rights" and subsequently the structure of the economic system (1981, p. 24).

A call for greater emphasis on political institutions is only recently being posed. Deeg and Jackson (2007) argue that a greater understanding of state structures and political institutions is an imperative challenge to the comparative capitalism literature. They call on scholars to focus on the ways in which political institutions and other "formal rule-making systems" shape the processes by which VOC are structured (Deeg & Jackson,

2007, p. 169). Amable and Palombarini (2009) call for greater emphasis on the ways in which states affect firm behavior. Specifically, they focus on the ways that state and political institutions constrain the behavior of actors operating within the political economy, or the ability of those controlling the state to autonomously institute changes in the institutional structures (Amable & Palombarini, 2009, pp. 126–129). Similarly, Hancké et al. call into question the VOC assumption that the state lacks the autonomy to implement policies capable of shaping the economic environment, especially in the presence of powerful business interests (Hancké, Rhodes, & Thatcher, 2007).

Political Regimes and Varieties of Capitalism

Scholars are in the early stages of developing a research program exploring the relationships between political institutions and capitalist structures. This section seeks to briefly illustrate some of the major studies conducted within the research program, examining the role political institutions play in shaping aspects of capitalist economies.

I begin with early studies of the effects of electoral system on degrees market coordination (Birchfield & Crepaz, 1998; Katzenstein, 1985; Lijphart & Crepaz, 1991). I then move on to examine the ways that political institutions affect the LME/CME dichotomy as posed by the VOC framework (Amable, 2003; Cusack, Iversen, & Soskice, 2007; Iversen & Soskice, 2006; Korpi, 2006; Martin & Swank, 2008).

Katzenstein (1985) finds that democratic corporatism is related to political parties and the party system. First, small states overwhelmingly have proportional representation (PR) systems and often minority governments. Both features promote coordination. Party unification is often weak in small states, resulting in coalition governments. This makes politicians less able to adopt zero-sum strategies. Furthermore, the PR system, coupled with a divided right, often leads to minority governments. Minority governments help ensure conciliation and compromise between actors. The sub-groups do not have a good chance of winning an outright majority. Many actors have influence over policy and there is much greater coordination, and corporatist arrangements emerge.

Similarly, Lijphart and Crepaz (1991) have examined the impact of consensus democracy on corporatism. Lijphart and Crepaz found that as the degree of consensus (as measured by macro-political institutions) increases, the level of corporatism increases. They define corporatism in a similar manner as Soskice defines CME production regimes; that is, CME production regimes are illustrated by cooperation between firms (monopolistic peak organization), industry-specific cooperation (specialization), and a national framework created by government (1999). As such, their research is of particular relevance in supporting the feasibility of the theory that institutions posed by the VOC literature are constrained by broader political institutions.

Birchfield and Crepaz (1998) find that consensus systems are related to lower levels of income inequalities while majoritarian systems are related to higher levels of income inequalities. The collective veto points found in consensus systems—PR systems, multi-party legislatures, multi-party governments, and parliamentary regimes—tend to promote compromise and negotiation. The consensus institutions themselves "not only provide access to political interests but also tend to include these interests in multi-party executive cabinets 'fused' to the legislature, ensuring representativeness on the one hand, and effectiveness on the other" (Birchfield & Crepaz, 1998, p. 179).

Amable examines the role of sociopolitical groups—the powerful coalition—and their preferences in shaping the economic institutions (2003). According to this logic, social groups are political actors operating "within [a] structured formal political process (e.g. majoritarianism)" and through their interaction are able to shape economic institutions in order to better pursue the interest of the relevant socioeconomic group (Deeg & Jackson, 2007, p. 160).

Iversen and Soskice (2006) examine the relationship between electoral and party systems on redistributive policies. The authors contend that electoral system type is associated with specific party systems. The party system, in turn, shapes the structure of class coalitions. They illustrate how such logic can be applied to capitalist divergence. They contend that "there exists a strategic complementarity between such insurance [stemming from redistributive policies] and individuals' decisions to invest in particular types of skills" (Iversen & Soskice, 2006). This suggests that different electoral systems can help shape at least one of the five arenas (labor relations) within which firms and labor interact.

Similarly, Cusack, Iversen, and Soskice attempt to explain "the close association between the current varieties of capitalism and electoral institutions" (2007, p. 373). In situations where production requires specific skills, the political right will accept PR, and consensual bargaining with the left in order to promote specific skill development. In nations with "adversarial industrial relations," the right will seek power over the left through majoritarian institutions. The authors suggest that once the PR system was adopted, "stable regulatory frameworks developed" which created incentives for asset-specific skills, which, through institutional complimentarily, led to the emergence of CME regimes.

Martin and Swank (2008) illustrate why some countries developed pluralist peak associations while others developed more corporatist employer associations. Martin and Swank (2008) contend that party systems and the structure of the state shape the type of business associations. In particular, they examine the effects of two-party versus multi-party systems on the structure of employer organizations. They find that PR and multi-party systems will lead to corporatist peak associations while two-party systems will lead to pluralist associations.

Similarly, Korpi (2006)—building on the power resources approach—argues that partisan politics, based on class divisions, are central to the divergence of production regimes. His explanatory variables include electoral institutions, state-corporatist structures, and the party orientation of cabinets. Korpi contends that PR systems are conducive to strong, leftist parties, while majoritarian systems tend to favor "secular center-right" parties. In short, the logic holds that states characterized by a combination of PR systems, state-corporatist structures, and "confessional party" coalitions are likely to promote CME production regimes, while states with an absence of such institutions are likely to have LME systems (Korpi, 2006).

Brady and Leicht (2007) contend that right-party power, as measured by long-term cabinet tenure, plays a significant role in increasing inequality in advanced industrial democracies. Specifically, the authors suggest that governments characterized by long-term right-party power seek smaller government, progressive taxation policies, and a retrenchment of the welfare state through three ways: legislative action, administrative office holding, and ideological influence (2007, pp. 7–9).

This book will expand on the current VOC literature by lending greater emphasis to competing interests, and the formal political institutions that shape and structure such competition. In doing so, this study will draw, in part, from power resources theory (PRT) to explain capitalist divergence. The power resources approach concentrates on the balance of power between classes—labor/left and capital/right—and the effects that the distribution of power has on economic policy. Although PRT has primarily been used in analyses of the welfare state, the concept will prove useful in discussing competing interests and variation between capitalist systems. Here I discuss current studies applying PRT to explain various political-economic outcomes.

Huber and Stephens write that the power resources approach:

> identifies the distribution of organizational power between labor and left-wing parties on the one hand, and center and right-wing parties on the other hand, as primary determinants of differences in welfare state development across countries and over time. (2000, p. 325)

Huber and Stephens (2000) find that social democratic governments—characterized by strong labor movements—have proved to be powerful political allies to women participating in the workforce, and subsequently have led to increases in social funding and the delivery of services in contrast to Christian democratic governments. The PRT approach suggests that disadvantaged classes will overcome collective action problems and mobilize politically—into political parties—and begin to demand welfare state development to modify the market-oriented distribution process.

Korpi (2006) has applied PRT to claim that divergence in capitalist systems is in part driven by the dispersion of power between competing classes. Korpi examines VOC and power resources explanations of capitalist divergence. The two approaches disagree on the causal factors leading to the divergence of production regimes. The VOC approach views variation in production regime as a result of employers' needs for either asset-specific skills or general skills (Estevez-Abe, Iversen, & Soskice, 2001; Mares, 2001, 2003).

Similarly, Swank illustrates that political institutions affect the ability of competing classes to pursue their interests (Swank, 2001, 2002). He argues that variation in the political institutions of developed democracies address global capital mobility, and subsequently welfare state pressures, in different ways. Swank argues that the consensus-oriented institutions are able to "blunt" the internationalization pressures, while the institutional structures of more liberal states will correspond with greater retrenchment. The main argument is that the impacts of the internationalization of capital will differ between nations based on presence of social corporatism versus pluralism, electoral interest representation, diverse versus concentrated power, and the structure of the welfare state.

For example, social corporatism and its corresponding political institutions grant power to those interests most negatively affected by the internationalization of capital. Corporatism grants labor interests veto power over policy changes, political power to leftist parties, and "cultivates a distinct constellation of norms and values that shape actor's behavior and the character of the policy process" (Swank, 2002, p. 43).

Furthermore, PR electoral systems and multi-party systems lend greater power to those adversely affected by globalization. They gain some control of institutional mechanisms with which to resist retrenchment policies. For example, greater inclusiveness will allow representation for ideological interests opposed to globalization, and liberal market policies.

Peter Hall has also recognized the role of politics in explaining variation in capitalist systems (1999, 2007). Hall contends that the ability of political economies to adjust to changes in the global economy is largely contingent upon political institutions and the dispersion of power within the system. Because adjustments affect people as well as firms, structural adjustments are political as well as economic. Hall writes:

> socioeconomic developments at the international or domestic level will tend to rearrange the social coalitions that divide the electorate or producer groups by shifting their underlying material interests. However, the extent of that arrangement and its impact on policy or organization of the political economy will be affected by the institutional structure of both the political economy and the polity. (1999, p. 159)

Hall contends that institutional structures affect adjustment paths through (a) a "power dimension" which provides disproportionate power to one group over another, and (b) through the emergence of collective action problems within groups. The effects of political institutions on adjustment paths are illustrated by the ability of Britain to rapidly pursue deregulation policies under the strong executive Margret Thatcher, while during the same time, the diffused power structure of Germany limited adjustment (Hall, 1986, 1999).

In conclusion, power, politics, and political institutions partly explain the divergence of economic structures, but the causal linkages must be examined further. For example, debate continues over the direction of causality between political institutions and economic institutions. The following section illustrates recent scholarship engaging in this debate, and suggests how this book will help address this question.

Debating the Causal Arrow

This section provides examples of the continuing debate within the VOC literature regarding the causal direction between political and economic institutions. Cusack et al. (2007) argue that economic institutions shape political structures, while Martin and Swank (2008) contend that political institutions shape economic structures.

Cusack, Iversen, and Soskice argue that economic interests drive the emergence of electoral systems (2007). They attempt to explain "the close association between the current varieties of capitalism and electoral institutions" (2007, p. 373). They contend that in situations of production which require asset-specific skills, the political right will accept PR systems, and subsequently form consensual agreements with labor and left parties, in order to guarantee the formation of the required skills. However, in countries where general, more transferable skills are required, the right will seek to maintain control over the left through majoritarian institutions. In short, the authors argue that in the early days of industrialization, in nations where cooperation developed between center and right parties versus the unions/left parties, "the benefits from the adoption of PR of consensual regulatory politics outweighed the cost of exclusion from minimum winning coalitions in redistributive politics" (2007, p. 306). However, in states where cooperation was weak, we see the emergence of minimal winning coalitions of center and right parties which form in opposition to the left. As such, the center and right will seek a majoritarian system to protect their interests against the left. The authors suggest that once the PR system was adopted "stable regulatory frameworks developed" which created incentives for asset-specific skills, which through institutional complementarity led to the emergence of CME regimes. Once such a framework was in place, a path dependency developed and created a disincentive to pursue majoritarian systems.

On the other hand, Martin and Swank contend that party systems and the structure of the state can shape the type of economic structures (2008). In particular, they examine the effects of two-party versus multi-party systems on the structure of employer organizations. They find that PR and multi-party systems will lead to corporatist peak associations while two-party systems will lead to pluralist/competitive associations. The logic contends that in PR/multi-party systems, we will find parties sympathetic to business interests. This results in cooperation between like-minded groups, and the formation of coalitions to support business interests.

Because it is unlikely that employer associations will gain majority control, they will seek other sources of influence outside of government. This can lead to more organized and centralized (coordinated) employer associations. In two-party systems, with two large "umbrella parties" business interests are dispersed. These big parties cross-cut class divides. "Employers have a harder time coming together, and have fewer reasons to negotiate with labor politically" (2008, p. 182).

As stated, within the VOC literature, the causal direction between political institutions and economic institutions remains unclear. This book seeks to lend clarity to the causal debate, and to further the understanding of how politics affects the formation of VOC. The following section describes the proposed causal explanation linking political institutional configurations and different types of capitalist economies.

A Proposed Causal Process

In proposing a theory explaining capitalist variation, I begin with the assumption that the political economy of advanced industrial societies is largely divided between two competing groups: capital holders and labor. The assumption proves useful in that the proposed labor-capital cleavage is a characteristic of all developed economies (Lijphart, 1984; Manow, 2009).[1] Within the political arena, groups will pursue the maximization of benefits through the formation of "social collectives" or "groups of individuals or families, who are tied to one another by virtue of shared traditions or because of their common interest and their common perspective" (Toennies, 1961, p. 49). This section illustrates the ways in which such "social collectives" have emerged into political vehicles in modern democratic capitalist economies. Specifically, I examine partisanship, political parties, electoral systems, and the organization of class competition and cooperation. I then discuss the ways that political institutions affect the political economy of a given state, namely, through a "power dimension" and through the facilitation of cooperation, or the propagation of competition.

Lipset and Rokkan contend that political parties and party systems develop over time. The authors find that party systems and parties develop from conflicting associations and cleavage groups in society seeking to promote their political agenda (1967a, 1967b). Whether or not social cleavages will develop into political parties depends on the threshold to be overcome in order to gain a representative voice. Depending on threshold levels, differing party systems emerge, that is, parliamentary multi-party systems, two-party or one-party systems, and so on. Thresholds are set by previous decision-making traditions, the channels by which political expression and mobilization occur, the payoffs and costs of various alliances, and the possibilities of majoritarian rule (1967a, 1967b, p. 29).

In electoral systems with high thresholds, it is difficult for new parties to break into the political arena unless they join forces with other, more established parties. For example, in systems where the capital holder class was cohesive, and confronted by a diffused labor class—communist versus social democratic—the capital holding class was able to use their existing political power to maintain control through majoritarian institutions. In general, systems with high thresholds are conducive to majoritarian government while lower thresholds will be more proportional (Lijphart, 1994; Seymour Lipset & Stein Rokkan, 1967a, 1967b, p. 29).

When demands for greater representation emerge among cleavage groups, we often see a move toward greater proportionality in the electoral system. Some have argued that as suffrage is extended, the newly enfranchised groups make greater demands for representation in the political system. That is, when class conflict and political struggle emerge over representation and the provision of social and economic rights we often see a move toward greater proportionality in the electoral system (Seymour Lipset & Stein Rokkan, 1967a, 1967b; Marshall, 1964; Orloff, 1993). On the one hand, the capital holder and managerial class has a great deal of power stemming from its strong position in the market, and will fight to limit the political and social rights of labor, as capital holders will bear disproportionate costs. On the other hand, workers are more numerous and can use their numbers to form political pressure groups and force the adoptions of political and social rights, thus weakening the power of the capitalists (Korpi, 1983).

In democratic systems, political parties based along the socioeconomic cleavage maintain power through a competitive electoral process. As such, according to Partisan Theory, parties have electoral incentives to pursue policies favorable to their constituent base. Quinn and Shapiro write, "At the root of the partisanship thesis is the idea that parties draw on different social bases of support and that the power of contending groups will fluctuate with the fortunes of their allied parties" (1991, p. 853).

The core constituency of the right is composed of capital holders, the managerial class, and others higher on the socioeconomic scale. The core constituency of the left is composed of those with commodified labor; that is, "their economic well-being depends almost entirely on earnings from labor" (Hibbs Jr., 1992, p. 362). Governments led by right parties often pursue policies conducive to the increased utility maximization of the core constituents, while governments led by parties of the left often pursue policies conducive to the interests of those in lower socioeconomic groups (Boix, 1998; Downs, 1957; Hibbs Jr., 1977, 1992).

In short, political parties are a major medium for the expression of class interest in advanced industrial democracies. Political parties largely tend to cluster around two categories: parties which generally represent the interests of the capital holder/managerial class, and parties generally representing the interests of the labor/lower class (Lijphart, 1984; Seymour Lipset & Stein Rokkan, 1967a, 1967b; Manow, 2009).

Capital interests can be classified as an exclusive group. In exclusive groups, the quantity of a collective good is finite. As such, the exclusive group maintains a minimum number of members so that each can attain a larger portion of the limited collective good. In this case, business will seek to exclude the interests of labor from the political process in order to achieve profit maximization for the oligopolistic business elite (Olson, 1965). Similarly, in their discussion on the sources of business power, Quinn and Shapiro write, "Other aspects of class (i.e. capitalist) organization might allow business to mobilize political resources. Interlinking corporate directorates, shared social ties, and shared ideology provide a basis for joint corporate activity and for overcoming collective action problems" (1991, p. 854). As such, by remaining exclusive, the capitalist class is able to lessen the need to address the concerns of labor.

Labor, on the other hand, will be considered an inclusive organization. An inclusive organization seeks to lower the costs of attaining a collective benefit by dispersing outlays across a larger number of actors. As such, labor will seek political mechanisms to check the power of business, and force business to contribute to the collective good of labor interests (Olson, 1965).

Here in lies the potential for inter-group class conflict. Each group competes for relative gains. In an environment where business is strong, the collective benefits of labor will decrease, and vice versa. The argument is illustrated by Orloff's discussion of class conflict and political struggle over social rights (1993). The "social citizenship perspectives emphasize the potential of social provision in democratic states, secured largely through the political struggles of citizens and others" (Orloff, 1993, p. 305).

On the one hand, capital has a great deal of power in the market and will fight to limit social rights as the capital holders will largely bear the costs. On the other hand, the workers are more numerous and can use their numerical superiority to use political pressure to force the adoptions of social rights and increased social policies.[2]

The difficulty of satisfying the "contradictory demands" of conflicting interests stems in part from asymmetries of power between groups. By power, I refer to what Dowding has described as "power over," that is, "the ability of an actor deliberately to change the incentive structure of another actor or actors to bring about or help bring about outcomes" (1996, p. 5). That is, groups with greater access to resources will find themselves in a stronger bargaining position than the rival, weaker group. The following section explores the role of power asymmetries within institutions in greater depth, and attempts to tie the concept to economic policymaking. This book assumes that social institutions emerge as a result of conflict between actors with differing interests and asymmetries of power (Knight, 1992; Knight & Sened, 1995). As such, the gains from interaction between players are not equitably distributed. According to Knight, social institutions are a way for "some to constrain the actions of others with whom they interact" (Knight, 1992, p. 19). Institutional development stems from the ongoing conflict between actors with competing interests. Korpi writes, "Social institutions and arrangements related to processes of distribution and decision-making can thus be seen as outcomes of recurrent conflicts of interests, where the parties concerned have invested their power resources in order to secure favorable outcomes" (1983, p. 19).[3]

In addition to institutional genesis, power asymmetries theory has been used to explain institutional change. Pontusson recognizes that institutional arrangements are designed to benefit one group at the expense of another. As a result, "institutional realignments occur when the interest and/or the power of relevant actors change" (Pontusson, 1995, p. 137). Such was the case in much of Europe with the expansion of suffrage, as well as the much more recent case of New Zealand and the subsequent move toward a more proportional electoral system (Mulgan, 1997; Vowles, 1995).

Huber and Stephens have also illustrated the role power asymmetries play on institutional development in regard to welfare state development. They contend that policy options are constrained by "power constellations," between business and labor (Huber & Stephens, 2001). As such, the group in power is able to constrain the feasibility of policy alternatives. In situations where labor is weak in the face of business, we are unlikely to see the expansion of welfare policies. However, changes in the balance of power will lead to changes in the ability of competing interests to shape policy.

Political institutions affect the structure of a given political economy in two main ways. First, political institutions contain a "power dimension" in which the institutional structures affect the dispersion of power between competing groups (Hall, 1986; Iversen & Soskice, 2006, 2009; Korpi, 1983, 2006). Second, within a political economy, coordination and collective action problems emerge between competing economic actors. Some political institutions are more conducive to an environment based on cooperation and creditable commitments, while others are more conducive to creating an environment of competition (Huber & Stephens, 2000; Iversen & Stevens, 2008; Manow, 2001a; Martin & Swank, 2008).

For example, majoritarian regimes create an intense competition between political and economic actors. Additionally, majoritarian regimes are characterized by a great deal of policy instability throughout the political economy. This in turn makes credible commitment to nonmarket coordination mechanisms difficult. This, coupled by the propensity of majoritarian systems to be governed by the right (Iversen & Soskice, 2006), leads majoritarian systems to adhere to the LME model. On the other hand, consensus-oriented political regimes create a political environment conducive to cooperation between political and economic actors. Due to the high numbers of political and economic actors granted access to the political and policy process—and the resulting institutional checks on the actions of competing interest groups—an environment of cooperation and credible commitment to nonmarket coordination mechanisms emerge. This, coupled by greater power of the left in consensus systems, is more conducive to a CME.

The main institutions by which political regimes (majoritarian or consensus) affect the dispersion of power and the ability of actors to cooperate or compete are political parties and the party system, the electoral system, the structure of governing cabinets, the number and type of constitutional constraints, and, subsequently, the partisanship and policy legacies of a given government. Broadly, this study seeks to explain the relationship between CMEs and LMEs and variation in political institutions. Within the CME/LME systems, the economic institutions to be explained—the dependent variables—include corporate governance, industrial relations, inter-firm relations, education and training systems, and employee structures. These economic institutions compose the core structures of production regime as illustrated by the VOC framework. The emergent complementarity configuration between economic institutions leads to a variety of capitalism: CMEs or LMEs. Table 2.1 provides a simplified illustration of the proposed logic.

The logic of the proposed causal model draws heavily on comparative political economy studies exploring the relationship between VOC and the welfare state. Soskice has illustrated complementarities between production regime, political system, and the welfare state (2007). Estevez-Abe et al. have illustrated complementarities between generous welfare states and asset-specific skill formation (2001). Mares examines the comparative institutional advantage of certain welfare policies for firms (2003). Iversen and Stephens find that education spending is largely the result of the partisan control of government (2008). Huber and Stephens have gone so far as to suggest that configurations of welfare states and production regimes can be categorized as particular "welfare regimes" (2001, p. 112). Nevertheless, as Soskice points out, only limited attention has been granted to understanding how production regimes and welfare states "tie into political systems" (2007, p. 92).

The major difference between the welfare state studies and my proposed model lies in the operationalization of the dependent variables. Whereas much of the scholarship on the welfare state uses government expenditures, social security transfers, government employment, or pen-

Table 2.1 The causal logic

Interests	*Power asymmetries*	*Political institutions*	*Economic institutions*	*VOC*
Capital	Right controlling resources	• Majoritarian • SMD • Center/right • Two-party • Right legacy	• Stakeholder • General skills • General education • Market coordination • Firm wage bargaining	LME
Labor	Left controlling resources	• Consensus • PR • Center/left • Multi-party • Left legacy	• Shareholder • Specific skills • Vocational education • Strategic coordination • Central wage bargaining	CME

sion spending as dependent variables in order to capture variation in welfare states, a similar model can be applied where industrial relations, inter-firm relations, skill system, and corporate governance serve as dependent variables which will capture variation in production regime.

Independent Variables and Hypotheses

The following section illustrates the political variables under investigation: partisanship and policy legacies, effective number of political parties, majoritarian cabinets, electoral systems, and constitutional structures. I also propose hypotheses regarding the causal relationships between political institutions and VOC. Capitalist variation is examined through an overarching dependent variable designed to measure market coordination over time. I then examine the economic arenas of the VOC framework: corporate governance, industrial relations, inter-firm relations, and education and training.

Partisanship and Policy Legacies

Partisanship and policy legacies matter in regard to shaping variation in capitalist economies. I hypothesize that where government is largely controlled by the interests of the right, the country's economic structures will likewise promote the interests of capital holders and the managerial class. In situations where labor parties control governments, economic structures will be more conducive to the interests of the lower classes (Esping-Andersen, 1990; Rothstein, Samanni, & Teorell, 2010). As such, long-term partisan policy legacies will affect variation in capitalist systems. By policy legacies I refer to long-term partisan control of the political process (Huber & Stephens, 2001). The importance of including measures of policy legacies is well illustrated in numerous studies of the welfare state, and is quite transferable to the current book.

Esping-Andersen has found policy legacies to play a significant role in the development of variation in welfare regimes (1990). In particular, he finds that policy legacies are important in that they establish the strength and weakness of class structures. Likewise, Hicks and Swank show that policy legacies—liberal, Christian democratic, or social democratic—can either maintain or minimize class "rigidities" and in turn affect welfare state policies, in this case variation in welfare state spending (1992). The logic is furthered by Huber and Stephens, who argue that long-term partisan governance is able to shape the ideology of the masses (2001). That is, ideology and policy preferences are the result of long-term class struggles. "Actors' intentions and desires are not self-generating but are products of social and political struggles over decades or even centuries" (Huber & Stephens, 2001, p. 30). Furthermore, left-leaning parties and governments tend to "bypass" or otherwise move away from market forces, while right-wing parties and governments tend to maintain a hands-off position, and rely heavily on the market (Huber, Ragin, & Stephens, 1993; Korpi, 1983, 2006).

In regard to variation in capitalist systems, I argue that where existing policies have been favorable to one interest over the other, changes to the status quo will be difficult at best. In part, this stems from the "ratchet effect" in which it becomes difficult to retrench or adjust policies once they are in place (Pierson, 1994). Furthermore, over a longer time span, not only will economic structures become more deeply entrenched, but they will represent stronger liberal market or coordinated market institutions.

In testing the impact of partisanship and policy legacies, I rely on Huber and Stephens's cumulative cabinet share index (2001). The cabinet variables measure the number of cabinet seats held by a political party as a proportion of all seats for each year. The proportions are then summed from 1946 to the year of the observation. The value of this measure lies in its ability to capture not only the partisan composition of the cabinet at a given year but also the effects of long-term partisan control of the cabinet. Huber and Stephens have pointed out that such effects should be included in the analysis because economic policies (for them, welfare state programs) have "long maturation periods" (2000, p. 329).

Long-term cabinet tenure and subsequent policy legacies of left-leaning governments are likely to be associated with (1) greater overall market coordination, (2) stakeholder models of corporate governance, (3) cooperative industrial relations policies, (4) greater investment in vocational training and education, (5) and greater degrees of cooperation between firms. In contrast, right-leaning governments are more likely to be associated with (1) limited market coordination, (2) shareholder models of corporate governance, (3) competitive industrial relations policies, (4) limited investment in vocational training and education, and lastly (5) limited cooperation between firms.

Effective Number of Political Parties

The number of political parties serves as an important variable in analyzing production regimes. Political parties affect the dispersion of political power, and the ways in which various parties interact. This, in turn, shapes the coordination capacities between players.

Following Lipset and Rokkan (1967a, 1967b), and Huber, Ragin, and Stephens (1993), I separate political parties from the overall state structure. Rather, political parties are "a product of the interaction between state structure and the underlying social cleavages" (Huber et al., 1993, p. 719). As stated previously, political parties vary along a socioeconomic spectrum (Lijphart, 1994). However, where a system is characterized by a higher number of political parties—at least greater than two—higher numbers of "interaction streams" emerge and subsequently increase the degree to which parties must cooperate in order to enact policy (Sartori, 1976).

The logic is further supported by Iversen and Stephens (2008), who found that cross-class bargaining and cooperation are furthered by the multiple political parties resulting from proportional electoral systems. The authors write that cross-class bargaining "is enabled by PR, because all major interests are represented through well-organized political parties, and because regulatory policies ... have to pass through committee systems typically based on PR and consensus bargaining" (2008, p. 606).

I argue that greater numbers of effective political parties will equate with a higher number of interests, and subsequently relevant players. In order for policy to be implemented, these various groups must compromise (Lijphart, 1999; Tsebelis, 1995). As such, multi-party systems are more likely to encourage cooperation and coordination, and subsequently lead to CMEs, while two-party systems create greater competition between interests and are likely to promote LMEs.[4] The number of effective parties in the legislature variable is drawn from the Comparative Politics Dataset I (CPDSI) data set (Armingeon, Gerber, Leimgruber, & Beyeler, 2008). Similar variables have been included in explanatory studies of welfare development (Iversen & Soskice, 2006; Martin & Swank, 2008). The effective number of political parties variable is an interval variable ranging from a low of 1.5 to 9.0 effective political parties.

I hypothesize that the existence of multiple political parties will be conducive to greater cooperation, and this cooperation will be represented by greater coordination across economic arenas. As such, we are likely to find

(1) greater degrees of market coordination, (2) a more cooperative shareholder model of corporate governance, (3) cooperative industrial relations policies, (4) greater emphasis on vocational training and education, and (5) greater cooperation between firms.

Cabinet Structures

Manow illustrates that electoral systems may reinforce asymmetries of power between competing socioeconomic groups (2009). In general, two-party systems are controlled by center-right governments, while multi-party systems are characterized by center-left dominance. He supports his claim by illustrating the strong correlation between majoritarian systems and liberal welfare states, and consensus systems and social democratic or Christian democratic welfare states.

Building on Iversen and Soskice (2006), Manow claims that the causal mechanism lies in the formation of class coalitions. The type of governing coalition largely structures the degree to which power is either concentrated or dispersed, who controls government and, subsequently, the policy arena. For example, rarely is the left-labor interest group capable of instituting policy alone. Rather, they must enter into coalitions with other groups (Huber & Stephens, 2000). As such, the majoritarian/consensus dichotomy deeply affects coalition formation and structures. Lijphart writes:

> The Westminster model concentrates executive power in a government supported by a relatively narrow parliamentary majority, whereas the consensus model favors broad coalitions in which all significant political parties and representatives of the major groups in society shape executive power. (1984, p. 46)

Iversen and Soskice's (2006) work empirically examines Lijphart's assumptions. Iversen and Soskice begin with the assumption of three classes: lower, middle, and upper, and either a proportional or plurality electoral system (2006). As Duverger has established, majoritarian systems lead to two parties, while proportional systems lead to multiple parties (1954). In a two-party system, composed of center-left and center-right parties, upper classes will support the center-right, while lower classes will support the center-left. The question emerges, however, as to the voting behavior of the middle class.

Assuming a system of regressive taxation, Iversen and Soskice contend that in two-party majoritarian systems, the middle class will align itself with the center-right (2006). Manow illustrates the logic clearly:

> If the left governs, the middle class has to fear that a left government will tax both the upper and middle classes for the exclusive benefit of the lower classes. If the right party governs, redistribution will be marginal, and the middle class hardly will be taxed. (2009, p. 104)

However, in a proportional system, the options of the middle class are less constrained. Because the left is unlikely to be able to govern by itself, it will seek to align with the middle class. Due to the necessity of maintaining the coalition, "both can agree and credibly commit to taxing the rich and sharing the revenue" (2009, p. 104). As such, center-right coalitions will likely support liberal market institutions, while center-left coalitions will likely support coordinated market institutions.

Furthermore, I draw on Riker's (1962) assumption of minimal winning coalitions, and subsequently Axelrod's (1970) theory of minimal connected winning coalitions (Lijphart, 1984). Riker's theory predicts that parties will enter into coalition in order to maximize their power in the form of holding cabinet positions. As such, they will seek to form a coalition in order to win the minimum number of parliamentary seats necessary to control the majority.

However, as Lijphart (1984) points out, Riker's theory is weakened by its lack of emphasis on the policy preferences of the parties. As such, Riker's theory must be supplemented by Axelrod's theory of minimal connected winning coalitions. Axelrod's theory contends that policy preferences matter in the formation of coalitions; that is, "coalitions will form that are both 'connected'—that is, composed of parties that are adjacent on the policy scale—and devoid of unnecessary partners" (Lijphart, 1984, p. 50).

As the majority of political parties are largely divided along socioeconomic lines (Seymour Lipset & Stein Rokkan, 1967a, 1967b), it is likely that the coalitions forming under Axelrod's assumption will also consist of similar socioeconomic interests, and subsequently possess similar economic policy preferences. Under conditions where the coalition takes the form of either single-party government, or minimal winning coalition, the dominant party will possess a greater concentration of power and thus be able to pursue their own policy aims. Under consensually oriented coalitions, namely, surplus coalitions or minority governments, power will be more dispersed, leading to greater agreement on the implemented policies. The cabinet structures measure is a dichotomous variable coded 0 and 1. A score of 1 indicates a single-party majority cabinet or a minimal winning coalition cabinet. A score of 0 indicates a minimal winning coalition, a surplus coalition, a single-party minority government, or multiparty government.

I hypothesize that majoritarian cabinet structures will represent the competition between the interests of capital and labor, while consensus cabinet structures will lead to a cooperation between capital and labor interests. As such, majoritarian cabinets are more likely to be associated with (1) limited market coordination, (2) shareholder models of corporate governance, (3) competitive industrial relations policies, (4) limited investment in vocational training and education, and lastly (5) limited cooperation between firms.

Electoral Systems

Following many comparative political economists, I contend that electoral systems matter in shaping economic structures (Cusack et al., 2007; Iversen & Soskice, 2006; Iversen & Stevens, 2008; Katzenstein, 1985; Korpi, 2006; Martin & Swank, 2008). Iversen and Soskice have illustrated that majoritarian systems are often governed by parties of the center-right, while proportional systems are governed by the center-left (2006). This is due largely in part to the middle class allying itself with the upper class in majoritarian systems, subsequently proving disadvantageous to parties of the left. The opposite bias holds true in proportional systems. Iversen and Stephens have illustrated how electoral system can shift power asymmetries through their discussion of the 1996 electoral changes in New Zealand (2008, p. 604).

First, adoption of the MMP system expanded the number of relevant political parties. Prior to the popular referendum of 1993, New Zealand politics was essentially a two-party system composed of the rightist National Party and the leftist Labour Party. However, as Duverger predicted, the move to a more proportional system brought additional parties into the political arena. For example, in 1993, the New Zealand Parliament added two additional parties: New Zealand First and Alliance.

Second, and partially a symptom of the new multi-party system, there is a much greater chance of coalition governments. Mulgan writes, "With

MMP, however, the chances that a single political party will secure a majority party have been greatly reduced" (1997, p. 102). As such, the electoral changes of 1996 correspond to an increasing number of left-led coalitions, and subsequent decline in governments led by the right (Iversen & Stevens, 2008).

In short, the New Zealand case shows that majoritarian electoral systems often favor interests of the political right, which may ultimately lead to LME systems, while proportional systems may prove conducive to the interests of the left, subsequently leading to CME systems.

The electoral systems data is drawn from the Comparative Welfare State (CWS) database (Huber, Ragin, Stephens, Brady, & Beckfield, 2004, p. 21). I examine proportional, mixed systems, and plurality systems. I create two dichotomous variables. The single-member district (SMD) variable is coded 0 and 1. A score of 1 indicates an SMD electoral system, while a score of 0 captures other electoral rules (PR or mixed). The PR variable is likewise coded 0 and 1. A score of 1 indicates PR rules, while 0 indicates other electoral rules (SMD or mixed). As such, the reference group will represent mixed electoral systems.

Constitutional Structures

Veto points can shape access to the political process. The logic posits that systems which are more encompassing of various interests, that is, those which provide greater power to the political process, will likely see competing interests use their political access to pursue utility maximization, through either negative power (halting change) or positive power (changing the status quo). Manow cites a growing literature which explains welfare state development as largely the result of veto point structures. This approach views "the institutional set-up of the political system as the decisive framework that constrains, supports, and shapes current welfare state reform" (Manow, 2001b, p. 13). I contend that a similar approach will prove conducive to explanations of economic policy preferences more broadly.

Tsebelis (1995) identifies two categories of veto players: partisan veto players and institutional veto players. Institutional veto players are those "specified by the Constitution" (Tsebelis, 1995, p. 302). Specifically, I examine federalism, bicameralism, presidentialism, the use of referenda, judicial review, and central bank independence. In political systems with multiple institutional veto players, policy change is difficult, while systems characterized by fewer institutional veto players tend to experience policy instability. I hypothesize that policy stability is an important indicator of production regime. Systems with high numbers of institutional veto players will likely produce a CME. Under such conditions actors must behave in a cooperative manner in order to address coordination problems. If actors' policy preference strays too far from the status quo, other actors with competing preferences will enact their veto power and the current state of affairs will remain.

Policy stability will lead to a decrease in the uncertainty that accompanies exchange, particularly in regard to exchange of information within the sector, corporate governance (particularly regarding investor security), and education and training systems (limiting the ability of firms to "poach" workers) (Hall & Soskice, 2001; North, 1990; Tsebelis, 1995). With the transaction costs of cooperation lowered through the existence of high numbers of institutional veto players, the interests of the economic actors to compromise and cooperate are increased. It is my contention that systems with large numbers of institutional veto players are likely to be more stable, and subsequently characterized by CMEs.

The opposite holds true for systems with few institutional veto points. Limited numbers of institutional veto points lead to policy instability which can promote increased pluralism and competition between interest groups participating in the political and economic arenas. Additionally, because of the fact that the system is based upon such deep-rooted competition, drastic changes in policy are likely, leading to instability. This instability makes competition and innovation necessary components to the functioning of the liberal market production regime.

Measures of constitutional constraints, or institutional veto points, are drawn from the Comparative Political Data Set I 1960–2006 (Armingeon et al., 2008). Specifically, I develop an additive index of constitutional structures. The measure consists of degrees of federalism, presidential versus parliamentary government, strength of bicameralism, the frequency of referenda, and degree of judicial review. The measure is coded 0–5. Lower scores indicate minimal constitutional constraints, while higher scores indicate increasing numbers of constitutional constraints.

Dependent Variables

This study broadly seeks to explain the relationship between political institutions and VOC. I hypothesize that political institutions shape economic structures. The VOC framework hypothesizes that variation in capitalist economies stems from institutional configurations which govern inter-firm relations. The logic posits that firms must interact with many different political and economic actors. Their ability to do so is largely constrained by institutional structures within four arenas: corporate governance, industrial relations, vocational training and education, and inter-firm relations (Hall & Soskice, 2001). Variation within these spheres will in turn lead to variation in the product market and innovation strategies of the firms operating within a given country. This analysis examines the effects of political institutions on these four spheres in order to better capture the effects of politics on capitalist variation.

Overarching Measures of Market Coordination

Broadly, this study seeks to identify the mechanisms linking political institutions to divergence between LMEs and CMEs. As such, the analysis begins with the examination of a dependent variable designed to measure variation between CMEs and LMEs over time. This measure will capture variation in the major arenas posed by the VOC framework, that is, corporate governance, internal firm structure, industrial relations, education and training systems, and inter-firm relations (Hall & Soskice, 2001). The variable is drawn from the CWS data set.

The variables composing the measure include the use of multi-divisional teams in firm structures, teamwork arrangements, employment security, competition between firms and suppliers, structure of firm ownership, corporatism as a function of the political system, levels of cooperation between government and interest groups, wage coordination, and the degree of business centralization. This is an interval variable coded 0–1. Higher scores indicate CME systems, while lower scores indicate LME systems. Such a measure improves upon existing measures of corporatism in regard to capitalist variation and production regime by including a number of firm-specific variables, as well as being applicable to panel data analysis (Hicks & Swank, 1992; Lijphart & Crepaz, 1991).

Following a similar strategy posed by Huber, Ragin, and Stephens's (1993) work on welfare state development, I move away from relying on one sole measure of capitalist variation. Rather, in addition to one overarching measure, I use a number of different indicators designed to capture the various aspects of VOC. The purpose here is to identify the possibility of differing causal processes affecting the component aspects of the overarching variety of capitalism. That is, it is possible that the political variables under investigation may cause different outcomes on the various aspects of VOC.

Economic Arenas of Varieties of Capitalism

The purpose of this book is to identify the relationship between political institutions and variation in capitalist systems or variation in production regimes. Soskice defines production regimes as:

> the organization of production through markets and market-related institutions. It analyzes the ways in which the microagents of capitalist systems—companies, customers, employees, owners of capital—organize and structure their interrelationships, within a framework of incentives and constraints or 'rules of the game' set by a range of market-related institutions within which the microagents are embedded. (1999, pp. 101–102)

Production regimes can be divided into two types: CMEs and LMEs. The VOC framework argues that differences between production regime stem from institutional variation within economic arenas: corporate governance, industrial relations, inter-firm relations, and education and training. This study tests the effects of the political institutions under investigation on the economic arenas. The purpose here is to identify the causal processes between political institutions and the individual economic arenas of coordinated and market economies.

Corporate Governance

By corporate governance, I refer to the ways by which firms garner financing, and how capital is "guaranteed" to investors. Corporate governance can largely be divided into two types: the shareholder model and the stakeholder model (Borsch, 2007; Hall & Soskice, 2001; Roe, 2003; Vitols, 2001). The shareholder model is characterized by individuals investing capital into a firm with the intent to reap profits through the maximization of the value of the share, usually in the short term. The stakeholder model, on the other hand, includes numerous actors, including workers, the government, and large shareholders (enterprises), who, in addition to financial goals, pursue strategic, long-term interests.

Vitols contends that the systems of corporate governance shape the product market and innovation strategies of political economies, thus leading to LME or CME regimes (2001). For example, ensuring shareholder value is crucial in LMEs. Investors demand high, rapid returns on capital, or will exit, and reinvest capital in more profitable enterprises. As such, CEOs of firms demand high levels of autonomy in order to make rapid, innovative decisions (e.g. job cuts, abandoning declining industries) in order to remain profitable in a highly competitive environment for attaining capital. In CMEs, on the other hand, pressures to produce rapid profits at higher risk are not as great as in LMEs. Dominant stakeholders, like labor, banks, and government, may demand more conservative profits in order to protect long-term strategic interests. As such, rapid changes to the status quo are difficult at best. Rather, shareholder systems will often pursue incremental improvements to existing product market strategies.

The variable capturing corporate governance is drawn from the CWS, and seeks to measure the "long-term voiced-based relationships between firms and their investors. 1 = large investors hold significant ownership shares for long periods; 0.5 = relatively decentralized ownership but with only moderate investor turnover; 0 = decentralized ownership with a high turnover rate" (Huber et al., 2004, p. 8). As such, lower scores will represent shareholder-focused LMEs, while higher scores represent stakeholder-focused CMEs.

Industrial Relations

Variation in industrial relations is an imperative aspect of the differentiation between CMEs and LMEs. Industrial relations refer to the ability of firms to "coordinate bargaining over wages and working-conditions with their labor force, the organization, the organizations that represent labor, and other employers" (Hall & Soskice, 2001, p. 7). CMEs are categorized by strong unions, which allow for "cooperative industrial relations with the company and coordinated wage bargaining across companies," (Soskice, 1999, p. 110). On the other hand, LMEs have less regulated labor markets, that is, a great deal of freedom to hire and fire employees, which leads to weaker unions and subsequently greater control of management over employees.

I hypothesize that countries with majoritarian political institutions are likely to have weaker labor coordination, less governmental involvement in labor relations, and subsequently LME political economies (Soskice, 2007). In measuring variation in industrial relations, I draw on the CWS data set variable measuring cooperation between government and interest groups, specifically labor and business. The measure is coded "1 = relatively cooperative interaction between cohesive government agencies and coordinated business and labor organizations; 0.5 = moderate cooperation; 0 = relatively combative, conflictual relationships between fragmented state agencies and interest group organizations" (Huber et al., 2004, p. 9). Higher scores indicate more cooperative industrial relations, while lower scores indicate more competitive industrial relations.

Vocational Training and Education

The vocational training and education arena examines coordination problems between firms and the workforce. That is, "firms face the problem of securing a workforce with suitable skills while workers face the problem of deciding how much to invest in what skills" (Hall & Soskice, 2001, p. 7).

Various types of skills are required by different product market strategies. Workers, acting rationally, will only invest in those required skills if there is a long-term guarantee in employment and wages. In order to ensure that workers invest in the necessary skill types—industry specific, firm specific, or general—there must be institutions in place that protect workers' skill investment in the face of uncertainty (Estevez-Abe et al., 2001).

In capturing employment protection I draw on a variable designed to measure "long-term employment security guaranteed by firms: 1 = long-term (in some cases lifetime) employment security common in large firms; 0.5 = some firms provide medium- or long-term security (facilitated by a relatively low unemployment rate); 0 = unemployment security relatively uncommon" (Huber et al., 2004).

Inter-Firm Relations

As Hall and Soskice point out, "inter-firm relations" is "a term we use to cover the relationships a company forms with other enterprises, and notably its suppliers or clients" (2001, p. 7). The variable, business confederation, is designed to capture the degree to which business confederations are centralized.

As Hicks and Kenworthy (1998) point out, under conditions in which business interests are highly decentralized, the potential of individual firms to pursue a strategy of "rent-seeking" is especially high. The authors write,

"The greater the fragmentation among firms and individual industry associations, the more likely it is that each will seek benefits only for itself rather than society as a whole" (Hicks & Kenworthy, 1998, p. 1636). Under such conditions, business interests largely operate as an exclusive group seeking to maintain a minimum number of members in order to attain a larger portion of finite collective goods (Olson, 1965).

However, where centralized business confederations are encouraged—possibly through institutional mechanisms—a larger share of society is represented in the overarching organization. The organization, here a centralized business confederation, is more representative of Olson's inclusive group (Olson, 1965). Hicks and Kenworthy write, "The more encompassing the organization—the larger the share of society that it represents—the greater its incentive to try to increase the size of its social product, since redistributive gains can be taken only at the expense of its own members (Olson 1982)" (1998, p. 1636).

In short, countries with high degrees of centralized business confederations are likely be associated with the more cooperative CMEs. Where business is largely decentralized, we are likely to find more competitive LMEs.

The inter-firm relations variable is designed to capture the degree to which business confederations are centralized. "1 = central business confederation with substantial authority over members and weakly contested by competing confederations, in some cases with government involvement; 0.5 central confederation with moderate authority and/or moderately contested by competitors; 0 = fragmentation among business federations and/or central federation with little authority over members" (Huber et al., 2004, p. 9). As such, higher scores represent CMEs, while low scores represent LMEs.

Conclusion

Since at least the 1960s, "The central question for comparative political economy ... has been how to explain the absence of convergence upon a common form of industrial society, and the continued distinctiveness of national capitalisms" (Howell, 2003, p. 241). One of the most recent and popular explanations of capitalist variation is the varieties of capitalist paradigm. This approach contends that variation within five economic institutional arenas shapes the behavior of firms and subsequently leads to either CMEs or LMEs.

I find this explanation lacking. The behavior of the firm does not occur in a political vacuum. Rather, behaviors are still constrained, or otherwise shaped, by the political institutions present in a country (Korpi, 1983). As such, I contend that capitalist diversity largely stems from variation between the macro-political institutions that characterize different countries. Specifically, I contend that political institutions shape and constrain the political and economic actors participating in a given political economy, and subsequently develop a specific capitalist economy.

Chapter 3 will explain my proposed methodology to be used to test the linkages between political institutions and capitalist economies. I will establish independent and dependent variables, proposed relationships, and illustrate the techniques—qualitative and quantitative—designed to test the proposed causal process.

Notes

1. I recognize that in the post-industrial era, the relationship between left and right and class divisions have become somewhat blurred. Esping-Andersen (1999) has argued that new types of cleavage structures are emerging in the post-industrial era. Specifically he cites cleavages between private and public sector employees, and between the privileged employed and the "other." Such cleavages may ultimately form what Esping-Andersen refers to as a "proto-class." However, I argue that such proto-classes remain largely divided between right and left, albeit with the right moving slightly left in order to protect their reputations in the face of necessary austerity programs in order to maintain a winning constituency.
2. Although the capital-labor dichotomy is useful, it is important to clarify my rejection of Marxian normative bias favoring labor. I adhere to a more empirical conception of competing interests. As such, I adopt a neorealist approach to class distinction. The neorealist conception of political economy is well illustrated by Amable and Palombarini (2009, p. 129).
3. However, we should not consider power asymmetries as committing solely zero-sum outcomes between rival groups. Rather, situations may arise during which cooperation between actors occurs, or at a minimum, actors are willing to adopt second-order preferences. Such was the case of the "historical compromise" between labor and employers in Sweden. (Korpi, 2006). It is important to note that

such a "historical compromise" was in part the result of the consensus of the political regime creating an environment conducive to coordination and cooperation between competing interests.

4. I recognize that multi-party systems have not always been equated with cooperation and compromise, that is, the French Fourth Republic and Weimar Germany. However, over the past 60 years, due in part to the adoption of voting thresholds following World War II, multi-party systems have proved much less polarized and more consensual and, thus, have largely avoided a replay of either the French or German experiences of the early twentieth century.

References

Amable, B. (2003). *The diversity of modern capitalism*. Oxford and New York: Oxford University Press.

Amable, B., & Palombarini, S. (2009). A neorealist approach to institutional change and the diversity of capitalism. *Socioeconomic Review, 7*(1), 123–143.

Armingeon, K., Gerber, M., Leimgruber, P., & Beyeler, M. (2008). *Comparative political data set 1960–2006*. Institute of Political Science, University of Berne. Retrieved from http://www.ipw.unibe.ch/content/team/klaus_armingeon/comparative_political_data_sets/index_ger.html

Axelrod, R. (1970). *Conflict of interest: A theory of divergent goals with applications to politics*. Chicago, IL: Markham.

Birchfield, V., & Crepaz, M. (1998). The impact of constitutional structures and collective and competitive veto points on income inequality in industrialized democracies. *European Journal of Political Research, 34*, 175–200.

Boix, C. (1998). *Political parties, growth, and equality: Conservative and social democratic economic strategies in the world economy*. New York: Cambridge University Press.

Boix, C. (2003). *Democracy and redistribution*. New York: Cambridge University Press.

Borsch, A. (2007). Institutional variation and coordination patterns in CMEs: Swiss and German corporate governance strategies. In B. Hancké, M. Rhodes, & M. Thatcher (Eds.), *Beyond varieties of capitalism: Conflict, contradictions, and complementarities in the European economy*. New York: Oxford University Press.

Brady, D., & Leicht, K. (2007). *Party to inequality: Right party power and income inequality in affluent western democracies*. Luxembourg Income Study Working Paper Series.

Coffey, D., & Thornley, C. (2009). *Globalization and varieties of capitalism: New labour, economic policy and the abject state*. Hampshire: Palgrave Macmillan.

Collier, D., & Mahon, J. (1993). Conceptual 'stretching' revisited: Adapting categories in comparative analysis. *American Political Science Review, 87*(4), 845–854.
Crouch, C. (2005). *Capitalist diversity and change: Recombinant governance and institutional entrepreneurs.* New York: Oxford University Press.
Cusack, T. R., Iverson, T., & Soskice, D. (2007). Economic interests and the origin of electoral systems. *American Political Science Review, 101*(3), 373–391.
Deeg, R., & Jackson, G. (2007). Towards a more dynamic theory of capitalist variety. *Socioeconomic Review, 5*(1), 149–179.
Dowding, K. (1996). *Power.* Minneapolis: University of Minnesota Press.
Downs, A. (1957). *An economic theory of democracy.* New York: Harper Collins.
Duverger, M. (1954). *Political parties.* New York: Science Editions.
Esping-Andersen, G. (1990). *The three worlds of welfare capitalism.* Princeton: Princeton University Press.
Esping-Andersen, G. (1999). Politics without class: Postindustrial cleavages in Europe and America. In H. Kitschelt, P. Lange, G. Marks, & J. Stephens (Eds.), *Continuity and change in contemporary capitalism.* New York: Cambridge University Press.
Estevez-Abe, M., Iversen, T., & Soskice, D. (2001). Social protection and the formation of skills: A reinterpretation of the welfare state. In P. A. Hall & D. Soskice (Eds.), *Varieties of capitalism: The institutional foundations of comparative advantage.* Oxford: University of Oxford Press.
Fukuyama, F. (2006). *The end of history and the last man.* New York: Free Press.
Gerber, L. G. (1995). Corporatism and state theory: A review essay for historians. *Social Science History, 19*(3), 313–332.
Hall, P. A. (1986). *Governing the economy: The politics of state intervention in Britain and France.* New York: Oxford University Press.
Hall, P. A. (1999). The political economy of Europe. In H. Kitschelt, P. Lange, G. Marks, & J. Stephens (Eds.), *Continuity and change in contemporary capitalism.* New York: Cambridge University Press.
Hall, P. A. (2007). The evolution of varieties of capitalism in Europe. In B. Hancké, M. Rhodes, & M. Thatcher (Eds.), *Beyond varieties of capitalism: Conflict, contradictions, and complementarities in the European economy.* New York: Oxford University Press.
Hall, P. A., & Gingerich, D. W. (2004). *Varieties of capitalism and institutionanl complementarites in the macroeconomy: An empirical analysis.* Max-Planck Institute for the Study of Societies, Cologne, Germany.
Hall, P. A., & Soskice, D. W. (2001). *Varieties of capitalism: The institutional foundations of comparative advantage.* Oxford, England and New York: Oxford University Press.
Hancké, B. (2009). Introducing the debate. In B. Hancké (Ed.), *Debating varieties of capitalism.* Oxford: Oxford University Press.

Hancké, B., Rhodes, M., & Thatcher, M. (2007). *Beyond varieties of capitalism: Conflict, contradictions, and complementarities in the European economy*. Oxford: Oxford University Press.

Hibbs Jr., D. A. (1977). Political parties and macroeconomic policy. *American Political Science Review, 71*, 1467–1487.

Hibbs Jr., D. A. (1992). Partisan theory after fifteen years. *European Journal of Political Economy, 8*, 361–373.

Hicks, A., & Kenworthy, L. (1998). Cooperation and political economic performance in affluent democratic capitalism. *American Journal of Sociology, 103*(6), 1631–1672.

Hicks, A., & Swank, D. (1992). Politics, institutions, and welfare spending in industralized democracies. *American Political Science Review, 84*, 658–674.

Hirschman, A. O. (1970). *Exit, voice, and loyalty: Responses to decline in firms, organizations, and states*. Cambridge, MA: Harvard University Press.

Hooghe, L., & Marks, G. (1999). The making of a polity: The struggle over European integration. In H. Kitschelt, P. Lange, G. Marks, & J. Stephens (Eds.), *Continuity and change in contemporary capitalism*. New York: Cambridge University Press.

Howell, C. (2003). Varieties of capitalism: And then there was one? *Comparative Politics, 36*(1), 103–124.

Huber, E., Ragin, C., & Stephens, J. (1993). Social democracy, Christian democracy, constitutional structure, and the welfare state. *American Journal of Sociology, 3*, 711–749.

Huber, E., Ragin, C., Stephens, J., Brady, D., & Beckfield, J. (2004). *Comparative Welfare Data Set*. http://www.nsd.uib.no/macrodataguide/set.html?id=8&sub=1

Huber, E., & Stephens, J. (2000). Partisan governance, women's employment, and the Social democratic service state. *American Sociological Review, 65*, 323–342.

Huber, E., & Stephens, J. (2001). *Development and crisis of the welfare state: Parties and policies in global markets*. Chicago: University of Chicago Press.

Iversen, T., & Soskice, D. (2006). Electoral institutions and the politics of coalitions: Why some democracies redistribute more than others. *American Political Science Review, 100*(2), 165–181.

Iversen, T., & Soskice, D. (2009). Distribution and redistribution: The shadow of the nineteenth century. *World Politics, 61*(3), 438–486.

Iversen, T., & Stevens, J. (2008). Partisan politics, the welfare state, and three worlds of human capital formation. *Comparative Political Studies, 41*(4–5), 600–637.

Judt, T. (2005). *Postwar: A history of Europe since 1945*. New York: The Penguin Press.

Katzenstein, P. J. (1985). *Small states in world markets: Industrial policy in Europe*. Ithaca, NY: Cornell University Press.
Kitschelt, H., Lange, P., Marks, G., & Stephens, J. D. (Eds.). (1999). *Continuity and change in contemporary capitalism*. New York: Cambridge University Press.
Knight, J. (1992). *Institutions and social conflict*. Cambridge: Cambridge University Press.
Knight, J., & Sened, I. (Eds.). (1995). *Explaining social institutions*. Ann Arbor: University of Michigan Press.
Korpi, W. (1983). *The democratic class struggle*. London: Routledge & Kegan Paul.
Korpi, W. (2006). Power resources and employer-centered approaches in explanations of welfare states and varieties of capitalism: Protagonists, consenters, and antagonists. *World Politics, 58*(2), 167–206.
Lehmbruch, G. (1979). Consociational democracy, class conflict, and the new corporatism. In P. Schmitter & G. Lehmbruch (Eds.), *Trends toward corporatist intermediation*. London: Sage.
Lijphart, A. (1984). *Democracies: Patterns of majoritarian and consensus democracies in twenty-one countries*. New Haven, CT: Yale University Press.
Lijphart, A. (1994). *Electoral systems and party systems: A study of twenty-seven democracies, 1945–1990*. New York: Oxford University Press.
Lijphart, A. (1999). *Patterns of democracy: Government forms and performance in thirty-six countries*. New Haven, CT: Yale University Press.
Lijphart, A., & Crepaz, M. M. L. (1991). Corporatism and consensus democracy in eighteen countries: Conceptual and empirical linkages. *British Journal of Political Science, 21*(2), 235–246.
Lipset, S., & Rokkan, S. (1967a). Cleavage structures, party systems, and voter alignments: An introduction. In S. Lipset & S. Rokkan (Eds.), *Party systems and voter alignments: Cross-national perspectives*. New York: The Free Press.
Lipset, S., & Rokkan, S. (Eds.). (1967b). *Party systems and voter alignments: Cross-national perspectives*. New York: The Free Press.
Manow, P. (2001a). *The political construction of a coordinated political economy*. Paper presented at the Business Interests and the Varieties of Capitalism: Historical Origins and Future Possibilities Meeting.
Manow, P. (2001b). Welfare state building and coordinated capitalism in Japan and Germany. In W. Streeck & K. Yamamura (Eds.), *The origins of nonliberal capitalism: Germany and Japan in comparison*. Ithaca, NY: Cornell University Press.
Manow, P. (2009). Electoral rules, class coalitions and welfare state regimes, or how to explain Esping-Andersen with Stein Rokkan. *Socio-Economic Review, 7*, 101–121.
Mares, I. (2001). Firms in the welfare state: When, why, and how does social policy matter to employers? In T. Iversen & D. Soskice (Eds.), *Varieties of capi-*

talism: The institutional foundations of comparative advantage. New York: Oxford University Press.

Mares, I. (2003). *The politics of social risk: Business and welfare state development*. New York: Cambridge University Press.

Marshall, T. H. (1964). *Class, citizenship, and social development*. Chicago: Chicago University Press.

Martin, C. J., & Swank, D. (2008). The political origins of coordinated capitalism: Business organizations, party systems, and state structure in the age of innocence. *American Political Science Review, 102*(2), 181–198.

Molina, O., & Rhodes, M. (2007). The political economy of adjustment in mixed market economies: A study of Spain and Italy. In B. Hancké, M. Rhodes, & M. Thatcher (Eds.), *Beyond varieties of capitalism: Conflict, contradictions, and complementarities in the European economy* (pp. 223–252). New York: Oxford University Press.

Mulgan, R. (1997). *Politics in New Zealand*. Auckland: Auckland University Press.

North, D. C. (1981). *Structure and change in economic history* (1st ed.). New York: Norton.

North, D. C. (1990). *Institutions, institutional change, and economic performance*. Cambridge: Cambridge University Press.

Olson, M. (1965). *The logic of collective action: Public goods and the theory of groups*. Cambridge: Harvard University Press.

Olson, M. (1982). *The rise and decline of nations: Economic growth, stagflation, and social rigidities*. New Haven: Yale University Press.

Orloff, A. S. (1993). Gender and the social rights of citizenship: The comparative analysis of gender relations and welfare states. *American Sociological Review, 58*, 303–328.

Phelps, E. (2006). Dynamic capitalism. *Wall Street Journal, 10*, A14.

Pierson, P. (1994). *Dismantling the welfare state?* New York: Cambridge University Press.

Pierson, P. (Ed.). (2001). *The new politics of the welfare state*. Oxford: Oxford University Press.

Pontusson, J. (1995). From comparative public policy to political economy: Putting political institutions in their place and taking interests seriously. *Comparative Political Studies, 28*(1), 117–147.

Przeworski, A., & Tenue, H. (1970). *Logic of comparative social inquiry*. New York: Wily-Interscience.

Quinn, D. P., & Shapiro, R. Y. (1991). Business political power: The case of taxation. *American Political Science Review, 85*(3), 851–874.

Riker, W. H. (1962). *The theory of political coalitions*. New Haven, CT: Yale University Press.

Roe, M. J. (2003). *Political determinants of corporate governance*. Oxford: Oxford University Press.

Rothstein, B., Samanni, M., & Teorell, J. (2010). Quality of government, political power and the welfare state. *The Quality of Government Institute, University of Gothenburg, 6*, 124.

Sartori, G. (1970). Concept formation in comparative politics. *American Political Science Review, 64*(4), 1033–1053.

Sartori, G. (1976). *Parties and party systems: A framework for analysis*. Cambridge, England and New York: Cambridge University Press.

Schmidt, V. A. (2007). *Changes in comparative political economy: Taking labor out, bringing the state back in, putting the firm front and center*. Paper presented at the European Studies Association Meeting.

Schmidt, V. A. (2009). Putting the political back into political economy by bringing the state back in yet again. *World Politcs, 61*(3), 516–546.

Schmitter, P. (1979a). Modes of interest intermediation and models of societal change in Western Europe. In P. Schmitter & G. Lehmbruch (Eds.), *Trends towards corporatist intermediation*. London: Sage.

Schmitter, P. (1979b). Still the century of corporatism? In P. Schmitter & G. Lehmbruch (Eds.), *Trends toward corporatist intermediation*. London: Sage Publications.

Schmitter, P., & Lehmbruch, G. (Eds.). (1979). *Trends towards corporatist intermediation*. London: Sage.

Shonfield, A. (1965). *Modern capitalism: The changing balance of public and private power*. London and New York: Oxford University Press.

Simmons, B. A. (1999). The internationalization of capital. In H. Kitschelt, P. Lange, G. Marks, & J. Stephens (Eds.), *Continuity and change in contemporary capitalism*. New York: Cambridge University Press.

Soskice, D. (1999). Divergent production regimes: Coordinated and uncoordinated market economies in the 1980s and 1990s. In H. Kitschelt, P. Lange, G. Marks, & J. D. Stephens (Eds.), *Continuity and change in contemporary captialism* (pp. 101–134). New York: Cambridge University Press.

Soskice, D. (2007). Macroeconomics and varieties of capitalism. In B. Hancké, M. Rhodes, & M. Thatcher (Eds.), *Beyond varieties of capitalism: Conflict, contradictions, and complementarities in the European economy*. New York: Oxford University Press.

Swank, D. (2001). Political institutions and welfare state restructuring: The impact of institutions on social policy change in developed democracies. In P. Pierson (Ed.), *The new politics of the welfare state*. New York: Oxford University Press.

Swank, D. (2002). *Global capital, political instiutions, and policy change in developed welfare states*. New York: Cambridge University Press.

Toennies, F. (1961). Estates and classes (R. Bendix, Trans.). In R. Bendix & S. M. Lipset (Eds.), *Class, status and power: A reader in social stratification* (5th ed., pp. 49–63). New York: The Free Press.

Tsebelis, G. (1995). Decision making in political systems: Veto players in presidentialism, parliamentarism, multicameralism and multipartyism. *British Journal of Political Science, 25*(3), 289–325.

Vitols, S. (2001). Varieties of corporate governance: Comparing Germany and the UK. In P. A. Hall & D. Soskice (Eds.), *Varieties of capitalism: The institutional foundations of comparative advantage*. New York: Oxford University Press.

Vowles, J. (1995). The politics of electoral reform in New Zealand. *International Political Science Review, 15*, 95–115.

CHAPTER 3

A Mixed-Method Approach to Capitalist Variation

This chapter will lay out the methodology to be used in testing the proposed relationships between political institutions and variation in capitalist systems. I begin by discussing the values of a mixed-method approach by illustrating the pros and cons of quantitative and qualitative research techniques. I then illustrate the added value of applying a combination of the two.

I then discuss the quantitative model to be used, and the subsequent research questions to be answered. These are: what political institutions are related to variation in capitalist systems, what political institutions serve as the strongest indicators of coordinated market or liberal market economies, and, what are the effects of specific political institutions on the characteristic arenas of the political economy which structure the CME and LME dichotomy. Additionally, I address quantitative case selection specifically focusing on members of Organisation for Economic Co-operation and Development (OECD). I then address the time frame under quantitative investigation, 1960 through 2006.

Next, I discuss the qualitative case studies which supplement the quantitative analyses. The qualitative approach is designed to answer three questions. First, do the proposed causal relationships between political institutions and varieties of capitalism exist in real-world cases? Second, how do the political institutions affect economic structures in reality? Third, what alternative or intervening variables become apparent through the qualitative research? I then move on to qualitative delimitations.

M.P. Arsenault, *The Effects of Political Institutions on Varieties of Capitalism*, DOI 10.1007/978-3-319-50892-4_3

Mixed-Methods

Inference is an imperative goal of social science research. The purpose of inference is to explain complex events. In doing so, inference can be divided into two categories: descriptive and causal. Descriptive inference refers to establishing generalizations from observed phenomena to a broader set of cases. Causal inference refers to the "process of reaching conclusions about causation on the basis of observed data" (H. E. Brady & Collier, 2004, p. 276). Generally speaking, well-structured social science research should not isolate descriptive and causal inference. Rather, all social science "involves the dual goals of describing and explaining" (G. King, Keohane, & Verba 1994, p. 34).

However, not all research methodologies are able to "describe and explain" social phenomena equally. Scholars must recognize that "strengths and weakness are to be found in both qualitative and quantitative methods" (H. E. Brady & Collier, 2004, p. 6). As such, I apply a mixed-method approach to analyze the relationship between political institutions and capitalist variation. A triangulation of methods will provide greater leverage over the phenomena under investigation (G. King et al., 1994; Tarrow, 1995). Quantitative techniques will be used to establish descriptive and causal inference, while case studies and process-tracing procedures will be applied to illustrate causal mechanisms, and further test theoretical propositions.

Quantitative Analysis

Quantitative analyses will be applied to establish which political variables shape variation in capitalist systems, ascertain the causal weight of the proposed variables, and, lastly, capture the effects of the proposed variables on the specific strategies of the firms in the various capitalist economies. The answers to these important questions will identify relevant causal variables, and thus structure the subsequent qualitative case studies designed to test the proposed causal processes.

Quantitative techniques prove useful in establishing causal and descriptive inference. Causally, quantitative analysis will prove constructive in establishing the effects of the political institution variables on the economic structures under investigation. Here, independent variables include partisanship and policy legacies, electoral system, the effective number of political parties, coalition structure, and constitutional constraints.

Dependent variables include overall degree of market coordination, as well as the arenas that characterize variation in production regime: corporate governance, internal firm structure, industrial relations, education and training, and inter-firm relations (Hall & Soskice, 2001). Subsequently, based on the constant effect assumption, the value of the dependent variable should fluctuate with changing values of the independent variable, lending credence to the proposed causal theory.

Descriptively, statistical techniques are used to establish that the proposed relationships exist across a broad number of observations. By transferring knowledge about a specific case or observation to the broader population, researchers develop a better understanding of unobserved cases, and add validity and reliability to the proposed theory.[1]

As stated previously, the main purpose of this study is to explore the relationships linking political institutions to variation in capitalist economic systems. However, the establishment "of causality is logically prior to the identification of causal mechanisms" (G. King et al., 1994, p. 86). In order to establish causality, the quantitative analysis seeks to answer three questions.

First, what political institutions are related to variation in capitalist systems? In answering this question, the analysis will "distinguish between the systematic component from the nonsystematic component of the phenomena we study" and assist in identifying the crucial independent variables with which to frame the qualitative case studies (G. King et al., 1994, p. 56).

Second, I seek to establish which political institutions serve as the strongest indicator of capitalist variation. The purpose is to assist in estimating causal effects and lend support to the causal theory.

Lastly, the analysis seeks to discover the relationship between specific political institutions, and the economic institutional arenas—corporate governance, internal firm structure, industrial relations, education and training systems, and inter-firm relations—which compose the CME/LME dichotomy. By examining the effects of political institutions on the disaggregated arenas of LMEs and CMEs, it is hoped that multiple causal processes, if evident, will be revealed.

Modeling Strategy

The analysis uses time-series cross-sectional (TSCS) data for 18 advanced industrial societies covering the years 1960–2000. The data are drawn from multiple sources: the Comparative Welfare Dataset (CWD) (Huber,

Table 3.1 Independent and dependent variables

Variables	*Source*
Dependent variables	
Neocorporatism scale based on 11 measures of business, labor, and government relations	Huber et al., 2004
Firm ownership capturing centralized or decentralized ownership and investment type	Huber et al., 2004
Wage coordination capturing centralized or firm-level wage negotiation	Huber et al., 2004
Job security capturing long-term versus short-term job security guarantees	Huber et al., 2004
Government cooperation with business and labor interest groups	Huber et al., 2004
Political variables	
Left cabinet as a cumulative measure of left seats in cabinet from 1946 to observed year	Huber et al., 2004
Center cabinet (see Left cabinet)	Huber et al., 2004
Right cabinet (see Left cabinet)	Huber et al., 2004
Proportional representation electoral system	Huber et al., 2004
Mixed electoral system	Huber et al., 2004
Single-member district/plurality	Huber et al., 2004
Effective number of parties in the legislature	Armingeon et al., 2008
Coalition structure	Armingeon et al., 2008
Constitutional structures/veto points	Armingeon et al., 2008
Controls	
Gross domestic product per capita	Huber et al., 2004
Unemployment as percentage of civilian labor force	Armingeon et al., 2008
Inflation as measured in annual percentage change in consumer price index	Huber et al., 2004
Gross public expenditures as a percentage of GDP	Huber et al., 2004
Economic openness as measured by sum of imports and exports as percentage of GDP	Armingeon et al., 2008

Ragin, Stephens, Brady, & Beckfield, 2004), the Database of Political Institutions (DPI) (T. Beck, Clarke, Groff, Keefer, & Walsh, 2001), and the Comparative Political Data Set I 1960–2000 (CPDSI) (Armingeon, Gerber, Leimgruber, & Beyeler, 2008). Table 3.1 illustrates the variables and sources to be used in the analysis.

Quantitative Case Selection and Time Frame

World War II left much of the globe in political and economic ruin. A return to political and economic stability proved a long and arduous process. It was not until the late 1950s to early 1960s that Europe and Japan regained a large degree of political and economic independence and stability, coupled with a solidification of democratic governance (Hall, 2007; Judt, 2005). Due to the political and economic turmoil that characterized the early post-war years, the quantitative analyses focus on the years 1960 through 2006. It was in this era, specifically in the earlier years, that the advanced industrial societies began to adopt modern and distinctive economic policy strategies and production regimes, or specific varieties of capitalism (Hall, 2007; Shonfield, 1965).

In exploring the advanced industrial societies, I focus on the 18 member states of the OECD.[2] The OECD, established in December 1960 (the starting point of this book), ushered in a new era of capitalism in the West. Countries moved away from the neomercantilist and protection policies of the past and adopted a greater system of economic liberalism designed to promote the goals of "economic growth, trade liberalization and development" (G. Evans & Newnham, 1998, p. 405). As such, the emergence of the OECD serves as a useful starting point in the development of modern capitalist systems. By concentrating on this era, this book can explain what led to the emergence of our current system, and suggest predictions for future behaviors.

Limitations of Quantitative Methods

Quantitative techniques are not without limitations. Specifically, statistical analyses are characterized by a degree of uncertainty in results, limited identification of complex causal processes, an imperfect understanding of the role of path dependency, and a lack of emphasis on "sequential interactions between individual agents" (George & Bennett, 2005, pp. 12–13).

A significant problem of establishing causal inference from quantitative analysis is that "We will never know a causal inference for certain" (G. King et al., 1994, p. 79). Uncertainty stems from a number of limitations of statistical approaches. Most importantly, quantitative analyses assume perfect model specificity, that is, all independent variables affecting the outcome are included in the model. The exclusion of relevant variables—omitted variable bias—can severely skew the inference proposed in the analysis. Second, quantitative methods are limited in the ability to recognize multiple causation, or "equifinality" (George & Bennett, 2005, p. 13). That is, the causal logic proposed by the model may fail to distinguish the effects of any number of intervening variables that lie between independent and dependent variables. This, again, can bias the inference proposed by the model.

In order to add validity and reliability to the quantitative assumptions of inference, it is useful to identify the causal mechanisms linking proposed cause and effect. Causal mechanisms are often established through an examination of a causal process, that is, “A sequence of events or steps through which causation occurs” (H. E. Brady & Collier, 2004, p. 277). The identification of causal mechanisms and the establishment of causal processes will be furthered through the use of case studies using process-tracing techniques.

Qualitative Analyses

Quantitative analyses are useful in answering “how much” questions, but are less applicable to answering inquiries into the “how or why” of social phenomena. David Laitin writes, “If statistical work addresses questions of propensities, narratives address the questions of process” (2002, p. 5). In order to more fully explain the causal linkages between political institutional configurations and variation in the capitalist systems, process-tracing techniques will be applied.

> [Process tracing] attempts to trace the links between possible causes and observed outcomes. In process-tracing, the researcher examines historics, archival documents, interview transcripts and other sources to see whether the causal process a theory hypothesizes or implies in a case is in fact evident in the sequence and values of the intervening variable. (George & Bennett, 2005, p. 6)

Process tracing consists of examining evidence within a case or cases selected to represent a specified complex social process. Process tracing can be inductive or deductive in nature. Inductive analyses largely seek to generate theory, while deductive analyses test existing theory.

The cases in this analysis will largely be deductive in nature, that is, I will use existing “theories and hypotheses to make empirical predictions, which are then … tested against [the qualitative] data” (H. E. Brady & Collier, 2004, p. 284). The deductive approach is especially pertinent for the current analyses in that rival hypotheses exist regarding the role of political institutions on variation in capitalist systems (Amable, 2003; Crouch, 2005; Hall, 2007; Iversen, 2007; Martin & Swank, 2008).

Andrew Bennett describes the process-tracing technique as consisting of a number of steps (2008). First, explanations and alternative explanations of a given phenomenon are developed. Second, the types of evidence—either present or absent—which will lend credence to, or call into question, the proposed explanation must be established. Third, "we seek out both the expected and the potentially surprising evidence from various sources, taking into account biases that these sources may reflect" (2008, p. 704). Fourth, based on the evidence, a new confidence level of the proposed explanation is developed. Lastly, depending on the strength or weakness of the evidence, the strength of the general theoretical assumptions underpinning the proposed relationship is reexamined.

In sum, the value of process-tracing techniques lies in the testing of proposed theory explaining the causal linkages between political institutions and political economies. As such, this approach will draw on Lijphart's conceptualization of theory-confirming or theory-infirming case studies (1971).

The cases are selected in order to apply Eckstein's conception of "tough tests" of theory. Such "tough tests" are applied to most-likely or least-likely cases. That is, cases "that ought, or ought not, to invalidate or confirm theories if any cases can be expected to do so" (Eckstein, 1975, p. 118). Specifically, I rely on most-likely cases. Most-likely cases are those in which "the independent variables posited by a theory are at values that strongly posit an extreme outcome" (George & Bennett, 2005, p. 121). Most-likely cases are largely used to invalidate the proposed theory. Here, if the proposed causal processes are not found to exist, then the theory that political institutional configurations shape economic structures must be called into question, and alternative explanations should be explored further.

Qualitative Case Selection and Time Frame

Case study techniques are often criticized for their quasi-experimental nature. Quasi-experimental designs resemble experimental designs, except that random selection is either not possible, or is not used. As such, case studies are susceptible to issues of selection bias.

Nonrandomized selection of cases can lead to a number of problems. First, the case selected may not be a generalizable sample of the population at large. Second, suitable degrees of variation may not be present to make valid inferences, and subsequently report inaccurate findings. I agree with King et al. that a more scientific approach to case selection is imperative in qualitative research (G. King et al., 1994; Laitin et al., 1995). However, I still recognize the trade-offs that must be made in case study analysis (Laitin et al., 1995; Przeworski & Tenue, 1970). As such, I rely on "purposive modes of sampling" as proposed by Seawright and Gerring (2008, p. 294).

The purpose of the case studies is largely to confirm the hypotheses proposed by the quantitative analysis. As such, I chose a combination of Seawright and Gerring's selection strategies (2008). I begin with diverse case selection. The goal of the diverse cases approach is to "represent the full range of values characterizing X, Y, or some particular X/Y relationship" (Seawright & Gerring, 2008, p. 300). As the objective of the analysis is largely confirmatory, I concentrate on the relationship between X and Y, specifically the relationship between relevant political institutions and variation in capitalist systems.

As the proposed variables are continuous in nature, Seawright and Gerring suggest selecting cases from both high and low values. In selecting cases, the sample of 18 OECD countries will be stratified into LME and CME regimes based on the Hall–Gingerich index of market coordination (Hall & Gingerich, 2004).

The Hall and Gingerich index measures a political economy's reliance on nonmarket forces for coordination. The measure is composed of a factor analysis of six variables: shareholder power, dispersion of control, size of stock market, level of wage coordination, degree of wage coordination, and labor turnover (Hall & Gingerich, 2004, p. 11). Shareholder power, dispersion of control, and stock market capitalization are designed to capture variance in the corporate governance arena. The level of wage coordination, degree of wage coordination, and labor turnover largely examine variation in the labor relations arena.

The index ranges from 0 to 1. High scores represent greater inter-firm coordination, while lower scores suggest greater reliance on market forces. The index confirms the basic premise of the varieties of capitalism framework, that is, economies can be divided between CME and LME production regimes. Most nations generally considered to be CMEs lie above 0.50, while most considered LMEs lie below 0.50 (Hall & Gingerich, 2004). Table 3.2 reports the Hall–Gingerich scores for the population of cases under investigation.

I select one extreme case from the CME category and one from the LME category. As the goal of the research design is to conduct most-likely

Table 3.2 Hall–Gingerich measures of market coordination

Country	*Hall–Gingerich score*
Austria	1
Germany	0.95
Italy	0.87
Norway	0.76
Belgium	0.74
Japan	0.74
Finland	0.72
Denmark	0.7
France	0.69
Sweden	0.69
The Netherlands	0.66
Switzerland	0.51
Australia	0.36
Ireland	0.29
New Zealand	0.21
Canada	0.13
United Kingdom	0.07
United States	0

tests of theory, I concentrate on those cases with either high or low values on the Hall–Gingerich scale. Specifically, I select Germany and the United Kingdom as strong CME and LME countries respectively.[3]

Furthermore, variation must exist within independent variables. By applying Lijphart's (1999) majoritarian versus consensus typology, variation in the independent variables—political institutions—can be established. Figure 3.1 illustrates a scatter plot of Vatter's (2009) updated measure of Lijphart's Executive-Parties dimension. I limit this initial analysis to the parties-executive dimension as my logic parallels that of Lijphart and Crepaz who argue that "the central element of this dimension of consensus democracy may well be described as *party concentration* or the concentration of partisan interests" (1991, p. 236). This better represents my prime concern with partisan legacies, and electoral systems.

As Fig. 3.1 illustrates, the United Kingdom is the extreme case located in the lower-left quadrant, suggesting a strong majoritarian system. Germany (FRG) is located in the upper-right quadrant, suggesting a much more consensual political regime. As such, Fig. 3.1 illustrates a great deal of

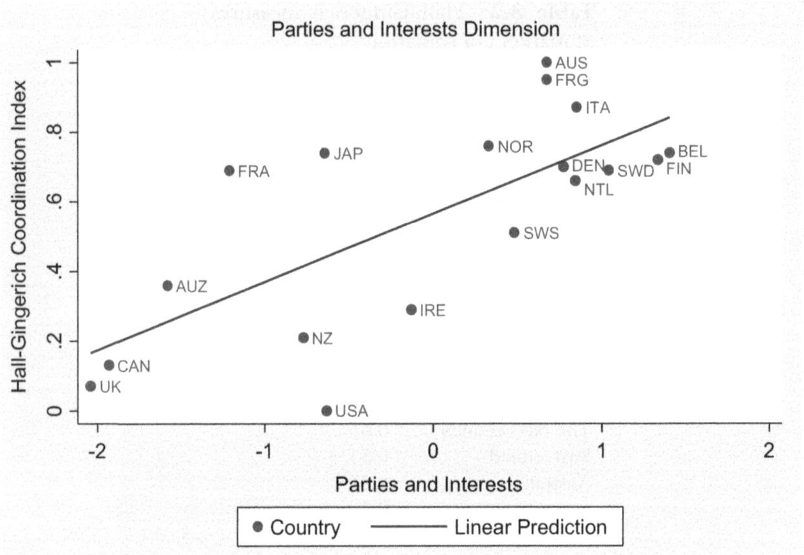

Fig. 3.1 Political institutions and market coordination

variation between the two cases on both the independent and dependent variables. Thus, the argument that Germany and the United Kingdom may be viewed as most-likely cases in testing the proposed causal argument holds.

In sum, as many VOC scholars have pointed out, and my purposive sampling confirms, Britain represents an ideal LME, while Germany represents CMEs (Hall & Soskice, 2001; Howell, 2007; Schmidt, 2009; Wood, 2001).

Britain maintains the typical aspects of a liberal market economy. As Howell writes:

> Britain has the main institutional elements of a liberal market economy as weakly organized employer and labor associations prevent wage or sill coordination in the labor market, and the dominance of equity markets in the provision of investment capital prevents coordination in financial markets. (2007, p. 203)

Politically, Britain serves as an ideal majoritarian democracy (Lijphart, 1984, 1994, 1999). Britain maintains an SMD electoral system, two major political parties, essentially a unicameral legislature, a strong executive, and generally minimum winning coalition governments (Mannin, 2010; Norton, 2007).

Germany, on the other hand, epitomizes CMEs (Hall & Soskice, 2001; Howell, 2003; Streeck & Yamamura, 2001; Vitols, 2001; Wood, 2001). That is, Germany tends to have nonmarket coordination, promotes an emphasis on skill formation, supports stakeholder corporate governance models, and upholds coordination among employer groups (Hall & Soskice, 2001; Howell, 2003). Furthermore, Germany possesses many of the characteristics of a consensus-oriented political system: a federated system, a proportional representational electoral system, multiple political parties, a bicameral legislature, and consensually oriented coalition structures.

Additionally, the German case provides a good deal of generalizability to other continental European advanced industrial countries. Manow writes:

> several recent contributions to the literature on comparative political economy have indicated that a number of European countries are in the process of converging their systems and have come to more closely resemble the 'German model with respect to wage-bargaining practices, macroeconomic management and the organization of the welfare state'. (2001, p. 150)

The German political economy epitomizes both consensus political regimes and CMEs. Britain, on the other hand, epitomizes both majoritarian political systems and LMEs. Additionally, these two states faced a tremendous amount of change to the international economic system in the 1980s (Kitschelt, Lange, Marks, & Stephens 1999). Convergence theories predicted that such changes would force the advanced industrial states to adopt, or converge on, neoliberal policies. Britain adopted the most radical neoliberal reforms of the European states, perhaps most readily illustrated by Margaret Thatcher's attack on organized labor, and the privatization of many state-run organizations (Hall, 1986; Schmidt, 2007). Germany, on the other hand, remained relatively unchanged, maintaining an overall system of cooperation between business, labor, and the state (Schmidt, 2007, pp. 5–6).

The pressures for neoliberal reforms of the 1980s can serve as a natural experiment to test the hypothesis that political institutions shape varieties of capitalism. Both countries faced exogenous economic changes to the world economy. Such changes were predicted to affect the domestic economies of different states. That is, states would ultimately be forced toward a convergence around neoliberal policies. However, these states reacted differently to these international pressures and maintained their particular variety of capitalism. I contend that the crucial independent variables that allowed Britain to adopt reforms, while German essentially maintained the status quo, lie in the institutional differences between the political regimes of both countries.

Institutional Change on Economic Structures: New Zealand

In addition to the British and German cases, I also examine the effects of political institutional change in New Zealand on economic structures. Like the German and British case—as well as many other OECD countries—New Zealand faced pressures to adopt neoliberal reforms in the 1980s. However, unlike the British and German cases, New Zealand made sweeping changes to its electoral system in 1996. Such changes to electoral institutions are an extremely rare event, and as such make the New Zealand case a unique natural experiment with which to test the effects of political institutions on economic structures (Lijphart, 1994; Vowles, Aimer, Banducci, & Karp, 1998).

In order to exploit this unique case, I apply a "before-after" design as suggested by George and Bennett (2005). That is, "Instead of trying to find two different cases that are comparable in all ways but one, the investigator may be able to achieve 'control' by dividing a single longitudinal case into two sub-cases" (George & Bennett, 2005, p. 166). Here the New Zealand case will be divided at the instrumental 1996 election, the first under new mixed-member proportional rules. I will examine a number of economic variables throughout the 1970s and 1980s prior the institutional reforms of 1996. I then reexamine the economic measures following the institutional change in order to identify the effects of political reform.

A Note on Qualitative Data

In addition to a tracing of historical processes, the case studies under investigation—Germany, the United Kingdom, and New Zealand—will be framed by the quantitative measures of economic structures drawn from Casey (2009). Casey's data seeks to establish comparable measures of various capitalist systems, thus filling a significant gap in the comparative political economy literature. The data examine 24 advanced industrial democracies from 1970 to 2005. Casey examines three major aspects of comparative capitalism, namely, the organization of labor, the organization of business, and state intervention. These three indices are then combined to form an overarching measure of comparative capitalism. This section will review the construction of Casey's indices, as well as the benefits and potential problems that accompany the use of said data.

Casey's first measure examines labor organization. The measure broadly examines "labor markets, labor-management relations, and skills" (2009, p. 264). Specifically, the measure captures trade union density, collective bargaining agreements, coordination of wage-setting, and education levels, including vocational training. As such, Casey's measure approximates an aggregate measure of the industrial relations, vocational training and education, and "employees" categories proposed by Hall and Soskice (2001).

The second measure examines business organization. Broadly, the measure examines corporate finance, corporate governance, and inter-firm relations. Specifically, the variable measures stock market capitalization, percentage of widely held firms, and an "'independence indicator' to characterize the degree of independence of a company in regard to its shareholders" (Casey, 2009, p. 266). Such a measure largely captures the structure of corporate governance types used by Hall and Soskice (2001) to differentiate liberal market and coordinated market production regimes.

The third measure examines the degree to which the state may intervene in the economy. The measure includes the size of the government, as measured by the degree of spending and taxation, the degree of business and labor regulation, unemployment benefits, and active labor market policies.

The underlining variables composing these three measures are normalized and the averaged scores generate a scaled variable ranging from 0 to 1. Lower scores represent more LMEs, while higher scores represent more CMEs. "The three sub-indices were than averaged into a single 'CC Index' [comparative capitalism index]" (Casey, 2009, p. 267).

Casey's data have made significant moves toward developing generalizable indicators of the most important aspects of comparative capitalism, and his measurements cover a significant time frame. As such, Casey has developed one of the only cross-national, time-variable measures of comparative capitalism. Still, for all its merits, the data does face some potential problems that will be addressed in the following section.

First, as Casey readily admits, the creation of a comparative capitalism index relies on publicly available comparable data across a large number of countries. However, some of the concepts that characterize the varieties of capitalism typology—corporate governance, industrial relations, vocational training, inter-firm relations—are not easily captured by the available data. Such issues are most readily apparent in the measures of education and training in the labor organization index, and measures of inter-firm relations in the business organization index. Education and training systems vary widely by country and are not easily comparable. Levels of inter-firm cooperation are equally problematic as many relationships are informal and not readily operationalized in generalizable data (Casey, 2009). As such, Casey's data will "offer an approximation—although a highly useful one—rather than a mathematically precise measurement" (2009, p. 262). Following Casey's advice, this study supplements the comparative capitalism measures with qualitative investigation.

Second, the Casey measure, like many comparative political economy datasets,[4] does suffer from some incidents of missing data. For most of the variables in Casey's measures, data was available beginning in 1970. In some cases, available data begins in or about 1980. For example, the years examining coverage of collective bargaining encompass the years from 1980 to 2000. As such, Casey's indices have "creat[ed] a workably complete data set back to the early 1980s," the starting point for the qualitative aspects of this investigation (Casey, 2009, p. 262).

Although the Casey data does pose some methodological problems, the benefits of using a comparable measure of changes in capitalist economies over time, and one that offers change in the subsequent components of the varieties of capitalism framework, far outweigh its limitations.

Conclusion

This study applies a mixed-method approach in order to best investigate the relationship between political institutions and variation in capitalist systems. The quantitative analyses—using OLS regression with PCSE—will identify (a) the relevant political institution causal variables, (b) the strength and direction of relationships, and (c) the causal effects of the political institution variables on the five arenas of firm relations.

The independent variables identified and confirmed through the quantitative chapter will then be used to structure the qualitative investigation into the causal mechanisms linking political institutions and varieties of capitalism. Specifically, I trace the ways in which the political institutions shape the behaviors of economic and political actors in Germany and Britain in the 1980s. Both countries faced significant pressures to adopt neoliberal policies in light of changes to the international political economy. However, only Britain—a strong majoritarian system—adopted significant neoliberal reforms. I contend that the variation in political institutions, majoritarian versus consensus, was crucial in shaping the ability of Britain to adopt neoliberal reforms, while Germany was able to maintain the status quo.

Lastly, I examine the effects of changes to political institutions on capitalist production regimes. Specifically, I examine the effects of electoral reform on the New Zealand economy in the 1980s and 1990s. By applying a "before-after" research design, I will shed light on the causal relationship between political institutions and production regime.

Notes

1. This study focuses on 18 of the oldest and most established members of the OECD. As such, the generalizability would largely apply to newly emerging democratic capitalist systems, possibly the former Eastern Bloc states, members of the European Union, or newly industrialized countries.
2. Countries include Australia, Austria, Belgium, Canada, Denmark, Finland, France, Germany, Italy, Ireland, Japan, the Netherlands, New Zealand, Norway, Sweden, Switzerland, the United Kingdom, and the United States.
3. Germany is selected over Austria for two reasons. First, as Manow points out, many European countries may be converging within the CME systems, toward a German model (2001). Second, Germany remains the most economically powerful nation in Europe. The United Kingdom is selected over the United States because although the United States does possess many of the dependent variable characteristics of a typical LME, the unique structure of its political institutions limits generalizability across cases. Britain, on the other hand, is much more similar to the other majoritarian systems under investigation.

4. See, for example, similar problems in the CWD (Huber et al., 2004), the Comparative Political Dataset (Armingeon et al., 2008), and DPI (T. Beck et al., 2001).

References

Amable, B. (2003). *The diversity of modern capitalism*. Oxford and New York: Oxford University Press.

Armingeon, K., Gerber, M., Leimgruber, P., & Beyeler, M. (2008). *Comparative political data set 1960–2006*. Institute of Political Science, University of Berne. Retrieved from http://www.ipw.unibe.ch/content/team/klaus_armingeon/comparative_political_data_sets/index_ger.html

Beck, T., Clarke, G., Groff, A., Keefer, P., & Walsh, P. (2001). New tools in comparative political economy: The database of political institutions. *The World Bank Economic Review, 15*(1), 165–176.

Bennett, A. (2008). Process-tracing: A Bayesian perspective. In J. Box-Steffensmeier, H. Brady, & D. Collier (Eds.), *Oxford handbook of political methodology* (pp. 702–721). New York: Oxford University Press.

Brady, H. E., & Collier, D. (Eds.). (2004). *Rethinking social inquiry: Diverse tools, shared standards*. Lanham, MD: Rowman & Littlefield.

Casey, T. (2009). Mapping stability and change in advanced capitalisms. *Comparative European Politics, 7*(2), 255–278.

Crouch, C. (2005). *Capitalist diversity and change: Recombinant governance and institutional entrepreneurs*. New York: Oxford University Press.

Eckstein, H. (1975). Case studies in political science. In F. Greenstein & N. Polsby (Eds.), *Handbook of political science* (Vol. 7). Reading, MA: Addison-Wesley.

Evans, G., & Newnham, J. (Eds.). (1998). *The Penguin dictionary of international relations*. London: Penguin Books.

George, A., & Bennett, A. (2005). *Case studies and theory development in the social sciences*. Cambridge, MA: The MIT Press.

Hall, P. A. (1986). *Governing the economy: The politics of state intervention in Britain and France*. New York: Oxford University Press.

Hall, P. A. (2007). The evolution of varieties of capitalism in Europe. In B. Hancké, M. Rhodes, & M. Thatcher (Eds.), *Beyond varieties of capitalism: Conflict, contradictions, and complementarities in the European economy*. New York: Oxford University Press.

Hall, P. A., & Gingerich, D. W. (2004). *Varieties of capitalism and institutionanl complementarites in the macroeconomy: An empirical analysis*. Max-Planck Institute for the Study of Societies, Cologne, Germany.

Hall, P. A., & Soskice, D. W. (2001). *Varieties of capitalism: The institutional foundations of comparative advantage*. Oxford, England and New York: Oxford University Press.

Howell, C. (2003). Varieties of capitalism: And then there was one? *Comparative Politics, 36*(1), 103–124.

Howell, C. (2007). The British variety of capitalism: Institutional change, industrial relations and British politics. *British Politics, 2*, 239–263.

Huber, E., Ragin, C., Stephens, J., Brady, D., & Beckfield, J. (2004). *Comparative Welfare Data Set.* http://www.nsd.uib.no/macrodataguide/set.html?id=8&sub=1

Iversen, T. (2007). Economic shocks and varieties of government response. In B. Hancké, M. Rhodes, & M. Thatcher (Eds.), *Beyond varieties of capitalism: Conflict, contradictions, and complementarities in the European economy.* New York: Oxford University Press.

Judt, T. (2005). *Postwar: A history of Europe since 1945.* New York: The Penguin Press.

King, G., Keohane, R. O., & Verba, S. (1994). *Designing social inquiry: Scientific inference in qualitative research.* Princeton: Princeton University Press.

Kitschelt, H., Lange, P., Marks, G., & Stephens, J. D. (Eds.). (1999). *Continuity and change in contemporary capitalism.* New York: Cambridge University Press.

Laitin, D. D. (2002). Comparative politics: The state of the subdiscipline. In H. Milner & I. Katznelson (Eds.), *Political science: The state of the discipline.* New York: Norton.

Laitin, D. D., Caporaso, J. A., Collier, D., Rogowski, R., Tarrow, S., King, G., et al. (1995). The qualitative-quantitative disputation: Gary King, Robert O. Keohane, and Sidney Verba's designing social inquiry: Scientific inference in qualitative research. *American Journal of Political Science, 89*(2), 454–456.

Lijphart, A. (1971). Comparative politics and the comparative method. *The American Political Science Review, 65*(3), 682–693.

Lijphart, A. (1984). *Democracies: Patterns of majoritarian and consensus democracies in twenty-one countries.* New Haven, CT: Yale University Press.

Lijphart, A. (1994). *Electoral systems and party systems: A study of twenty-seven democracies, 1945–1990.* New York: Oxford University Press.

Lijphart, A. (1999). *Patterns of democracy: Government forms and performance in thirty-six countries.* New Haven, CT: Yale University Press.

Lijphart, A., & Crepaz, M. M. L. (1991). Corporatism and consensus democracy in eighteen countries: Conceptual and empirical linkages. *British Journal of Political Science, 21*(2), 235–246.

Mannin, M. L. (2010). *British government and politics: Balancing Europeanization and independence.* Lanham, MD: Rowman & Littlefield.

Manow, P. (2001). Welfare state building and coordinated capitalism in Japan and Germany. In W. Streeck & K. Yamamura (Eds.), *The origins of nonliberal capitalism: Germany and Japan in comparison.* Ithaca, NY: Cornell University Press.

Martin, C. J., & Swank, D. (2008). The political origins of coordinated capitalism: Business organizations, party systems, and state structure in the age of innocence. *American Political Science Review, 102*(2), 181–198.
Norton, B. F. (2007). *Politics in Britain.* Washington, DC: CQ Press.
Przeworski, A., & Tenue, H. (1970). *Logic of comparative social inquiry.* New York: Wily-Interscience.
Schmidt, V. A. (2007). *Changes in comparative political economy: Taking labor out, bringing the state back in, putting the firm front and center.* Paper presented at the European Studies Association Meeting.
Schmidt, V. A. (2009). Putting the political back into political economy by bringing the state back in yet again. *World Politcs, 61*(3), 516–546.
Seawright, J., & Gerring, J. (2008). Case selection techniques in case study research: A menu of qualitative and quantitative options. *Political Research Quarterly, 61*(2), 294–308.
Shonfield, A. (1965). *Modern capitalism: The changing balance of public and private power.* London and New York: Oxford University Press.
Streeck, W., & Yamamura, K. (Eds.). (2001). *The origins of nonliberal capitalism: Germany and Japan in comparison.* Ithaca, NY: Cornell University Press.
Tarrow, S. (1995). Bridging the quantitative-qualitative divide in political science. *American Political Science Review, 89*(2), 454–481.
Vatter, A. (2009). Lijphart expanded: Three dimensions of democracy in advanced OECD countries? *European Consortium for Political Research, 1*(1), 125–154.
Vitols, S. (2001). Varieties of corporate governance: Comparing Germany and the UK. In P. A. Hall & D. Soskice (Eds.), *Varieties of capitalism: The institutional foundations of comparative advantage.* New York: Oxford University Press.
Vowles, J., Aimer, P., Banducci, S., & Karp, J. (1998). Expectations of change. In J. Vowles, P. Aimer, S. Banducci, & J. Karp (Eds.), *Voters' victory?: New Zealand's first election under proportional representation* (pp. 1–27). Auckland: Auckland University Press.
Wood, S. (2001). Business, government, and patterns of labor market policy in Britain and the Federal Republic of Germany. In P. Hall & D. Soskice (Eds.), *Varieties of capitalism.* New York: Oxford University Press.

CHAPTER 4

Quantitative Analysis of Varieties of Capitalism

The purpose of this book is to examine and explain the relationship between political institutions and variation in capitalist economies. The literature suggests that a relationship exists between political regime—here majoritarian and consensus democracies—and LMEs and CMEs (Gourevitch, 2003; Roe, 2003). However, the literature has underemphasized the causal processes and causal directions linking these two institutional systems (Amable, 2003; Amable & Palombarini, 2009; Deeg & Jackson, 2007; Schmidt, 2009). This chapter seeks to quantitatively investigate the association between political and economic institutions and lend greater clarity to the causal relationships between the two.

The purpose of this chapter is fourfold. First, the chapter will confirm the relationship between political regime and VOC, and identify the direction of the relationship. Second, this chapter will quantitatively establish which political institutions serve as the strongest indicators of capitalist variation and lend support to the estimation of causal effects. Third, this chapter will investigate the relationship between specific political institutions and the economic arenas posed by the VOC framework. Lastly, this chapter will synthesize the quantitative findings, and subsequently lay the groundwork—through the establishment of relevant causal variables—for the qualitative investigation of Chaps. 5 and 6.

M.P. Arsenault, *The Effects of Political Institutions on Varieties of Capitalism*, DOI 10.1007/978-3-319-50892-4_4

Chapter Outline

The chapter begins by broadly examining the relationship between market coordination and political regime through a cross-sectional OLS regression. Measures of political regime are drawn from Lijphart's (1999) aggregated scores for both the executive-parties and federal-unitary dimensions, and Vatter's (2009) expanded measures of democracy. Measures of market coordination—here capturing capitalism type—are drawn from Kenworthy (2006) and Hall and Gingerich (2004). This section is designed to lend support to the guiding hypothesis that a significant relationship exists between political regime and capitalist type and identify the direction of this relationship.

I next disaggregate Lijphart's measures into select constituent elements, namely, electoral system, number of political parties, constitutional structures, and cabinet structures. Additionally, I include measures of partisanship and policy legacies as established throughout the literature (D. Brady & Leicht, 2007; Huber, Ragin, & Stephens, 1993; Huber, Ragin, Stephens, Brady, & Beckfield, 2004; Huber & Stephens, 2001; Rothstein, Samanni, & Teorell, 2010; Stephens, Huber, & Ray, 1999).

Using time-series, cross-sectional data, I apply an OLS model with PCSE in order to test the relationship between these independent variables and an aggregate measure of market coordination. By examining the individual independent variables, I will establish which variables prove to be the strongest indicators of capitalist variation.

Lastly, I apply the model citied above to four economic arenas that compose the VOC framework: corporate governance, industrial relations, inter-firm relations, and education and training. The purpose here is to identify the effects of individual political institutions on the multiple components of the production regime. In doing so, multiple causal processes may be revealed which may ultimately affect the overall structure of the capitalist type.

Cross-Sectional Analysis

This initial analysis confirms that political institutions are related to capitalism type. Specifically, majoritarian systems cluster with LMEs, and consensus system with CMEs. The dependent variables are indices which measure market coordination across countries. To maintain the coherence of the

VOC approach, these indices are aggregate measures of coordination along the arenas of corporate governance, industrial relations, education and training, inter-firm relations.[1]

The Hicks–Kenworthy variable seeks to measure a nation's "degree of cooperation between spheres" (Kenworthy, 2006, p. 75). These spheres include:

> (a) relations among firms across industries; (b) relations among unions; (c) relations between the state and interest groups; (d) relations among firms and investors; (e) relations among firms and suppliers; (f) relations among competing firms; (g) relations between labour and management; (h) relations among workers; (i) relations among functional departments within the firm. (Kenworthy, 2006, p. 75)

Each sphere is coded as 0, 0.5, or 1, representing weak, moderate, or strong cooperation. "The scores are then averaged to form the index, which ranges from 0 to 1" (Kenworthy, 2006, p. 75).

The Hall and Gingerich index seeks to measure a nation's reliance on nonmarket means of coordination. The index is based on a factor analysis of six variables: shareholder power, dispersion of control, size of stock market, level of wage coordination, degree of wage coordination, and labor turnover (Hall & Gingerich, 2004, p. 11).

The first three indicators—shareholder power, dispersion of control, and size of the stock market—illustrate variance in the corporate governance arena. This arena includes a firm's access to financial capital as well as guarantees on investor capital. The Hall and Gingerich logic holds that in situations where "influence tilts toward dominant shareholders, ownership is relatively concentrated, and equity markets are small, securing access to external finance and negotiating corporate control is more likely to involve firms in strategic interaction within corporate networks" (Hall & Gingerich, 2004, p. 12). Thus the economy is likely to be characterized by a high degree of coordination. Where the reverse holds true, we are likely to find liberal market economy production regimes.

The remaining three indicators—level of wage coordination, degree of wage coordination, and labor turnover—examine coordination in the labor relations arena. According to Hall and Gingerich, the logic contends that high degrees of wage coordination and low levels of labor turnover indicate coordinated economies, while the reverse holds true for LMEs (2004).

Both indices range between 0 and 1. The higher the score, the more coordinated the economy. Lower scores illustrate a greater reliance on market forces and, hence, are representative of LMEs. The indices confirm the basic argument of the VOC approach which holds that economies cluster around CME and LME production regimes. The CME nations generally lie above 0.50, while most LME nations lie below 0.50 (Hall & Gingerich, 2004). In order to establish an encompassing measure of relevant macro-political institutions, I draw on the majoritarian/consensus variables developed by Lijphart (1984, 1999).

A major distinction between these systems lies in the division along the executive-parties, and federal-unitary dimensions. The executive-parties dimension includes the variables: number of political parties, minimal winning cabinets, executive dominance, disproportionality, and group pluralism. The federal-unitary dimension includes bicameralism, constitutional rigidity, judicial review, and central bank independence (Lijphart, 1999). Scores for each of the 18 countries are found in Table 4.1.

Table 4.1 Hicks–Kenworthy, Hall–Gingerich indices, and the executive-parties dimension

Country	*Hicks–Kenworthy*	*Hall–Gingerich*	*Exec-parties*	*Fed-unitary*
Austria	0.7	1	0.26	1.08
Germany	0.66	0.95	0.23	2.53
Italy	0.42	0.87	1.16	−0.11
Norway	0.75	0.76	0.92	−0.65
Belgium	0.56	0.74	1.42	0.21
Japan	0.82	0.74	0.85	0.22
Finland	0.68	0.72	1.66	−0.83
Denmark	0.58	0.7	1.45	−0.38
France	0.28	0.69	−0.93	−0.17
Sweden	0.74	0.69	1.04	−0.79
The Netherlands	0.43	0.66	1.16	0.35
Switzerland	0.44	0.51	1.87	1.67
Australia	0.14	0.36	−0.67	1.72
Ireland	0.08	0.29	0.12	−0.42
New Zealand	0.13	0.21	−1.12	−1.77
Canada	0.06	0.13	−1.07	1.88
United Kingdom	0.1	0.07	−1.39	−1.19
United States	0.07	0	−0.52	2.36

These two measures—the executive-parties dimension and the federal-unitary dimension—capture two different aspects of the political regime. The two measures are very weakly correlated at −0.0599.

The first measure, the executives-parties dimension, captures the primary variables under investigation and captures the political arena in which competing interests vie for the power to either compete or cooperate in the development and implementation of policy outcomes (Amable, 2003; Cusack, Iverson, & Soskice, 2007; Iverson & Soskice, 2006; Korpi, 1983, 2006; Lijphart & Crepaz, 1991; Martin & Swank, 2008).

The second measure, the federal-unitary dimension, captures a number of constitutional veto points extant in a given political regime. The measures are largely stable, and are less susceptible to the influence of partisan interests (Tsebelis, 1995).

I hypothesize that the executive-parties dimension, capturing the interaction of various interests within the political arena, will serve as the strongest indicator of market coordination. Such a hypothesis is confirmed through an OLS regression comparing the impact of the dimensions on market coordination. The executive-parties dimension is a significant indicator of market coordination when applied to both the Hicks–Kenworthy and Hall–Gingerich indices, and the coefficients are in the predicted direction. This suggests that countries with more consensus-oriented political institutions are likely to have associated higher scores along the market coordination indices. The federal-unitary dimension does not prove statistically significant. Regression results regarding the relevant dimensions are illustrated in Table 4.2.

Table 4.2 Market coordination as a function of the executive-parties dimension

Variable	*Hicks–Kenworthy*	*Hall–Gingerich*
Executive-parties	0.1841***	0.1845**
	(0.031)	(0.048)
Federal-unitary	−0.0138	0.0041
	(0.0384)	(0.0649)
Constant	0.3629***	0.4933***
	(0.0516)	(0.0649)
Adj. R^2	0.4648	0.3311
N	18	18

p *** < 0.001

p ** < 0.01

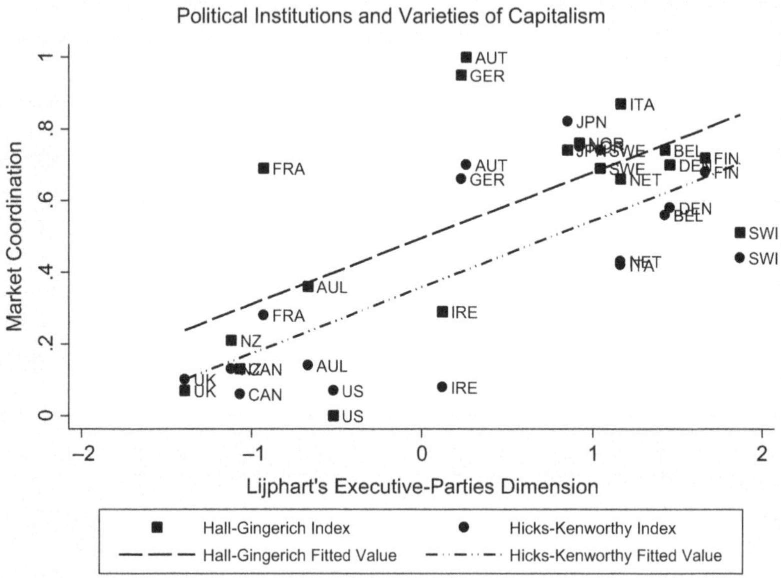

Fig. 4.1 Political institutions and VOC: executive-parties dimension

Building upon the significance of the executive-parties dimension, Fig. 4.1 provides an overlaid scatterplot diagram illustrating the clustering of political systems around their respective production regimes. As the figure illustrates, a clear relationship exists between political institutions and degree of market coordination. Countries considered majoritarian cluster around LME production regimes, while consensus countries cluster around CME production regimes.

Political Institutions and Market Coordination

As the above analysis indicates, a relationship exists between the political institutions captured by the executive-parties dimension and market coordination. The next step, then, is to disaggregate the executive-parties measure in order to identify which specific political institutions are related to variation in capitalist systems.

Here I begin with a dependent variable designed to measure degrees of variation between CMEs and LMEs over time. The variable,

"Neocorporatism Index," is drawn from the CWS data set (Huber et al., 2004). It is a scaled variable, measured from 0 to 1. It is based on the scores of 11 independent variables also from the CWS. The variables composing the measure include the use of multi-divisional teams in firm structures, teamwork arrangements, employment security, competition between firms and suppliers, structure of firm ownership, corporatism as a function of the political system, levels of cooperation between government and interest groups, wage coordination, and the degree of business centralization. Higher scores indicate CME systems, while lower scores indicate LME systems. This measure improves upon existing measures of corporatism in regard to capitalist variation and production regime by including a number of firm-specific variables, as well as being applicable to panel data analysis (Hicks & Swank, 1992; Lijphart & Crepaz, 1991). Figure 4.2 provides a histogram of the neocorporatism index.

The histogram illustrates a U-shaped pattern. Like the Hall–Gingerich (2004), and the Hicks–Kenworthy (1998) indices, this suggests a clustering of observations around the lower end of the scale, representing LMEs,

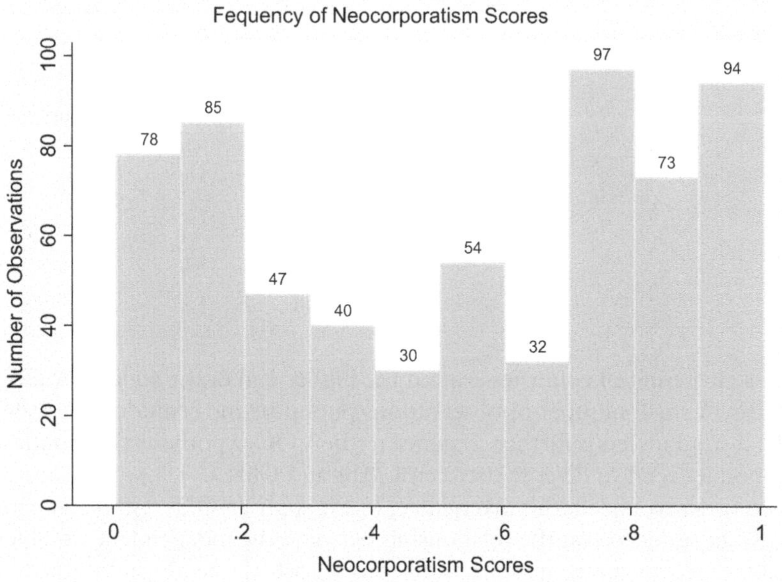

Fig. 4.2 Neocorporatism index frequencies

Table 4.3 Political institutions and the neocorporatism index

Left cabinet	0.0077***
	(0.0016)
Center cabinet	−0.0069***
	(0.0013)
Right cabinet	−0.0036**
	(0.0012)
Effective number of parties	0.0098*
	(0.0042)
Majoritarian cabinet	−0.0008
	(0.0059)
PR system	0.1147***
	(0.0243)
SMD system	−0.3438***
	(0.0268)
Constitutional structures	−0.0037
	(0.0046)
Price level of GDP	−0.0003
	(0.0007)
Unemployment	−0.0089***
	(0.0022)
Consumer price index	−0.0003
	(0.0007)
Social security transfers	0.0024
	(0.0016)
Economic openness	−0.0006
	(0.0005)
CONSTANT	0.6024***
	0.0346
ADJ R^2	0.6537

p *** < 0.001
p ** < 0.01
p * < 0.05

and a clustering of countries around the higher end of the scale indicating CMEs. A small number of observations pool near the center of the scale. The histogram lends further credence to the VOC hypothesis that political economies tend to diverge between LMEs and CMEs.

In order to explain this divergence, I next apply an OLS regression with PCSE in order to test the relationship between the independent variables and the neocorporatism index. Table 4.3 reports the regression output. The political institutions of primary interest are partisanship and policy legacies, the effective number of political parties in the legislature, cabinet structure, and electoral system. The results suggest that partisanship and policy

Table 4.4 Correlation matrix for right-, center-, and left-cabinet variables

	Right cabinet	*Center cabinet*	*Left cabinet*
Right cabinet	1.00		
Center cabinet	−0.3956	1.00	
Left cabinet	−0.1952	−0.2895	1.00

legacies, effective number of political parties, along with electoral system, affect overall market coordination as measured by the neocorporatism index.

The three cabinet variables are designed to capture the cumulative power of political parties.[2] Specifically, the variables measure the number of cabinet seats held by a political party as a proportion of all seats for each year. The proportions are then summed from 1946 to the year of the observation. Data is drawn from the CWD (Huber et al., 2004). Following Brady and Leicht (2007), I sum parties considered "right," "right, Christian," and "right, Catholic" as coded by Huber et al. (2004).[3] Similarly, I sum the Huber et al. measures for "center," "center, Christian," and "center, Catholic" parties. Table 4.4 illustrates the correlation between the three cabinet variables.

All three cabinet variables are statistically significant, and the coefficients are in the predicted direction. Cumulative center-party power is negatively related to the neocorporatism index and proves the strongest indicator of the three cabinet variables.[4] As the strength of center-party power moves from the 25th to the 75th percentile, there is a corresponding −0.1267 decrease on the neocorporatism scale. Cumulative left-party power serves as the second strongest indicator and is positively related to the neocorporatism index. As left-party power moves from the 25th percentile to the 75th percentile, there is a corresponding 0.1006 increase on the neocorporatism scale. Cumulative right-party power is also negatively related to the neocorporatism index, but with a weaker association than both center-controlled and left-controlled cabinets. As right-party power moves from the 25th to the 75th percentile, there is a −0.059 decrease on the neocorporatism measure.

Both electoral systems variables proved statistically significant, and the coefficients are in the predicted directions. SMD electoral systems were found to have a strong, negative relationship to the neocorporatism index. Countries with SMD electoral systems scored −0.3438 points lower than countries with other types of electoral system. PR systems are positively related to higher scores along the neocorporatism index. Countries with PR system score 0.1147 points higher than countries with other electoral systems.

The effective number of parties variable also proved statistically significant, and in the predicted direction. As the number of political parties increases, there is an associated increase in scores along the neocorporatism index. As the number of political parties moves from the 25th to the 75th percentile, there is an associated increase of 0.0188 on the index.

The majoritarian cabinet variable was not statistically significant, but the coefficient was in the predicted direction. This finding may call into question the hypothesis that majoritarian control of cabinets should lead to decreased levels of market coordination. It is likely that the ideology of the cabinet does not matter as a majoritarian cabinet could be ruled by a social democratic government that may avoid or retrench neoliberal policies.

The control variable capturing levels of unemployment is statistically significant and in the predicted direction. Higher levels of unemployment are associated with higher scores on the neocorporatism index, while lower levels of unemployment are associated with lower scores along the index. As unemployment moves from the 25th to the 75th percentile, scores along the neocorporatism index decrease by −0.0641. However, the causal direction remains to be seen. That is, a spurious relationship may exist. It is unclear whether higher rates of unemployment are a result of LMEs, or whether higher rates of unemployment lead to more liberal policies. Iversen, however, offers an interesting and reasonable explanation (2007).

Increasing levels of unemployment will affect the income distribution of a given country. In majoritarian system, rising income inequality should move the preferences of the median voter toward greater social protection and redistribution. Left parties may attempt to capture the median voter constituency by arguing for increasing taxation on the upper classes, for example. However, in majoritarian systems, party platforms are largely nonbinding, in part due to the stability of parliament or, like the case of Britain, the concept of parliamentary sovereignty (Mannin, 2010; Norton, 2007). If the left party gains majority of control of parliament, there is no guarantee to the median voter that more radical redistributive policies may be implemented to placate the lower-class constituency which may ultimately harm the median voter. At the same time, the upper-class constituency will demand lower taxation across the board which makes the likely effects on the median voter much more stable. As such, the effect of changes to income inequality:

> in a majoritarian system is therefore ambiguous: stronger preferences for redistribution but greater fear of what an 'ideological' left party might do. In a multiparty PR system, by contrast, a rise in inequality will increase the incentives for the centre and left to form a coalition to tax the rich. (Iversen, 2007, pp. 279–280)

As such, in a majoritarian system, higher rates of unemployment, and the likely resulting income inequality, may not garner a political response as readily as in a system characterized by proportional representation, and multiple political parties, thus the relationship between higher rates of unemployment in liberal market economies.

Other control variables—the federal-unitary dimension, GDP, consumer price index, and social security transfers, and economic openness—are not statistically significant.

In sum, all but one—majoritarian cabinets—of the political variables proved statistically significant and in the predicted directions. Electoral systems proved to be the strongest indicator of overall market coordination. Specifically, SMD systems had the greatest effect, followed by PR systems.

Additionally, long-term partisan control of cabinets affects market coordination. Surprisingly, center-party power was the strongest indicator, followed by left-party power. Right-party power, although statistically significant, was the weakest indicator of the cabinet variables. Of the political variables, the effective number of parties in the legislature had the weakest effect. The adjusted R-squared is 0.6537, suggesting that approximately 66 percent of the variance of the neocorporatism index is explained by the model.

Political Institutions and Economic Arenas

Production regimes can be divided into two types: CMEs and LMEs. The VOC framework argues that differences between production regimes stem from institutional variation within the various economic arenas, including corporate governance, industrial relations, inter-firm relations, and education and training. The purpose here is to establish the relevant political institutions for the individual economic arenas of coordinated and market economies in order to test hypotheses through the qualitative case studies. Table 4.5 illustrates the regression output, and is followed by interpretation for each of the four arenas.

Corporate Governance

By corporate governance, I am referring to the ownership and management structure of the firms. As Hall and Soskice point out, corporate governance concentrates on access to financing, and how "investors seek assurances of returns on their investment" (2001, p. 7). Corporate governance can largely be divided into two types: the shareholder model and the stakeholder model (Borsch, 2007; Hall & Soskice, 2001; Roe, 2003; Vitols, 2001). LMEs are characterized by a shareholder model in which the individuals make short-term investments in a firm in order to maximize profits through rising share values. Under such a system, firm ownership is largely dispersed, with management beholden to shareholders. CMEs, on the other hand, are characterized by stakeholder models of corporate governance. Stakeholders may include a wide variety of actors—workers, government, large shareholders, employers, banks, and institutional investors—who, in addition to financial goals, pursue long-term strategic interests (Hall & Soskice, 2001; Roe, 2003; Vitols, 2001).

The variable capturing corporate governance (INVFIRMS) is drawn from the CWS, and seeks to measure the "long-term voiced-based relationships between firms and their investors. 1 = large investors hold significant ownership shares for long periods; 0.5 = relatively decentralized ownership but with only moderate investor turnover; 0 = decentralized ownership with a high turnover rate" (Huber et al., 2004, p. 8). As such, lower scores will represent shareholder-focused LMEs, while higher scores represent stakeholder-focused CMEs.

Of the three cabinet variables both left-party power and right-party power are statistically significant and in the predicted direction. That is, cumulative power of the left is associated with increasing levels of stakeholder corporate governance, while cumulative right-party power is associated with shareholder systems. Center-party power was not statistically significant, but the coefficient was in the predicted direction.

The effective number of political parties variable also proved statistically significant and the relationship is in the predicted direction. The relationship suggests that systems with higher numbers of effective political

Table 4.5 Regression output: four economic arenas

Independent variables	*Corporate governance*	*Industrial relations*	*Vocational training*	*Inter-firm relations*
Left cabinet	0.0064*	0.0065***	0.0022	0.0089***
	(0.0026)	(0.0014)	(0.0029)	(0.0018)
Center cabinet	−0.0044	−0.0048**	−0.0051	−0.004**
	(0.0035)	(0.0014)	(0.0031)	(0.0013)
Right cabinet	−0.007[a]	−0.0015*	−0.0064*	0.0001
	(0.0036)	(0.0008)	(0.003)	(0.0014)
Number of parties	0.1729*	0.0041	0.0154	0.0169**
	(0.0073)	(0.003)	(0.0085)	(0.007)
Majoritarian cabinets	−0.0035	−0.0082	0.0042	0.0032
	(0.0082)	(0.0054)	(0.0135)	(0.0069)
PR electoral system	0.0563[b]	0.0224	0.1477**	0.1631***
	(0.029)	(0.0183)	(0.0493)	(0.0379)
SMD electoral system	−0.4633***	−0.6589***	−0.2315***	−0.4333***
	(0.0631)	(0.0147)	(0.032)	(0.0454)
Constitutional structures	0.0055	−0.0075	−0.0215**	0.0029
	(0.0081)	(0.0061)	(0.0079)	(0.0066)
GDP per capita	0.0002	0.00001	−0.0004	0.0002
	(0.0003)	(0.0006)	(0.0005)	(0.0002)
Unemployment	−0.0025	−0.005*	−0.0345***	−0.0053**
	(0.0045)	(0.002)	(0.0048)	(0.002)
Inflation	0.0023	−0.0007	−0.0024	−0.0005
	(0.0016)	(0.0006)	(0.0021)	(0.0006)
Social security transfers	0.0003	0.0083***	−0.0017	0.0016
	(0.0025)	(0.0018)	(0.0028)	(0.0019)
Economic openness	0.0047***	0.0001	−0.0009	−0.0019**
	(0.001)	(0.0005)	(0.0009)	(0.0006)
CONSTANT	0.9649***	0.6523***	0.9061***	0.4427***
	(0.0907)	(0.0346)	(0.091)	(0.059)
ADJ R^2	0.508	0.631	0.540	0.499
N	604	604	604	604

[a]Right-party power approaches generally held thresholds for statistical significance at $p > 0.052$

[b]PR electoral system approaches generally held thresholds for statistical significance at $p > 0.052$

p *** < 0.001

p ** < 0.01

p * < 0.05

parties in legislatures are likely to be associated with stakeholder corporate governance structures.

The relationships between both electoral system variables are in the predicted direction. SMD electoral systems are associated with shareholder corporate governance structures, and the relationship proves statistically significant. PR electoral systems are positively related to stakeholder corporate governance, and the relationship approaches generally held thresholds for statistical significance at the $p > 0.052$ level.

The coefficients of both the majoritarian cabinet variables and the constitutional constraints variables were in the predicted direction. Majoritarian cabinets were negatively related to the corporate governance measure, while the constitutional constraints variable was positively related to the corporate governance measure. However, both variables did not meet traditionally held thresholds for statistical significance.

Of all the control variables—price level of GDP, unemployment rate, consumer price index, social security transfers, and economic openness—only economic openness proved statistically significant. The relationship suggests that greater degrees of economic openness are associated with shareholder corporate governance structures.

As stated above, electoral system has the strongest effect on the market coordination variable. PR systems are associated with stakeholder corporate governance models, and SMD systems are associated with shareholder corporate governance models. The relationship is largely explained through the level of policy stability and the structure of interest associations in a given country.

First, policy stability is conducive to CMEs, while instability is conducive to LMEs. PR systems tend to allow only moderate changes to existing policy, while SMD systems tend to allow for much more rapid policy changes. Policy stability decreases the uncertainty of exchange, while instability increases uncertainty. Where policy stability exists, economic actors are more likely to make long-term credible commitments and investments. In an environment where policy can change quickly, like in a majoritarian system, actors are less likely to make long-term commitments, and tend to favor short-term investments (Wood, 2001).

Second, CMEs are characterized by peak interest associations, while LMEs are characterized by much more pluralistic interest associations (Hall & Soskice, 2001). PR and multi-party systems are conducive to the development of corporatist peak associations and stakeholder corporate governance structures, while SMD and two-party systems are conducive to more pluralistic interest associations and stakeholder corporate governance structures (Martin & Swank, 2008).

In shareholder corporate governance systems, CEOs of firms require autonomy to make rapid, innovative decisions—like job cuts, abandoning declining industries, and so on (Deakin, Hobbs, Konzelmann, & Wilkinson, 2006; Roe, 2003; Vitols, 2001). The ability for a CEO to implement such measures likely stems from his or her freedom from the constraints of peak associations. On the other hand, CEOs in stakeholder systems are constrained by the necessity of interacting and consulting with labor, industry, employer, and other associations.

Industrial Relations

Variation in industrial relations is an imperative aspect of the differentiation between CMEs and LMEs. Industrial relations refer to the ability of firms to "coordinate bargaining over wages and working-conditions with their labor force, the organization, the organizations that represent labor, and other employers" (Hall & Soskice, 2001, p. 7). CMEs are categorized by strong unions, which allows for "cooperative industrial relations with the company and coordinated wage bargaining across companies" (Soskice, 1999, p. 110). On the other hand, LMEs have deregulated labor markets, that is, a great deal of freedom to hire and fire employees, which leads to weaker unions, and subsequently greater control of management over employees. As majoritarian systems tend to favor the political right over the political left, I hypothesize that countries with majoritarian political institutions are likely to have weaker labor coordination, less governmental involvement in labor relations, and subsequently LME production regimes (Soskice, 2007).

In operationalizing variation in industrial relations, I draw on the CWS Dataset, GOVTINTS variable which measures cooperation between government and interest groups, specifically labor and business. The measure is coded "1 = relatively cooperative interaction between cohesive government agencies and coordinated business and labor organizations; 0.5 = moderate cooperation; 0 = relatively combative, adversarial relationships between fragmented state agencies and interest group organizations" (Huber et al., 2004, p. 9). Higher scores indicate more cooperative industrial relations, while lower scores indicate more competitive industrial relations.

All three cabinet variables are statistically significant and in the predicted directions. Cumulative left-party power is positively associated with the industrial relations measure suggesting that countries with higher levels of left-party power over time will likely have more cooperative industrial relations systems. Both center-party power and right-party power were negatively related to the industrial relations measure. That is, countries with higher levels of center- or right-party power are associated with more adversarial industrial relations systems.

The coefficients for both the effective number of parties in the legislature, majoritarian cabinet, and constitutional constraints variables were in the predicted direction, but the measures were not statistically significant.

The coefficients of both electoral systems variables were in the predicted direction, but only SMD proved statistically significant. SMD electoral systems are negatively related to the industrial relations variable suggesting that SMD systems are associated with more competitive and adversarial industrial relations systems. Here I find two major issues at play. First, PR and multi-party systems tend to favor the interests of the left. As the major constituency of the left is labor, we are likely to find policies that encourage greater cooperation between labor and business. Second, PR and multi-party systems are conducive to the development of peak labor and business association which improve coordination between labor and business interests (Martin & Swank, 2008).

Of the control variables, unemployment rate and social security transfer payments were statistically significant. Unemployment is negatively related to the industrial relations measure, implying that higher rates of unemployment are associated with adversarial industrial relations systems. Social security transfers are positively related to the measure suggesting that states with higher levels of social security transfer payments are associated with more cooperative industrial relations system.

Vocational Training and Education

The vocational training and education arena examines coordination problems between firms and the workforce. That is, "firms face the problem of securing a workforce with suitable skills while workers face the problem of deciding how much to invest in what skills" (Hall & Soskice, 2001, p. 7).

Various types of skills are required by different product market strategies. Workers, acting rationally, will invest only in those required skills if there is a long-term guarantee in employment and wages. In order to ensure workers invest in the necessary skill types—industry specific, firm specific, or general—there must be institutions in place that protect workers' skill investment in the face of uncertainty (Estevez-Abe, Iversen, & Soskice, 2001; Soskice, 1999).

In capturing employment protection I draw on a variable (LABMGMT) designed to measure "long-term employment security guaranteed by firms. 1 = long term (in some cases lifetime) employment security common in large firms; 0.5 = some firms provide medium- or long-term security (facilitated by a relatively low unemployment rate): 0 = unemployment security relatively uncommon" (Huber et al., 2004).

All coefficients for the cumulative party-power variables were in the predicted direction. However, only cumulative right-party power proved statistically significant. The relationship suggests that in countries with higher levels of cumulative right-party power, there is likely to be low levels of unemployment security.

Both electoral systems variables proved statistically significant, and relationships were in the predicted direction. PR electoral systems are positively related to the employment protection variable, while SMD electoral systems are negatively related. As such, countries with PR systems are likely to have higher levels of long-term employment security, while SMD systems are likely to have much more limited unemployment security. These findings support the work of Cusack, Iversen, and Stephens (2007), who examine the relationship between electoral system and VOC, focusing specifically on the vocational training and education arena. Cusack et al. contend that in situations where production requires specific skills, the political right will accept PR and consensual bargaining with the left in order to promote specific skill development. On the other hand, where countries require generalizable skills, the right will maintain control over the left through majoritarian institutions.

Additionally, the constitutional constraints variables proved statistically significant and were in the predicted direction. The relationship suggests that a country with higher numbers of constitutional constraints is likely to also have higher levels of long-term employment security. Interestingly, this is the only model of the four economic arenas in which the constitutional constraints variable proved statistically significant.

Of all the control variables, only unemployment rate proved statistically significant. Unemployment is negatively related to the employment security variable. That is, countries with higher rates of unemployment are likely to be associated with lower levels of long-term unemployment security.

Inter-Firm Relations

As Hall and Soskice point out "inter-firm relations" is "a term we use to cover the relationships a company forms with other enterprises, and notably its suppliers or clients" (2001, p. 7). The variable (BUSCONF) is designed to capture the degree to which business confederations are centralized. "1 = central business confederation with substantial authority over members and weakly contested by competing confederations, in some cases with government involvement; 0.5 central confederation with moderate authority and/or moderately contested by competitors; 0 = fragmentation among business federations and/or central federation with little authority over members" (Huber et al., 2004, p. 9). As such, higher scores represent CMEs, while low scores represent LMEs.

Both left-party and center-party power proved statistically significant and were in the predicted direction. That is, countries with long-term left-party power will be associated with higher levels of centralized business confederations. On the other hand, countries with long-term center-party power are associated with more fragmented business federations. Cumulative right-party power was not statistically significant, and the coefficient was opposite of the predicted direction.

The effective number of political parties' variable proved statistically significant, and the relationship with the level of business confederation was in the predicted direction. Countries with higher numbers of effective parties in the legislature are associated with more coordinated business interests.

Both electoral systems variables were statistically significant and in the predicted direction. Countries with PR systems are associated with greater degrees of business coordination than countries with SMD electoral systems. Majoritarian cabinets and constitutional constraints did not approach generally held thresholds of statistical significance. The main mechanism here is the relationship between political institutions and employer associations. Such findings support the work of Martin and Swank (2008) who find that electoral system and party system shape peak interest associations. The logic contends that in PR systems, we are likely to find parties sympathetic to business interests. This results in cooperation of like-minded groups and the formation of coalitions to support business interests (like ACT NZ and National in New Zealand) (Castles, Gerritsen, & Vowles, 1996). However, because such parties are unlikely to gain majority control of government, they will seek other sources of influence outside of government, namely, centralized business and employer associations.

Of the control variables, both unemployment and economic openness proved statistically significant and in the predicted direction. That is, countries with higher levels of unemployment and greater degrees of economic openness area associated with political economies characterized by less coordinated business interests.

Conclusion

This chapter was designed to answer three questions. First, what political institutions are related to variation in capitalist systems? Second, what political institutions serve as the strongest indicator of CMEs and LMEs? Third, what are the effects of specific political institutions on the economic arenas that characterize the CME and LME dichotomy?

First, the above findings illustrate a strong relationship between political regime and VOC. Majoritarian systems are strongly correlated with LMEs, while consensus political systems are strongly correlated with CMEs. However, when disaggregating the political regime into its constituent executive-parties and federal-unitary dimensions, the findings suggest that variables in the executive-parties dimension play a more significant role.

Second, partisanship and policy legacies, the effective number of political parties, and electoral system all prove to be significant indicators of capitalist variation. Left-cabinet governments are positively related to CMEs; center- and right cabinets are negatively related to CMEs. The number of political parties is positively related to CMEs. PR electoral rules are positively related to CMEs, while SMD or FPP systems are negatively related to CMEs. The analysis suggests that most prescient variable is the type of electoral system present in a given state. It is likely that the robustness of the measure lies in the fact that electoral system is instrumental in structuring many other political institutions. Electoral system shapes the number of political parties, the structure of cabinets, and the strength of the executive. Although the other political variables play a significant role in shaping the degree to which competing interests either cooperate or compete, it is the electoral system that establishes the groundwork and institutional structure of the other variables.

Third, across all four economic arenas—corporate governance, industrial relations, vocational training and education, and inter-firm relations—the role of politics matters. However, the effects of different political institutions vary across arenas. Left-cabinet governments are positively associated with greater coordination across the four arenas, achieving statistical significance in corporate governance, industrial relations, and inter-firm relations. Center cabinets are negatively associated with all four arenas and meet thresholds for statistical significance in industrial relations and inter-firm relations. Right cabinets, as expected, are negatively related to corporate governance, industrial relations, and vocational training. The right-cabinet variable approaches generally held thresholds of statistical significance in corporate governance, industrial relations, and vocational training and education.

The number of political parties variable was positively related to all economic arenas, and proved especially strong in regard to the corporate governance measure. However, the number of political parties variable proved statistically significant in only two of the economic arenas: corporate governance and inter-firm relations.

By far, the most robust indicator of variation in capitalist economies is the type of electoral system within a given state. PR systems were positively related to all four economic arenas, and approached generally held thresholds of statistical significance in corporate governance, vocational training and education, and inter-firm relations. SMD electoral systems were negatively associated with all four economic arenas and, in general, proved to have the strongest relationships of all political institutions investigated.

Based upon the above findings, the major political institutions to be explored in the qualitative case studies of Chaps. 5 and 6 are partisanship and policy legacies, the numbers of political parties, and electoral systems. Additionally, the qualitative chapters will seek to identify other relevant political and economic variables that may not have been found in the statistical analyses.

Notes

1. Although useful measures of market coordination, the indices are flawed in some regards. The Hicks–Kenworthy index proves problematic in that "These scores are subjective. They are created based

on the authors' reading of secondary and primary sources." The subjective nature of this measure may decrease its reliability, but, as Kenworthy points out, may increase its validity (Kenworthy, 2006, p. 75). The Hall–Gingerich measure fails to adequately examine all five arenas posed by the VOC literature, concentrating solely on corporate governance, training and education, and, to a lesser extent, employer–employee relations. Limiting the analysis to these select spheres may exclude relevant components of market coordination. However, I find consistency in the direction and strength of the selected independent variables when applied to both measures lending credence to their ability to gauge the overall relationship between political institutions and market coordination (see Table 4.2).

2. The CWD cabinet variables have been used extensively to capture partisanship and policy legacies throughout the political economy literature, specifically in studies addressing welfare state development (D. Brady & Leicht, 2007; Huber et al., 1993; Huber et al., 2004; Huber & Stephens, 2001; Rothstein et al., 2010; Stephens et al., 1999). I find the variables equally appropriate here.
3. As Brady and Leicht (2007) point out, some controversy may emerge as to the coding of some centrist parties as "right." The authors specifically cite the potentially problematic German Christian Democrats (CDU) and the Italian Christian Democrats (ICD). I agree with the authors—building on Allan and Scruggs (2004)—in the justification of the coding of CDU and ICD as "right" due to the fact that both parliaments do not have effective parties to the right of either the CDU or ICD.
4. The fact that cumulative center-party power appears a stronger indicator of LMEs than cumulative right-party power deserves some explanation. In continental Europe, many parties considered "centrist" have adopted a more neoliberal policy stance (Kitschelt, 1994). This, coupled with a generally limited "right," may lead the resulting regression results to indicate a greater influence of centrist parties than right parties.

References

Allen, J. B., & Scruggs, L. (2004). Political partisanship and welfare state reform in advanced industrial societies. *American Journal of Political Science, 48*(3), 496–512.

Amable, B. (2003). *The diversity of modern capitalism*. Oxford and New York: Oxford University Press.

Amable, B., & Palombarini, S. (2009). A neorealist approach to institutional change and the diversity of capitalism. *Socioeconomic Review, 7*(1), 123–143.

Borsch, A. (2007). Institutional variation and coordination patterns in CMEs: Swiss and German corporate governance strategies. In B. Hancké, M. Rhodes, & M. Thatcher (Eds.), *Beyond varieties of capitalism: Conflict, contradictions, and complementarities in the European economy*. New York: Oxford University Press.

Brady, D., & Leicht, K. (2007). *Party to inequality: Right party power and income inequality in affluent western democracies*. Luxembourg Income Study Working Paper Series.

Castles, F., Gerritsen, R., & Vowles, J. (1996). Conclusion: The great experiment in perspective. In F. Castles, R. Gerritsen, & J. Vowles (Eds.), *The great experiment: Labour parties and public policy transformation in Australia and New Zealand*. St. Leonards, Australia: Allen and Unwin.

Cusack, T. R., Iverson, T., & Soskice, D. (2007). Economic interests and the origin of electoral systems. *American Political Science Review, 101*(3), 373–391.

Deakin, S., Hobbs, R., Konzelmann, S. J., & Wilkinson, F. (2006). Anglo-American corporate governance and the employment relationship: A case to answer? *Socioeconomic Review, 4*(1), 155–174.

Deeg, R., & Jackson, G. (2007). Towards a more dynamic theory of capitalist variety. *Socioeconomic Review, 5*(1), 149–179.

Estevez-Abe, M., Iversen, T., & Soskice, D. (2001). Social protection and the formation of skills: A reinterpretation of the welfare state. In P. A. Hall & D. Soskice (Eds.), *Varieties of capitalism: The institutional foundations of comparative advantage*. Oxford: University of Oxford Press.

Gourevitch, P. A. (2003). Review: The politics of corporate governance regulation. *The Yale Law Journal, 112*(7), 1829–1880.

Hall, P. A., & Gingerich, D. W. (2004). *Varieties of capitalism and institutionanl complementarites in the macroeconomy: An empirical analysis*. Max-Planck Institute for the Study of Societies, Cologne, Germany.

Hall, P. A., & Soskice, D. W. (2001). *Varieties of capitalism: The institutional foundations of comparative advantage*. Oxford, England and New York: Oxford University Press.

Hicks, A., & Kenworthy, L. (1998). Cooperation and political economic performance in affluent democratic capitalism. *American Journal of Sociology, 103*(6), 1631–1672.

Hicks, A., & Swank, D. (1992). Politics, institutions, and welfare spending in industralized democracies. *American Political Science Review, 84*, 658–674.

Huber, E., Ragin, C., & Stephens, J. (1993). Social democracy, Christian democracy, constitutional structure, and the welfare state. *American Journal of Sociology, 3*, 711–749.

Huber, E., Ragin, C., Stephens, J., Brady, D., & Beckfield, J. (2004). *Comparative Welfare Data Set*. http://www.nsd.uib.no/macrodataguide/set.html?id=8&sub=1

Huber, E., & Stephens, J. (2001). *Development and crisis of the welfare state: Parties and policies in global markets*. Chicago: University of Chicago Press.
Iversen, T. (2007). Economic shocks and varieties of government response. In B. Hancké, M. Rhodes, & M. Thatcher (Eds.), *Beyond varieties of capitalism: Conflict, contradictions, and complementarities in the European economy*. New York: Oxford University Press.
Iversen, T., & Soskice, D. (2006). Electoral institutions and the politics of coalitions: Why some democracies redistribute more than others. *American Political Science Review, 100*(2), 165–181.
Kenworthy, L. (2006). Institutional coherence and macroeconomic performance. *Socio-Economic Review, 4*(1), 69–91.
Kitschelt, H. (1994). *The transformation of European social democracy*. Cambridge: Cambridge University Press.
Korpi, W. (1983). *The democratic class struggle*. London: Routledge & Kegan Paul.
Korpi, W. (2006). Power resources and employer-centered approaches in explanations of welfare states and varieties of capitalism: Protagonists, consenters, and antagonists. *World Politics, 58*(2), 167–206.
Lijphart, A. (1984). *Democracies: Patterns of majoritarian and consensus democracies in twenty-one countries*. New Haven, CT: Yale University Press.
Lijphart, A. (1999). *Patterns of democracy: Government forms and performance in thirty-six countries*. New Haven, CT: Yale University Press.
Lijphart, A., & Crepaz, M. M. L. (1991). Corporatism and consensus democracy in eighteen countries: Conceptual and empirical linkages. *British Journal of Political Science, 21*(2), 235–246.
Mannin, M. L. (2010). *British government and politics: Balancing Europeanization and independence*. Lanham, MD: Rowman & Littlefield.
Martin, C. J., & Swank, D. (2008). The political origins of coordinated capitalism: Business organizations, party systems, and state structure in the age of innocence. *American Political Science Review, 102*(2), 181–198.
Norton, B. F. (2007). *Politics in Britain*. Washington, DC: CQ Press.
Roe, M. J. (2003). *Political determinants of corporate governance*. Oxford: Oxford University Press.
Rothstein, B., Samanni, M., & Teorell, J. (2010). Quality of government, political power and the welfare state. *The Quality of Government Institute, University of Gothenburg, 6*, 124.
Schmidt, V. A. (2009). Putting the political back into political economy by bringing the state back in yet again. *World Politcs, 61*(3), 516–546.
Soskice, D. (1999). Divergent production regimes: Coordinated and uncoordinated market economies in the 1980s and 1990s. In H. Kitschelt, P. Lange, G. Marks, & J. D. Stephens (Eds.), *Continuity and change in contemporary captialism* (pp. 101–134). New York: Cambridge University Press.

Soskice, D. (2007). Macroeconomics and varieties of capitalism. In B. Hancké, M. Rhodes, & M. Thatcher (Eds.), *Beyond varieties of capitalism: Conflict, contradictions, and complementarities in the European economy*. New York: Oxford University Press.

Stephens, J., Huber, E., & Ray, L. (1999). The welfare state in hard times. In H. Kitschelt, P. Lange, G. Marks, & J. Stephens (Eds.), *Continuity and change in contemporary capitalism*. New York: Cambridge University Press.

Tsebelis, G. (1995). Decision making in political systems: Veto players in presidentialism, parliamentarism, multicameralism and multipartyism. *British Journal of Political Science, 25*(3), 289–325.

Vatter, A. (2009). Lijphart expanded: Three dimensions of democracy in advanced OECD countries? *European Consortium for Political Research, 1*(1), 125–154.

Vitols, S. (2001). Varieties of corporate governance: Comparing Germany and the UK. In P. A. Hall & D. Soskice (Eds.), *Varieties of capitalism: The institutional foundations of comparative advantage*. New York: Oxford University Press.

Wood, S. (2001). Business, government, and patterns of labor market policy in Britain and the Federal Republic of Germany. In P. Hall & D. Soskice (Eds.), *Varieties of capitalism*. New York: Oxford University Press.

CHAPTER 5

Political Institutions and Economic Reforms: Britain and Germany

The 1970s and 1980s were an era characterized by significant changes to the global economy. Changes included increased liberalization of capital markets, increased power of global business, weakened power of the state, deindustrialization, high rates of unemployment and inflation, and increasing competition from newly industrialized countries (Kitschelt, Lange, Marks, & Stephens, 1999). OECD countries faced significant pressures to adopt (and ultimately did adopt, albeit to a greater or lesser degree) neoliberal economic policies designed to address changing economic conditions (Casey, 2009; Kitschelt, 1994). However, as the comparative capitalism literature suggests, there were a number of ways by which countries adapted to changing global markets (Kitschelt et al., 1999; Martin & Thelen, 2007; Thelen, 2001).

For example, we did not see a convergence to a single institutional framework based on deregulation and a strict adherence to neoclassical economic principles (Thelen, 2001). Rather, we saw a continued "bifurcation" between LME and CME frameworks (Kitschelt et al., 1999; Soskice, 1999).

LMEs, such as Britain and the United States, deregulated much of the economy, while CMEs "by contrast appear to be seeking flexibility through controlled decentralization (not deregulation but reregulation) of various issues at lower bargaining levels, but along with a continued commitment to coordination (especially wage bargaining)" (Thelen, 2001, p. 78). Many of the previous approaches to political economy

M.P. Arsenault, *The Effects of Political Institutions on Varieties of Capitalism*, DOI 10.1007/978-3-319-50892-4_5

proved useful in explaining continuity in the face of economic challenges, but have failed in their attempt to examine the diverse strategies adopted by various states in regard to the changing economic conditions (Hall, 1999).

This chapter explores the ways that countries with differing political institutions, namely, majoritarian and consensus systems, adapted to the new economic environment. I hypothesize that majoritarian systems were conducive to the continuation and/or expansion of liberal economic structures. On the other hand, consensus political systems limited the implementation of neoliberal policies, and allowed for a continuation of coordinated market production regimes.

The structure of political institutions likely affects the adjustment paths of the political economy for two reasons. First, there may be a "power dimension" involved in the institutional structure that gives power to one group at the expense of another (i.e. capital vs. labor), as evidenced by the propensity of majoritarian systems to favor parties of the center-right and consensus systems to favor parties of the center-left (Iversen & Soskice, 2006, 2009; Korpi, 1983, 2006). In part, this supports Korpi's power resources theory in which partisan power affects economic policy (2006).

Second, collective action problems may emerge and some institutions are better suited to fomenting cooperation than others (Huber & Stephens, 2000; Iversen & Stevens, 2008; Manow, 2001a; Martin & Swank, 2008). Majoritarian systems lead to more adversarial politics, while consensus systems lead to greater cooperation. For example, Britain was able to undertake more rapid structural adjustments in the 1980s because of the institutionalized strong executive and the concept of parliamentary sovereignty (Hall, 1986; Norton, 2007). In Germany, the diffused power structure allows for many groups to veto—or at least slow—adjustments (Hancock & Krisch, 2009). As such, "we can expect the institutional structures of the polity and political economy to have an impact on the adjustment paths at several levels" namely, the power of a given interest group, and the coordination capacity of competing interests (Hall, 1986, p. 161). Such is evidenced by the continuing desire for both labor and employers to "manage new pressures for flexibility within traditional institutions" (Thelen, 2001, p. 85).

This hypothesis builds upon the VOC conception of institutional complementarity in that institutions shape and constrain the opportunities of firms (Hall & Soskice, 2001). As Casey points out, "Institutions are complementary to each other when the presence of one raises the returns of the other" (2009, p. 257). In this case, the argument posits that the majoritarian political institutions, which characterized Britain, proved complementary to more radical neoliberal reforms, while the consensus-oriented German system retarded or slowed the implementation of neoliberal policies and allowed Germany to maintain a more coordinated market economy. As such, the process is in part associated with a path-dependence logic which suggests that "Early institutional developments serve to facilitate or constrain (if not close) certain institutional options for the future" (Casey, 2002, p. 8). As this chapter will illustrate, the legacy of political institutions ultimately led to the overall maintenance of existing production regimes in face of a changing global economic environment.

Chapter Outline

This chapter begins by discussing the institutional differences between the political systems of Germany and Britain in regard to electoral system, number of political parties, coalition structures, and constitutional structures. I illustrate the consensus structure of the German political regime and the converse structures of the British majoritarian system.

I next discuss the pressures to adopt neoliberal reforms facing both Germany and Britain in the 1980s. Specifically, I discuss the radical reforms of the Thatcherite Conservative governments in Britain, and the less far-reaching reforms of the German case. I illustrate the ways in which German political institutions proved conducive to an environment in which the interests of various actors are integrated into the political process, thus leading to greater cooperation and consensus.

Germany was able to mitigate the pressures to adopt neoliberal reforms, and subsequently maintain a CME by constraining the first-order preferences of economic and political actors—largely divided along socioeconomic lines. Conversely, I illustrate how the British Westminster system promotes an environment of adversarial politics in which competing interests—largely divided along socioeconomic lines—vie for control of the political and policy process with little or no consultation between groups. As such, the British model creates an environment of strong competition between competing groups which in turn allowed the British system to adopt the radical reforms of the 1980s.

Then, I examine the effects of the changing international economic environment on the politico-economic structures of both Germany and

Britain. It will become apparent that the German system retained many of the corporatist facets present in the pre-1980 period, while the British case adopted a much more neoliberal approach. Additionally, I illustrate the ways in which the pre-existing political institutions affected the "adjustment paths" available to political and economic actors, as well as the state's "capacities to adjust" to changing international economic conditions (Hall, 1999, p. 158).

Institutional Differences: Germany and Britain

The majoritarian system, or Westminster model, is generally characterized by a two-party system, and a strong one-party executive and cabinet with the executive exercising more power than its legislative counterparts. Furthermore, a majoritarian system adheres to SMD electoral rules which can lead to disproportional representation. Also, majoritarian systems often possess a highly competitive pluralist interest group system. Additionally, the Westminster system is characterized by a strong, centralized government and a unicameral legislature. Furthermore, most majoritarian systems possess a flexible constitution that can readily be amended or changed (Lijphart, 1984, 1999). Lastly, the British majoritarian system is characterized by "parliamentary sovereignty." That is, the legislature holds the final word in the constitutionality of legislation, and, as such, majoritarian systems tend not to have a strong system of judicial review (Norton, 2007). Lijphart cites Britain and pre-1996 New Zealand as typical examples of majoritarian democracies (1999).

Consensus democracy varies institutionally from the Westminster model. First, under the consensus model, the executive is often composed of a multi-party power-sharing cabinet or coalition government. In addition, power-sharing exists between the executive branch and the legislature, and the electoral system is often characterized by proportional representation. Unlike the highly competitive special interest group system of the Westminster model, a consensus democracy promotes a system of interest group compromise. The consensus model has a decentralized government characterized by a federated system and bicameral legislature. In addition, the constitution is often rigid, making change difficult. Lastly, the consensus system often has a strong institution of judicial review to monitor the legality of legislation. Lijphart cites Switzerland and Germany as examples of consensus democracy (1999).

Table 5.1 Institutional variations between Germany and Britain

Political institutions	*Germany*	*Britain*
Electoral system	MMP (PR)	SMD
Party system	Multi-party	Two party
Cabinet structure	Coalition	Single party
Executive structure	Weak	Strong
Federalism	Federal	Unitary
Bicameralism	Strong	Weak
Form of government	Parliamentary	Parliamentary
Constitutional rigidity	Rigid	Flexible
Judicial review	Strong	Weak
Central bank independence	High	Low

Note: Data drawn from Lijphart (1999)

Table 5.1 illustrates the major institutional differences between Germany and Britain. As can be seen, Germany typifies Lijphart's consensus democracies, while Britain represents the quintessential majoritarian system. The table illustrates that Germany and Britain differ in all institutional areas except one, the presidential/parliamentary dimension.

Following the quantitative findings in Chap. 4, the institutions of particular interest to this study are variations in electoral system, party system, coalition structure, and constitutional structures. Specifically, I examine how such institutions can potentially shape variation in capitalist systems. The following sections explore the major differences between the German and British institutions in greater depth.

Electoral Systems

Electoral systems play a decisive role in shaping the structure of the political and economic regimes of various states (Cusack, Iverson, & Soskice, 2007; Katzenstein, 1985; Martin & Swank, 2008). Electoral systems influence the number of effective political parties, the strength of the executive, and the structure of governing cabinets. Electoral systems are largely divided between proportional representation, here represented by Germany, and SMD plurality, represented by Britain (Lijphart, 1994).

The German electoral system is based on MMP rules. That is, German voters are granted two votes. The first vote—the constituency candidate vote—is based on SMD electoral rules in which voters select a representative from within the district where he or she resides. The second vote—the party vote—is based on party list rules. The party vote is counted first. The total percentage of party votes in each federal state (Land) establishes how many seats are due to a specific party in a specific Land (Hancock & Krisch, 2009; James, 2003; Roberts, 2006).

The MMP system, due to the proportional distribution of legislative seats, and the possibility of split-ticket voting, allows for an increase in the number of political parties in the legislature. Additionally, split-ticket voting allows for strategic voting which “allows electors to support two parties at the same time; for example, in the hope that two parties together can garner enough strength to form a coalition” (Hancock & Krisch, 2009, p. 119). This is evidenced by the Free Democrats and the Green Party’s strategy of attempting to woo the second ballot of voters who traditionally supported either the CDU-CSU or SPD in order to gain legislative seats according to party list vote percentages (Roberts, 2006, p. 88).

The British electoral system is based on SMD and plurality or FPP voting rules. That is, within a given district, the candidate who wins the most votes of all competing candidates is granted a parliamentary seat. Such a “winner-take-all” system allows for a candidate to win a parliamentary seat, even though he or she may have not earned a majority of the popular vote in a given district.

An extreme, yet illustrative example is found in the 1992 election in which Sir Ian Russell Johnston earned a parliamentary seat by garnering only 26 percent of the popular vote (Norton, 2007, pp. 172–173). The Russell Johnston example illustrates that the plurality rules lead to significant levels of disproportionality in parliament. Particularly, the party winning a majority of constituency seats will often be overrepresented in parliament when compared to earned percentage of the popular vote (Lijphart, 1999, p. 143).

Electoral systems matter in regard to shaping economic structures (Cusack et al., 2007; Iversen & Stevens, 2008; Katzenstein, 1985; Korpi, 2006; Martin & Swank, 2008). Majoritarian systems are generally governed by parties of the right, while PR systems are governed by coalitions of center-left parties (Iverson & Soskice, 2006). This is due, in part, to the role of the middle class. In majoritarian systems the middle class often allies itself with parties of the right which proves disadvantageous to left. The opposite holds true in proportional systems (Iversen, 2007; Iversen & Soskice, 2006; Iversen & Stevens, 2008).

In the German case, the Christian Democratic Union/Christian Social Union (CDU/CSU) largely occupy the center of the political spectrum with no effective political parties falling right of the CDU/CSU bloc (J. B. Allen & Scruggs, 2004; D. Brady & Leicht, 2007; Roberts, 2006). In Britain, on the other hand, as a result of the SMD plurality rules, the two major parties—Conservative and Labour—occupy the political right and left respectively.

Party Systems

As Duverger points out, electoral systems are instrumental in structuring the number of effective political parties in legislatures. PR systems led to multiple political parties gaining representation in legislatures, while SMD electoral rules usher in two dominant political parties (1954).

From Germany's first independent post-war election in 1949 until 1980, the German political system has been characterized by four parties: Social Democrats (SPD), CDU, CSU, and the Free Democrats (FDP) (Hancock & Krisch, 2009).[1] SPD and CDU/CSU are the largest, while the FDP often becomes a "third force" which has the potential to ultimately give one of the big parties control of parliament (Matthew Allen, 2006; James, 2003; Roberts, 2006). However, following unification, Germany has witnessed a rise in the number of smaller parties who gain legislative representation. Most dominant of these smaller parties are the Greens who emerged in 1980, and formed a coalition government with the SPD at the national level in 1998 (Hancock & Krisch, 2009; Roberts, 2006).[2]

Since 1945, the British government has been dominated by two major parties: the right-leaning Conservatives and the left-leaning Labour Party. However, since 1974, the role of smaller, third parties has increased and some have argued that Britain is characterized as a "two-party dominant system" in which minority parties garner between 5 and 10 percent of seats, but one or the either of the two dominant parties still control government through majority rule (Norton, 2007, p. 78).[3] Still, due to the SMD electoral rules, and the subsequent disproportional allocation of legislative seats, the smaller parties remain largely unable to garner the necessary support to ensure legislative representation and subsequently remain in a peripheral position within British politics. However, in cases where a fractionalization occurs within one of the two major parties—as was the case with Labour in 1983 and 1987—we may find a disproportional victory of the unfractionalized party (D. King & Wood, 1999).

The number of political parties affects the dispersion of power in government, and the ways in which various political and economic actors interact, specifically in regard to the coordination capacities of relevant players. As such, the number of political parties proves an important element in the analysis of production regimes. In the case of multiple political parties—largely the result of electoral system—cross-class bargaining and cooperation emerge, whereas two-party systems are much more closely divided along socioeconomic lines (Iversen & Stevens, 2008).

In part, this is the result of the higher number of "interaction streams" that accompany greater numbers of political parties, and the subsequent necessity of cooperation between parties in order to enact policy (Sartori, 1976). Iversen and Stephens argue that cross-class bargaining "is enabled by PR, because all major interests are represented through well-organized political parties, and because regulatory policies … have to pass through committee systems typically based on PR and consensus bargaining" (2008, p. 606).

The German case, characterized by multiple effective political parties, equates with higher numbers of interests, and subsequently higher numbers of relevant actors. In order for policy to be implemented, these various groups must compromise (Lijphart, 1999; Tsebelis, 1995). In the face of the growing necessity to adopt neoliberal reforms, the relevant actors in the German system would have to come to a more consensual agreement in regard to the extent of neoliberal initiatives and subsequently would likely adopt more moderate policy measures.

The British two-party system lacks the institutional constraints of the German model. The ruling government has very little incentive to consult with or cooperate with opposing economic and political actors. As such, the Thatcher government, and subsequently the Major government, were able to drive through the neoliberal reforms with little or no input from competing interests (Gamble, 1988).

Coalition Structures

As a result of the electoral rules and subsequent number of political parties, England has traditionally been governed by single-party majority governments, while the German system has largely been governed by coalition governments. Single-party majority or minimal winning coalition governments allow for the dominance of one party. The party is largely beholden to no entity other than the electorate during an election season (Mannin, 2010; Norton, 2007). As such, it is increasingly likely to see radical changes in situations in which parliament is governed by single-party majority. Such was the case under Margaret Thatcher's Conservative Party (Gamble, 1988), and New Zealand under the Labour government of 1984 (Castles, Gerritsen, & Vowles, 1996).

Systems which promote coalition governments—namely, surplus coalitions or minority governments—are characterized by a greater diffusion of power. Issues of parliamentary sovereignty are greatly mitigated by the multiple political parties participating in the cabinet and the subsequent possibility of either a split in a given party and or a vote of no confidence. Under such conditions a change to existing structures will be likely slowed in comparison with systems promoting majoritarian governments.

In discussing the potential for policy change, Horst Teltschik, Helmut Kohl's national security advisor, stated, "'The difference between Britain and Germany was that Margaret Thatcher has a clear majority government, while Germany always has a coalition government, and within the big parties, even the Christian Democrats, you always have a left wing [a result of the cross-class alliances characteristic of the CDU]'" (Bering, 1999, p. 15).

The German political system has long been characterized by coalition governments, with the FDP usually being an essential partner for government formation (Matthew Allen, 2006; Hancock & Krisch, 2009, p. 121). In modern German history, parliament has been ruled by absolute majority only once. The CDU maintained an absolute majority between 1957 and 1961. Coalition governments have been the norm ever since. "The need to form coalition governments at the federal level is often seen as the driving force behind the search for consensus rather than confrontation" (James, 2003, p. 25). Because of the necessity of coalition governments, cabinet assignments are drawn from not only the party of the Federal Chancellor but also—through extensive consultation—from the party of any and all coalition partners, thus furthering the necessity of cooperation (Allen, 2006, p. 68; Hancock & Krisch, 2009, p. 85).

Unlike the German case, Britain is characterized by majoritarian cabinet structures. That is, the party garnering the majority of seats in the legislature is able to form a one-party government. The structure of British coalition governments leads to conflict between the ruling party and the opposition "because the ruling party usually commands an overall majority and party discipline in the House of Commons is robustly enforced, the government of the day almost always has its way while the Opposition merely has its say" (Norton, 2007, p. 74). As the British system is characterized by competition between two major parties—Conservatives and Labour—government is largely distinguished by the ideological divide between the right and left. In general, there is very little in the way of policy consultation between the ruling government and the opposition.

In this study, I build upon Iversen and Soskice (2006) and Manow (2009) who contend that the necessity of coalition governments (the result of electoral system and subsequent number of political parties) shapes the degree to which power is concentrated or dispersed, the ideological control of government, and, subsequently, who has greater influence of the policy process. Under the British majoritarian system, even when a ruling government is tacitly controlled by the left, as was Tony Blair's Labour Party, the interests of the right still carry significant weight (Mannin, 2010). This phenomenon is a result of the two-party, SMD system where center-left parties, in order to secure the support of the median voter, must illustrate that they are committed "to a moderate platform by concentrating power in a leader with a reputation for being moderate or even slightly right of centre (think Tony Blair or Bill Clinton). When they succeed, they are competitive with centre-right parties" (Iversen, 2007, p. 284). Such was the case with the increasingly radicalization of British labor in the 1970s. Due to the two-party system, such radicalization made the electoral success of the Labour Party problematic as "centripetal competition around vote- and office-seeking objectives" favored a more moderate policy (Kitschelt, 1994, p. 39).

Constitutional Structures

Veto points/players can shape access to the political process. Tsebelis identifies two types of veto players: partisan veto players and institutional veto players. Institutional veto players are largely guided by the constitutional structures of a given state (Tsebelis, 1995, p. 302). Constitutional structures "have to do with the presence or absence of explicit restraints on the legislative power of parliamentary majorities" (Lijphart, 1999, p. 216). Constitutional structures may include federalism, bicameralism, presidentialism, the use of referenda, judicial review, and central bank independence. The veto points within the political system constrain or promote the ability of minorities to veto policy proposals. Immergut's case study examining socialized medicine illustrates that countries with fewer veto points are able to make more radical policy changes than countries with greater numbers of veto points (1990).

Veto points are important in that they affect policy stability, and policy stability affects production regime. As Wood points out:

> the stability of policy regimes over time is largely determined by the power of governments to initiate reform or reversals. In each case, the degree of constraint on central government is fundamental to employers' ability to pursue those production strategies that distinguish each variety of capitalism. (2001, p. 248)

I contend that policy stability is conducive to CMEs, while instability is conducive to LMEs. Policy stability will decrease the uncertainty in the exchange of information between economic and political actors, specifically in regard to issues like corporate governance, education and training systems, inter-firm relations, and industrial relations (Hall & Soskice, 2001; North, 1990). If transaction costs are lowered, the interests of political and economic actors to compromise and cooperate are increased.

The opposite holds true for political systems characterized by fewer institutional veto points. Limited numbers of institutional veto points and the accompanying increased level of policy instability create an environment of increased pluralism and competition between political and economic actors. The fact that such a system is then based upon deep-rooted competition between competing actors can lead to radical policy change. This instability makes competition and innovation necessary components to the functioning of the liberal market political economy (Iversen, 2007).

The German political system is characterized by a high number of constitutional constraints. Most notably, the German system maintains a rather rigid written constitution in the Basic Law ratified following World War II (Hancock & Krisch, 2009; Roberts, 2006). Germany maintains a strong federalist system with state and local governments maintaining a significant degree of autonomy from the central government. Germany also maintains a bicameral legislature consisting of a first chamber, the *Bundestag*, and a second chamber, the *Bundesrat* which consists of delegates appointed by *Lander* governments. Both houses must cooperate in order to pass legislation as the *Bundesrat* "exercises coequal powers with the lower house, the *Bundestag*, over most important policy issues" (Wood, 2001, p. 254).[4] Additionally, Germany has a strong tradition of judicial review, with the Federal Constitutional Court acting "as an independent institution with sweeping legal authority" (Hancock & Krisch, 2009, p. 95). Of particular note here is the Federal Constitutional Court's upholding of codetermination agreements in the face of strong business pressure.

The British case maintains significantly fewer constitutional constraints than Germany. Although maintaining an upper house, the House of Lords, Britain is considered for all intents and purposes a unicameral system. Unlike the German case which allows for significant input from constituent federated elements (largely represented in the *Bundesrat*), the British government remains highly centralized.[5] In the British case the executive-legislative functions are largely fused which allows for the ruling government to largely act on preferred policies without the consent of the opposition (Mannin, 2010, p. 70). Most important, however, is the fact that the British system adheres strongly to the concept of parliamentary sovereignty, that is, "'Parliament ... has ... the right to make or unmake any law whatever; further, that no person or body is recognized by the law as having a right to override or set aside the legislation of Parliament'" (Norton, 2007, p. 60).[6] The lack of constitutional constraints in the British system was instrumental to the ability of the Conservative ruling government to implement "unbridled liberalism" in the 1980s and 1990s, and retrench many Labour policies of the 1970s, including the 1975 Industrial Relations Act (Coates, 2000, p. 51).

Due to the strong adherence to parliamentary sovereignty, the British system maintains a weak institution of judicial review, partly a result of the unwritten British Constitution.[7]

> In their rulings, judges were barred from straying beyond what Parliament provided for in law unless there were inconsistencies in the law or the law lacked clarity. Because judges were expected to rule in scrupulous accord with what Parliament said the law was, the judiciary did not emerge as an independent force poised to engage in political struggles with Parliament and the government of the day. (Norton, 2007)

The high number of constitutional constraints encourages policy stability and cooperation in German politics. Such constraints led to the maintenance of the coordinated market production regime in the face of pressures to adopt more neoliberal policies (Wood, 2001). The low numbers of constitutional constraints promote an environment of adversarial politics in Britain and potentially allow for rapid policy changes. This is readily evidenced by the rapid adoption of neoliberal reforms under British Conservative regimes (Gamble, 1988; Mannin, 2010; Norton, 2007). As Wood points out:

> in the German case, the presence of institutional guarantees that limit the degree and type of government intervention is central to the logic of supply side coordination. In Britain, the absence of such guarantees makes institutions of non-market coordination difficult to sustain. (2001, pp. 248–249)

As such, the case studies support the contention that systems with higher levels of constitutional constraint will likely favor maintenance of a CME, while systems with fewer constitutional constraints will likely favor a continuation and expansion of liberal market economic policies.

Summation and Discussion of Political Institutions

As a result of the differing structures of political institutions, interest group representation varies between Germany and Britain. The German case, characterized by consensus-oriented structures, allows for greater interest group participation through social partnerships and in the policymaking process, higher numbers of veto players, and subsequently more consensual policy outcomes. On the other hand, the majoritarian structures of Britain are much more adversarial, with interest groups—to a great degree divided by political party, and subsequently socioeconomic class—vying for total control of the legislative and, subsequently, the policy process.

The remainder of this chapter will examine the effects of these institutional differences on the abilities of Germany and Britain to either adopt or limit neoliberal reforms beginning in the 1980s.

Neoliberal Reforms of the 1980s: Germany and Britain

The economic crises of the 1980s and the subsequent challenges to social democracy were truly global events (Castles et al., 1996; Kitschelt, 1994; Norton, 2007). Such changes include greater openness of trade, increasing competition from foreign markets, and the liberalization of capital controls. Such changes have led many OECD countries to adopt neoliberal policies in order to address the changing global economy. However, the degree of liberalization has varied between OECD states, particularly between those states considered majoritarian democracies and those considered consensus democracies. In reference to the 1980s, Wood writes:

> In Great Britain this was a decade of unprecedented neo-liberal reform, propelled by the combination of employers agitating for the restoration of a liberal market economy and a powerful central government under Margaret Thatcher. In West Germany, however, the 1980s were a decade in which reform impulses were frustrated. (2001, p. 249)

Figure 5.1 illustrates the variation in market coordination between Germany and Britain compared to the OECD average from 1970 to 2005. The figure depicts a scaled index, drawn from Casey (2009) coded 0–1. A score of 0 represents highly uncoordinated regimes, while a score of 1 represents a significant degree of coordination. The measure is derived

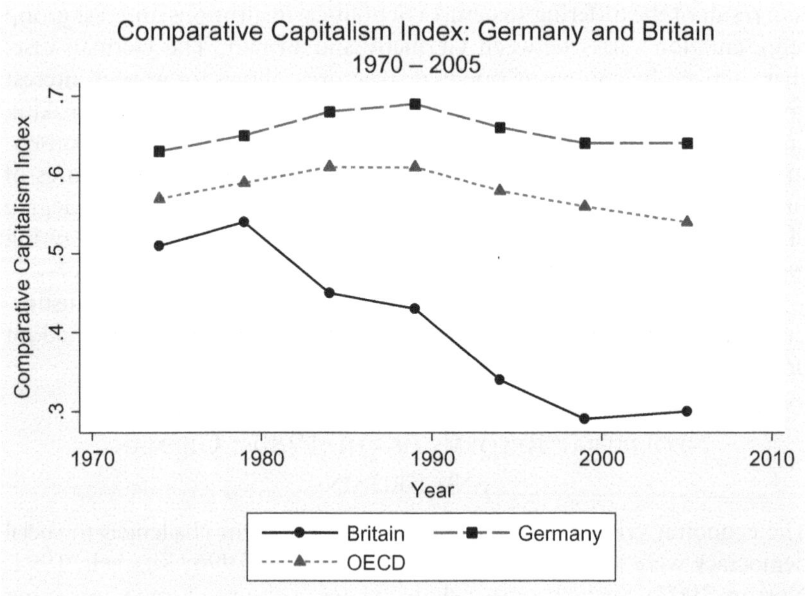

Fig. 5.1 Trends in the comparative capitalism index over time in Germany and Britain. *Note*: Data from Casey (2009)

from three sub-indices capturing labor coordination, business coordination, and state intervention.

The graph illustrates a significant difference between the level of liberalization between Germany and Britain between 1980 and 2006. The German case began with a higher level of coordination than the OECD average and continued to be quite high through the 1980s and relatively stable through 2006. The findings are especially interesting in light of Germany's continued economic difficulties between 1973 and 1998 (Manow, 2001c). Germany has faced high unemployment, "low levels of inward direct investment, high levels of investment abroad by German companies" and a continually problematic welfare state (Matthew Allen, 2006, p. 3). The level of coordination in Britain, on the other hand, began slightly lower than the OECD average between 1974 and 1980, but declined sharply through the 1980s and continued to decline through 2005, the end point of this data.

The findings lend credence to two major hypotheses. First, Peter Hall finds that the ways in which political economies are able to adjust to changes in the global economy depend on the type of political institutions and dispersion of power in a given state (Hall, 1999, 2007). Second, Swank argues that the consensus-oriented institutions are able to "blunt" the pressures for change stemming from an evolving international economy. The main argument is that the impacts of internationalization will differ between nations based on the presence of social corporatism versus pluralism, variations in electoral representation, diverse versus concentrated power, and the structure of the welfare state (Swank, 2001, 2002).

The following section will examine the divergent strategies that led to the relative stability of German market coordination, and the much more radical neoliberal reforms of Britain. Specifically, I inspect the roles that the political regimes—consensus in the case of Germany, and majoritarian in the case of Britain—played in the ability of Germany and Britain to adopt or limit neoliberal reforms. By doing so, I will shed light on the relationship between political institutions and variation in capitalist systems.

Changing Political Power: Germany and Britain in the 1980s

In the late 1970s and early 1980s, ideological change in government occurred in both Germany and England. Following ten years of social democratic governance, the 1982 vote of no confidence saw the German center-left coalition, led by the SPD, replaced by a center-right Christian Democratic regime led by Helmut Kohl (Bering, 1999). Similarly, the 1979 election in England saw the British Labour Party soundly defeated and replaced by the Conservative Party led by Margaret Thatcher (Gamble, 1988; Kitschelt, 1994, p. 2).

Both the newly elected British and German governments, and their subsequent policies, were the result of a continuing series of economic crises. In 1981, Germany "saw record unemployment, firms heading into the bankruptcy courts, falling investment, and a rise in inflation to 5 percent" (Bering, 1999, p. 4). Following the 1982 collapse of the German SPD–FDP coalition (the result of conflicting opinions regarding how to address increasing economic difficulties [Bering, 1999, p. 13]), the Conservative Democrat coalition (CDU/CSU and FDP) "played on the worsening economic situation, promising a change of direction" from the previous Social Democrat policy positions (Roberts, 2006, p. 87).

Similarly, throughout the 1970s, British labor possessed significant political power exercised through the Labour Party (Coates, 2000, p. 88). However, faced with increasing strikes, low productivity, and decreasing international competitiveness, the Labour Party lost the confidence of the electorate, and the Thatcherite government came to power. As such, the rise of the British Conservatives is "associated with economic decline and electoral unpopularity for those responsible" (D. King & Wood, 1999, p. 378).

However, although facing similar economic difficulties, the ways in which the German and British governments addressed the economic problems differed dramatically. For example, the Thatcher government

> set out to end British economic decline by smashing the corporatist, Keynesian 'post-war consensus.' The Tories implemented a free market reform programme intended to unleash British entrepreneurialism, which they argued had been suppressed by both the Labour Party and 'one nation' Tory moderates. (Casey, 2002, p. 3)

In Germany, with the election of Helmut Kohl's CDU-CSU/FDP coalition, and its slogan of "less state, more freedom" it appeared that Germany was on the verge of adopting its own neoliberal policies (Wood, 2001, p. 266). However, Germany maintained many of the corporatist bargaining structures—through encompassing labor, business, and state organizations—that characterized much of the post-war period (Hassel, 2007).

The ability of the governments to adopt neoliberal reforms—in the case of Britain, or less far-reaching policy measures in the case of Germany—depended largely on the differing political regimes of the two states. To a large extent it was the political institutions that explain the variation in the economic coping strategies of Germany and Britain.

As stated previously, the Thatcher government abandoned traditional Keynesian policies, severely weakened labor, denationalized many state-owned businesses, and in general, "[set] the market free" (Howell, 2007, p. 249). The question, of course, must be asked, how were such economic reforms, and the subsequent negative impacts on a significant proportion of population not only politically feasible but also conducive to a sustained Conservative government? King and Wood (1999) provide a highly plausible explanation by citing the unique features of the British electoral and party systems.

First, the negative effects of neoliberal reforms were most concentrated in the industrial north of the country (Casey, 2002), the results of which limited the electoral costs of reforms to predominately safe Labour districts, thus not affecting, to a great degree, the existing Conservative electoral standing (D. King & Wood, 1999, p. 382).

Second, "the single member plurality electoral system rewarded the Conservatives for the division of the Labour Party and the formation of the Social Democratic Party (SDP)" (D. King & Wood, 1999, p. 382; Wood, 2001). Majoritarian systems are widely known for limiting the power of small, third parties (Duverger, 1954; Lijphart, 1994; Sartori, 1976). The British case is no exception. "The three-way electoral race robbed a potential 'unified' opposition of seats" supporting labor interests, thus ushering in the continuation of Conservative government (D. King & Wood, 1999, p. 382). This supports power resource theory assumptions that disadvantaged classes will seek to overcome collective action problems and mobilize politically—often into political parties—and begin to demand economic policies designed to mitigate the negative effects of market-oriented distribution policies (Korpi, 1983, 2006). However, political institutions shape the ability for such disadvantaged classes to effect political change (Swank, 2001, 2002). Under majoritarian systems, workers have limited ability to exit "the socialist camp" (Kitschelt, 1994, p. 61).

Additionally, business sided strongly with the Conservative Party's reforms when it became evident that "the government's *electoral* prospects would not be harmed by the resolute pursuit of its economic and industrial-relations goals" (Wood, 2001, p. 263).

Table 5.2 Disproportionality of British politics: fractionalization of Labour 1983 and 1987

Party	*Vote %*	*Total seats*	*Percentage of seats*
1983 election			
Conservative	42.4	397	62.7
Labour	27.6	209	33.1
Liberal/SDP	25.4	23	3.6
1987 election			
Conservative	42.2	375	59.2
Labour	30.8	229	36.2
Liberal/SDP	22.6	22	3.4

Note: Data drawn from www.ukpolitical.info

Table 5.2 illustrates the results of the fractionalization of the Labour Party, and the subsequent effects on the electoral victory of the Conservative Party. Had Britain adhered to PR rules, it is likely that a coalition would have formed between Labor and the Liberal/SDP bloc which may, in turn, have led to a much less severe neoliberal reform policy package.

Germany addressed the political crises in significantly different ways than its British counterpart. Germany became aware of its declining economic status in the mid-1960s. However, unlike the radical neoliberal reforms engaged by the Conservative-majority government in Britain, the unique political institutions led to a much more moderate economic policy. The 1967 grand coalition of CDU-SPD created "a tripartite system of economic policy consultation involving meetings between high-level government officials and representatives of private capital and organized labor" (Hancock & Krisch, 2009, p. 165). Such policies, in part, institutionalized cooperation and coordination regarding economic issues within the political environment as evidenced by much more moderate political party behavior.

> "'Both major German parties have been committed to expansive social protection and to politics promoting job security and codetermination … in enterprise.' Their common goal has been to institutionalize a social partnership between private capital and labor to avoid the class conflict that characterized the Imperial and Weimar systems." (Hancock & Krisch, 2009, p. 161)

Here we see that the consensus institutions "not only provide access to political interests but also tend to include these interest in multi-party executive cabinets 'fused' to the legislature, ensuring representativeness on the one hand, and effectiveness on the other" (Birchfield & Crepaz, 1998, p. 179). As such, these findings support the proposition that as the degree of consensus (created by macro-political institutions) increases, so does the level of corporatist arrangements (Lijphart & Crepaz, 1991).

Labor Organization: Germany and Britain

Changes in the global economy—beginning in the 1970s—led to pressure for structural changes in advanced industrialized economies, specifically in regard to labor relations (D. King & Wood, 1999, p. 373). In many OECD countries, employers required greater flexibility to address changing market conditions (Thelen, 2001). Some argued that such changes would lead to labor deregulation and a subsequent convergence between CME and LME institutional structures.

> From the early 1980s to the early 1990s, socialist, social democratic, and labor ideologies underwent more change than in any decade since World War II. Parties everywhere began to withdraw from old programmatic priorities, yet the pace extent and direction of that strategic transformation have varied across countries. (Kitschelt, 1994, p. 3)

The differences in political institutions between Germany and Britain led to significant variation in the power resources of organized labor.

In measuring variation in labor organization, I draw on Casey's measure capturing trade union density, coverage of collective bargaining agreements, the centralization and coordination of wages, and levels of educational attainment (2009). Higher scores indicate greater strength of organized labor, while lower scores indicate weaker labor power.

Figure 5.2 indicates that between the 1970 and 1980, Germany and Britain maintained similar degrees of labor organization. However, a significant divergence occurred in 1980. The power of German labor increased between 1980 and 1984 before reaching a rough plateau between 1984 and 2000. Labor power in Britain, on the other hand, declined significantly over the same time period. Such divergence is largely the result of the political strength of labor in the two countries which ultimately is structured by the electoral system, the subsequent number of political parties, and the structure of governing coalitions.

Fig. 5.2 Trends in the labor organization index over time in Germany and Britain. *Note*: Data from Casey (2009)

Between 1940 and 1979, British politics was characterized by a degree of consensus between the Conservative and Labour parties (Howell, 2007). In part, such consensus was driven first by the need mobilize the homeland against an aggressive Germany, and second, to rebuild Britain following the tremendous destruction of World War II (Judt, 2005). In the 1960s and 1970s such cooperation between parties led to corporatist system consisting of "compromise worked out between the representatives of labour, capital, and the central bureaucracy" (Gamble, 1988, p. 17).

However, in the late 1970s, as result of increasing economic difficulties and an overburdened welfare state, the corporatist arrangements—which were becoming increasingly viewed as problematic by the public—began to fragment and the cooperation between the Conservatives and Labour began to dissolve. The labor movement, historically strong in Britain, began to make increasing demands on the government in the face of rising economic crises leading to the "Winter of Discontent" in 1979 (Gamble, 1988; Norton, 2007). The disproportionate strength of labor grew increasingly unpopular. "The unions were holding the government hostage—at least that is how the public saw it" (Norton, 2007, p. 134).

The result of the radicalization of labor created electoral difficulties for the Labour Party. Due to the two-party system, and the subsequent necessity of capturing the median voter, the Labour Party adopted a much more moderate series of reforms. This led to a significant disillusionment with the Labour Party on the part of its traditional labor constituency (Kitschelt, 1994, p. 39). However, due to the lack of exit options on the part of labor from the Labour Party, labor largely had to tacitly accept the policies of the party (Kitschelt, 1994, p. 61).

In part, the unpopularity of the British unions within the British electorate led to a significant split in the Labour Party and the emergence of the Social Democratic Party—a more militant wing of Labour—in 1981. As illustrated above, within an SMD electoral system the fractionalization of the Labour Party diluted the overall power of labor and ushered in a continuation of Thatcherite government and neoliberal policies.

The Conservative Party, first under Margaret Thatcher, and latter under John Major, controlled the British government from 1979 to 1997 (Mannin, 2010; Norton, 2007). The Thatcherite government was a dramatic move away from the British conservativism of post-war period, and rejected the social compromises that characterized the 1950s and 1960s (Gamble, 1988; Wood, 2001). Legislation passed by the ruling government in the 1980s and 1990s "included measures that made it more difficult for unions to initiate industrial action and secure collective bargaining rights" (Thelen, 2001, p. 95).

Furthermore, the structure of British labor made it especially difficult to form a unified bloc in opposition to the Thatcherite legislation.

> The organization of British labour also mitigated against coordinated restructuring. Political influence was assured through formal affiliation with the Labour Party and a national voice in the form of the Trades Union Congress (TUC), but the TUC was never more than a loose confederation of member unions, and national leaders lacked real control over member unions. (Casey, 2002, p. 14)

As such, Britain lacked a strong peak labor organization. The lack of peak organization was likely the result of the limitations of interest groups to participate in the political process under a majoritarian system (Soskice, 2007b, p. 93), as well as the cited fractionalization of the Labour Party. A lack of peak organizations representing labor interests made efficient collaboration and cooperation between business and labor difficult. In part, the lack of peak labor associations is the result of the necessity of labor to maintain general skills as a result of possibility of rapid policy changes. "Under majoritarian institutions ... the difficulty of parties making commitments, both to particular constituents and to the future, means that there is less political protection of specific assets and greater incentives to invest in general skills as an insurance against labour market risks" (Iversen, 2007, p. 288). The requirement to maintain transferable, general skills makes commitment to large labor organizations difficult.

Unlike the British model, Germany possesses strong, unified, peak labor organizations, specifically the German Trade Union Confederation. The German Trade Union Confederation "identifies itself 'as the voice of trade unions in relation to political decision makers, parties and associations ... [Its role] is to coordinate union activities" (Hancock & Krisch, 2009, p. 139). Although reporting to be nonpartisan, the German Trade Union Confederation is closely tied with the SPD. "In exchange for political support for central labor objectives, the [German Trade Union Confederation] and its member unions have pursued a strategy of general wage and strike restraint to bolster Germany's economic growth and stability" (Hancock & Krisch, 2009, p. 140).

Additionally, German labor relations include a strong adherence to the concept of industrial citizenship. "Industrial citizenship refers to the status rights and obligations that are reciprocal between the rights of workers and the obligations of employers and asymmetric in addressing the unequal power of the two parties in exchange" (Jackson, 2001, p. 121). In the German case, industrial citizenship is most often illustrated through the constitutionally protected codetermination policies which ensure labor representation in managerial decisions (Roe, 2003; Streeck & Yamamura, 2001).

Under the German consensus regime, the interests of business and labor were much more similar than under the British system. The consensus political systems

> provide a framework for interest groups to take part in the policymaking. The importance of this is reflected in the many areas of institutional policymaking in which the major business and union groups have broadly shared

> goals (training systems, employee representation, collective bargaining, etc.) but often sharply different ideal points within those areas; and where some degree of standardization national is called for. (Soskice, 2007a, p. 93)

In part, this can be explained by the role of interest mediation—stemming from consensus political institutions—that characterize Christian democracies, governments, and coalitions. Such interest group mediation took on a political mantle with the creation of the grand CDU/CSU-SPD coalition in 1967 which

> created a tripartite consultative process known as concerted action ... in which federal officials and representatives of both the [German Trade Union Confederation] and employer associations agreed to meet on a regular basis to discuss measures to exercise wage and price restraint. (Hancock & Krisch, 2009, p. 140)

Additionally, the role that constitutional constraints play on the role of policy stability must be addressed. German codetermination laws are constitutionally binding, making drastic reforms to existing policies untenable (Hancock & Krisch, 2009). This differs dramatically from the British system in which the concept of parliamentary sovereignty makes the repeal of existing agreements much less difficult (D. King & Wood, 1999, p. 380; Mannin, 2010; Norton, 2007).

Furthermore, Germany possesses "deeply ingrained attitudes—about unemployment, business, work, the role of the state—that have evolved over decades" (Bering, 1999, p. 220). Swank contends that such attitudes are the result of corporatist structures which grant labor interests veto power over policy changes, political power to leftist parties, and "cultivates a distinct constellation of norms and values that shape actor's behavior and the character of the policy process" (Swank, 2002, p. 43).

Additionally, German political parties are much more encompassing than their British counterparts. As such, in Germany, workers "can exit from the socialist coalition [or the moderate right coalition] given the cross-class appeals of the differing parties" (Kitschelt, 1994, p. 61). In part this is the result of the necessity of coalition formation in order to govern. Such a relationship is well illustrated by the CDU's "links with trade unions [which] have been crucial in counterbalancing the more economically liberal agenda of these groups and of the FDP" (Wood, 2001, p. 254). This was especially prevalent in the 1980s, when the support of the FDP was imperative to coalition formation, but the CDU was unwilling to alienate a significant segment of its electoral support and thus adopted much more moderate policies with labor.

These findings support the work of Martin and Swank who contend that party systems and the structure of state shape the development of peak interest organizations. Specifically, these findings support the premise that PR and multi-party systems support the development of corporatist peak associations, while two-party, majoritarian systems are conducive to pluralist peak associations (Martin & Swank, 2008).

Business Organization: Germany and Britain

The ways in which business organizations are structured play a major role in shaping capitalist systems. Drawing on Casey, business organization is measured as a scaled variable capturing corporate finance, corporate governance, and inter-firm relations (2009, p. 265). Specifically, the variable measures the level of stock market capitalization, the percentage of widely held firms, and the degree to which firms are able to operate independently from shareholders. Such a measure parallels Hall and Soskice's internal structure of the firm, financial system and corporate governance, and inter-company relations (2001). Higher scores represent greater degrees of business coordination, while lower scores indicate less business coordination (Fig. 5.3).

The German case maintained much more static scores along the business index, remaining above the OECD average during the time frame under investigation. Although beginning with scores significantly lower than Germany and the OECD average, the British case experienced a much more precipitous decline between 1980 and 1999, albeit with a slight increase between 1999 and 2004, possibly as a result of Tony Blair's New Labour policies.

The German state has long provided support for various manufacturing sectors. "From the 1970s they showed what Porter called a 'stubbornly persistent tendency to subsidize ailing sectors' (Porter, 1990, p. 378) not least shipbuilding, railways, coal, steel, and agriculture" (Coates, 2000, p. 212). In part, continued government subsidies are the result of strong peak employer organizations; the most notable is the Federal Union of German Employer Associations. This peak employer organization consists of a large number of firms "primarily responsible for labor market relations," specifically in regard to "collective bargaining responsibilities with

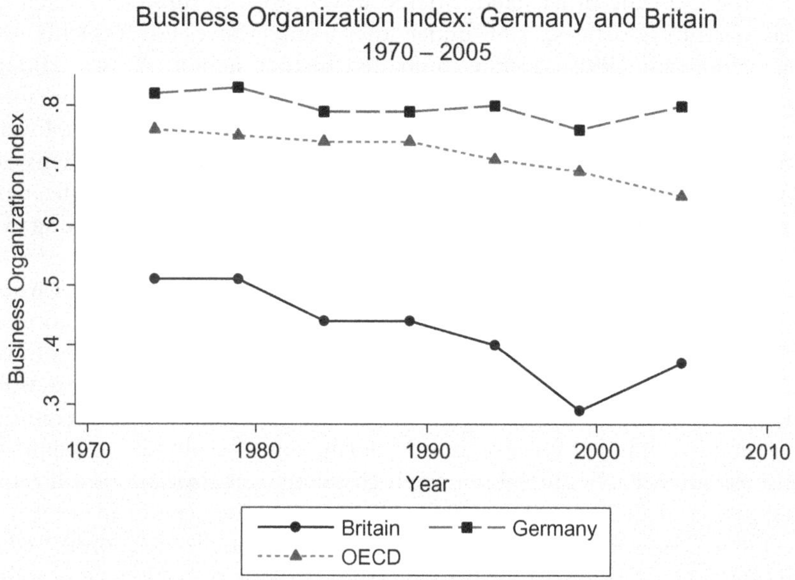

Fig. 5.3 Change in business organization: Germany and Britain. *Note*: Data from Casey (2009)

unions" (Hancock & Krisch, 2009, pp. 144–145). As such, the German case likely represents a continuation of the traditional stakeholder-based financial system which focuses on strategic goals rather than the British market-based system concerned with short-term investment returns (Vitols, 2001).

Additionally, German business interests are constrained by the existing policies favoring coordination. The weakness of the German state—the result of the consensus nature of the political regime—makes the possibility of abandoning existing policies of coordination difficult. Due to the institutional constraints placed on the German state, and the subsequent policy stability, German business is more likely to make the long-term investments in industry-specific skills, for example, that characterize a coordinated market production regime, and "provide an additional assurance that these investments are safe" (Wood, 2001, p. 257). As such, once such policies are in place, it is likely that such policies will continue.

Britain, on the other hand, offered lower levels of subsidies to major manufacturing sectors, and under the Conservative governments of the 1980s and 1990s, all but eliminated further support (Casey, 2002; Gamble, 1988). In part, this is the result of few peak employer organizations in the British political economy. As such, the lack of employer organizations leads to "the inability of business to solve basic problems of collective action [which] undermines any public policy effort predicated on concentration between the social actors and the state" (D. King & Wood, 1999, p. 375).

This lends credence to the work developed by Martin and Swank who find that PR and multi-party system lead to corporatist peak associations, while two-party systems will lead to pluralist/competitive organizations (2008). The logic contends that in PR/multi-party systems, we will find parties sympathetic to business interests. This results in cooperation between like-minded groups, and the formation of coalitions to support business interests. Because it is unlikely that employer associations will gain majority control, they will seek other sources of influence outside of government. This can lead to more organized and centralized (coordinated) employer associations. In two-party systems, with two large "umbrella parties" business interests are dispersed. These big parties cross-cut class divides. Employers have a harder time coming together, and have fewer reasons to negotiate with labor politically (2008, p. 182).

Additionally, the structure of the British political system creates an environment of policy uncertainty. "Because governments have the capacity to introduce radical changes of policy at will, companies are unwilling to make the risky long-term investments that would be necessary for constructing networks of coordination [either between employers themselves, or between employers and organized labor]" (Wood, 2001, p. 259). As such, it is in the interests of business to maintain the economic structures characterized by LMEs and their subsequent production regimes. Such a system differs quite dramatically from the German model, in which constitutional constraints and electoral requirements of more encompassing political parties make radical policy change difficult.

State Organization: Germany and Britain

The degree to which a state intervenes in the economy proves a significant factor in shaping variation in capitalist systems. In LMEs, the state largely maintains a "hands-off" relationship with business and labor, relying largely on market forces to address coordination problems between relevant actors. In CMEs, on the other hand, the state plays a much more interventionist role, relying on nonmarket mechanisms to address coordination problems (Hall & Soskice, 2001).

In both Britain and Germany, the 1960s and 1970s were an era characterized by corporatist political-economic arrangements (Gerber, 1995; Schmidt, 2007). Under such arrangements "the legitimacy and functioning of the state is primarily or exclusively dependent on the activity of singular, noncompetitive, hierarchically ordered representative 'corporations'" (Schmitter, 1979, p. 20). In the cases of both Germany and Britain, the major "corporations" were business, labor, and the state (Gamble, 1988; Hancock & Krisch, 2009; Mannin, 2010; Norton, 2007; Schmidt, 2009). However, the 1980s saw significant changes to the corporatist arrangements of Britain and relative stability in the case of Germany. As will be shown below, the degree to which the state involves itself in the political economy is largely structured by the political institutions which characterize a particular country's political regime.

Figure 5.4 illustrates the level of state involvement in the economies of Germany, Britain, as well as an average of OECD scores. The measure is scaled 0–1 with high scores representing greater involvement and low scores illustrating less involvement. The measure is an aggregate of variables capturing the size of government, levels of employment protection legislation, levels of unemployment benefits, and the degree of active labor market policies (Casey, 2009, p. 263).

As Fig. 5.4 illustrates, Germany and Britain maintained very similar levels of state involvement in the economy between 1970 and 1980 with both countries maintaining levels slightly above the OECD average. However, between 1980 and 1990, a significant divergence emerges between the two states, with an even greater diverging trend between 1990 and 2005.[8] The remainder of this section will attempt to highlight some of the major causes of the divergence between British and German levels of state intervention, paying particular attention to the role of political institutions.

The German state has a long history of involving itself an in the economy (Coates, 2000; Streeck, 2001). In the early stages of industrialization, the German state played an overarching role in structuring the German economy by channeling finances to the "commanding heights of the economy" in order to "catch up" to its early industrializing rivals (Gershenkron, 1962). This historical trend and its subsequent structural aspects have led to the propensity for continued state involvement

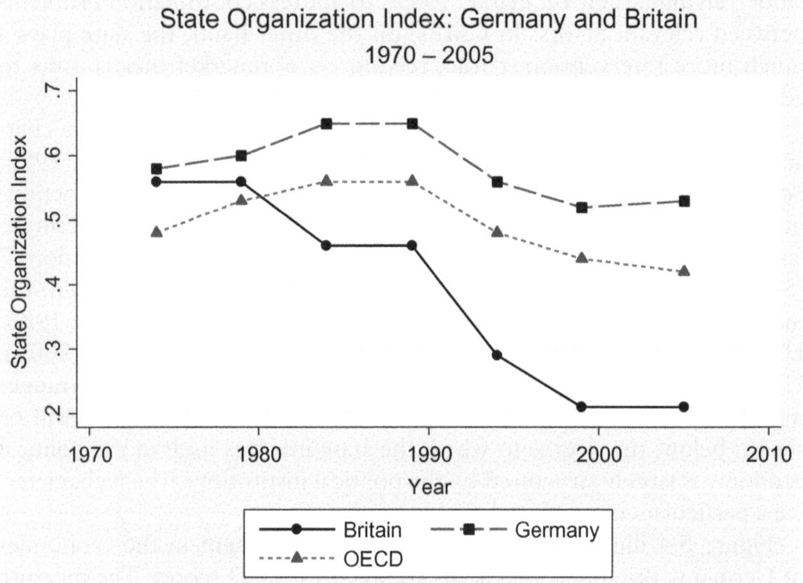

Fig. 5.4 Change in state organization: Germany and Britain. *Note*: Data from Casey (2009)

between business and labor. To a large degree such involvement served to ensure support from those most necessary for the modernization process, including both employer groups and, at times, a rather militant labor movement (Coates, 2000, p. 112; Manow, 2001b; Thelen, 2001). Such political involvement continued through the 1980s and 1990s. Schmidt describes the modern structure of German state involvement well:

> In a CME like Germany, the state is enabling because it takes action not only to arbitrate among economic actors but also facilitate their activities; it often leaves the rules to be jointly administered by them, while acting as a coequal (or bystander) with management and unions in labor regulation and wage bargaining and generally acting to protect the production system's nonmarket coordinating institutions. Adjustment here is led by firms and jointly negotiated cooperatively between business, labor, and the state. (2009, pp. 521–522)

Interestingly, Britain, on the other hand, maintains a quite different structure affecting government intervention in the economy. Schmidt writes:

> In an LME like Britain, the state is liberal because it takes an arm's length approach to business and labor, limiting its role to setting rules and settling conflicts; it often leaves the administration of the rules to self-regulating bodies or to regulatory agencies and generally acts as an agent of market preservation. Adjustment is driven by the financial markets and led by autonomous firms acting on their own, with comparatively little input—whether positive or negative—from state or labor. (2009, p. 521)

In Britain, the extreme deregulation of the market involved strong state intervention. However, the strength of the state largely stemmed from the political institutions existent in the country. "A combination of the doctrine of parliamentary sovereignty, a first-past-the-post electoral system, internally hierarchical political parties gives Britain enormously powerful single-party governments" (Wood, 2001, p. 255). To a large degree, the ability of a state to adopt neoliberal reforms, or maintain existing nonmarket coordination mechanisms, stems from the power of the state. In the case of Germany, a large number of political constraints exist which limit the state's ability to change existing policies that shape the production regime.

Conclusion

The ways in which states were affected by pressures to adopt neoliberal reforms in the 1980s allow for a closer examination of the relationship between political regime and VOC. Both Germany and Britain faced exogenous pressures—as a result of changes to the international economy—to reexamine their political-economic systems. Although at first glance it may have appeared that a convergence toward LMEs was on the horizon, Germany and Britain reacted differently to these international pressures and maintained, to a large extent, their pre-existing variety of capitalism.

I contend that the crucial independent variables that allowed Britain to adopt reforms, while German essentially maintained the status quo, lie in the differences between the political systems of each. That is, consensus institutions are conducive to creating an environment of cooperation and credible commitment to nonmarket mechanisms of coordination between political and economic actors with competing interests. On the other hand, majoritarian systems lead to an adversarial political-economic environment characterized by limited cooperation, high levels of competition, and a heavy reliance on market mechanisms for coordination.

As such, the political institutions of Germany—namely, mixed-member proportional electoral rules, a multi-party system, the necessity of a coalition government, and rather strict constitutional constraints—constrained the "adjustment paths" available to political and economic actors, and the state's "capacities to adjust" to changing conditions in the world economy (Hall, 1999, p. 158). Under the consensus political regime, a large number of actors—representing both business and labor—were institutionally compelled to enter into cooperative agreements, thus leading to the maintenance of a CME.

Britain, on the other hand, with a majoritarian political regime characterized by an adherence to SMD electoral rules, an entrenched two-party system, a majoritarian cabinet structure, and very loose constitutional constraints, allowed for much more rapid policy changes. The failure of the majoritarian political institutions to provide a credible commitment to nonmarket mechanisms for coordination between business and labor led a significant degree of competition between business and labor. Due to the fact that majoritarian systems tend to favor the power of the right over labor (Iversen & Soskice, 2006; Martin & Swank, 2008), the Thatcherite neoliberal policies were allowed to be implemented.

As stated in chapter three, the purpose of the qualitative case studies was to supplement and test the statistical relationships between political institutional variation in capitalist economies established in the quantitative chapter. As such, this chapter was designed to answer three questions. First, do the proposed causal relationships between political institutions and VOC exist in real-world cases? Second, how do the political institutions affect economic structures in reality? Third, what alternative variables become apparent through the qualitative research?

First, in answer to question one, this book has supported the argument that political institutions matter in regard to variation in capitalist systems (Cusack et al., 2007; Gourevitch, 2003; Iversen & Stevens, 2008; Katzenstein, 1985; D. King & Wood, 1999; Korpi, 1983, 2006; Martin & Swank, 2008; Roe, 2003). The German consensus political regime maintained many of the aspects of CME that characterized its production regime prior to changes in the global economy in the 1970s and

1980s. The British majoritarian political regime adopted a radical increase in levels of liberalization during the same time period. Furthermore, this chapter supports the quantitative findings of Chap. 4 which suggest that partisanship and policy legacies, the number of political parties, and the type of electoral system all possess a significant relationship with varieties of capitalist systems.

Second, in answer to question two—how do the political institutions affect economic structures in reality—this chapter finds that that pre-existing institutions affect the "adjustment paths" available to political and economic actors, as well as the state's "capacities to adjust" to changing international economic conditions (Hall, 1999, p. 158). The German political regime, characterized by long-standing influence of Christian democracy, multiple political parties, and a PR electoral system, adopted much more neoliberal reforms than the British system characterized by a two-party system, an SMD electoral system, and parliamentary sovereignty.

Proportional electoral systems, through the promotion of multiple political parties, allow greater numbers of interests to participate in the policymaking process. Subsequently, coalitions, in order to garner enough electoral support to form a government, must maintain a system of integration, accommodation, and mediation in order to implement policy (Van Kersbergen, 1999). SMD electoral rules and the consequent two-party system lead to more adversarial politics. This is most readily evidenced by majoritarian cabinet structures and, in the British case, parliamentary sovereignty. Here, the ruling party is allowed to enact policy with little to no consultation with the opposition (Mannin, 2010; Norton, 2007).

Third, in answer to question three, constitutional constraints play a significant role in shaping VOC. Although Chap. 4 found a weak, non-statistically significant relationship between constitutional structures and VOC, the relationship appears much more significant upon closer examination of the German and British cases. Germany, with a more rigid written constitution, possessed significant checks not only from constitutional statutes like codetermination policies but also through a federated system which allowed for regional governments to play a significant role in policy development and implementation. The British case, on the other hand, is governed largely by the sovereignty of parliament and the tight relationship between executive and parliament.

Notes

1. Some called Germany a "two-and-a-half" party system, largely due to the FDP's size (Hancock & Krisch, 2009). A two-and-a-half party system "is a party system in which there are two large parties, neither of which has won an overall majority of seats, plus one or more smaller, minor parties" (Norton, 2007, p. 78). However, "In terms of size, membership, and electoral support, the Liberals were certainly no more than a 'half' compared to the two major parties, yet in terms of political influence and government participation they could be regarded as a 'full' party" (James, 2003, p. 32). In addition to the FDP, the Greens have also shown themselves to be a valuable coalition partner. As such, following unification, Germany is generally considered a five-party system.
2. The election of October 1990, the first under German unification, saw five political parties gaining, and generally holding, representation in the German parliament (Hancock & Krisch, 2009, p. 124; Roberts, 2006, p. 4).
3. Those nondominant parties are generally regionally based, stemming from Northern Ireland, Scotland, and Wales. They hold very few parliamentary seats, and British politics remains dominated by the Labour and Conservative parties.
4. Such was the case in 2003 when debate between the *Bundesrat* and *Bundestag* over possible changes to collective bargaining laws essentially led to a maintenance of the status quo (Hassel, 2007, p. 263).
5. Similarly, Easton and Gerritsen contend that the federated structure of Australia was instrumental in preventing the radical neoliberal reforms which occurred in New Zealand in the 1980s (1996).
6. A.V Dicey's *An Introduction to the Study of the Law of the Constitution*, cited in Norton (2007, p. 60).
7. In 2009, the traditional highest court in the land, the Appellate Committee of the House of Lords, was replaced by a Supreme Court (Mannin, 2010; Norton, 2007). Still, for the time frame under investigation, Britain was characterized by little or no judicial review.
8. It is interesting to note that Fig. 5.4 illustrates the continuance of the neoliberal reforms under *New Labour* led first by Tony Blair, and continued under Gordon Brown in that "the current Labour government is best understood as a consolidation, rather than a radical

departure, from Thatcherism" (Howell, 2007, p. 258). Such a trend lends support to the idea that partisanship and policy legacies play a significant role in shaping capitalist structures.

References

Allen, J. B., & Scruggs, L. (2004). Political partisanship and welfare state reform in advanced industrial societies. *American Journal of Political Science, 48*(3), 496–512.

Allen, M. (2006). *The varieties of capitalism paradigm: Explaining Germany's comparative advantage?* Hampshire: Palgrave Macmillian.

Bering, H. (1999). *Helmut Kohl.* Washington, DC: Regnery Publishing.

Birchfield, V., & Crepaz, M. (1998). The impact of constitutional structures and collective and competitive veto points on income inequality in industrialized democracies. *European Journal of Political Research, 34*, 175–200.

Brady, D., & Leicht, K. (2007). *Party to inequality: Right party power and income inequality in affluent western democracies.* Luxembourg Income Study Working Paper Series.

Casey, T. (2002). *The social context of economic change in Britain: Between policy and performance.* Manchester: Manchester University Press.

Casey, T. (2009). Mapping stability and change in advanced capitalisms. *Comparative European Politics, 7*(2), 255–278.

Castles, F., Gerritsen, R., & Vowles, J. (Eds.). (1996). *The great experiment: Labour parties and public policy transformations in Australia and New Zealand.* St. Leonards, Australia: Allen and Unwin.

Coates, D. (2000). *Models of capitalism: Growth and stagnation in the modern era.* Cambridge: Polity Press.

Cusack, T. R., Iverson, T., & Soskice, D. (2007). Economic interests and the origin of electoral systems. *American Political Science Review, 101*(3), 373–391.

Duverger, M. (1954). *Political parties.* New York: Science Editions.

Easton, B., & Gerritsen, R. (1996). Economic reform: Parallels and divergences. In F. Castles, R. Gerritsen, & J. Vowles (Eds.), *The great experiment: Labour parties and public policy transformation in Australia and New Zealand.* St. Leonards, Australia: Allen and Unwin.

Gamble, A. (1988). *The free economy and the strong state: The politics of Thatcherism.* Durham: Duke University Press.

Gerber, L. G. (1995). Corporatism and state theory: A review essay for historians. *Social Science History, 19*(3), 313–332.

Gershenkron, A. (1962). Economic backwardness in historical perspective. In A. Gershenkron (Ed.), *Economic backwardness in historical persepective.* Cambridge: Harvard University Press.

Gourevitch, P. A. (2003). Review: The politics of corporate governance regulation. *The Yale Law Journal, 112*(7), 1829–1880.

Hall, P. A. (1986). *Governing the economy: The politics of state intervention in Britain and France.* New York: Oxford University Press.

Hall, P. A. (1999). The political economy of Europe. In H. Kitschelt, P. Lange, G. Marks, & J. Stephens (Eds.), *Continuity and change in contemporary capitalism.* New York: Cambridge University Press.

Hall, P. A. (2007). The evolution of varieties of capitalism in Europe. In B. Hancké, M. Rhodes, & M. Thatcher (Eds.), *Beyond varieties of capitalism: Conflict, contradictions, and complementarities in the European economy.* New York: Oxford University Press.

Hall, P. A., & Soskice, D. W. (2001). *Varieties of capitalism: The institutional foundations of comparative advantage.* Oxford, England and New York: Oxford University Press.

Hancock, M. D., & Krisch, H. (2009). *Politics in Germany.* Washington, DC: CQ Press.

Hassel, A. (2007). What does business want? Labour market reforms in CMEs and its problems. In B. Hancké, M. Rhodes, & M. Thatcher (Eds.), *Beyond varieties of capitalism: Conflict, contradictions, and complemetarities in the European economy.* Oxford: Oxford University Press.

Howell, C. (2007). The British variety of capitalism: Institutional change, industrial relations and British politics. *British Politics, 2*, 239–263.

Huber, E., & Stephens, J. (2000). Partisan governance, women's employment, and the Social democratic service state. *American Sociological Review, 65*, 323–342.

Immergut, E. M. (1990). Institutions, veto points, and policy results: A comparative analysis of health care. *Journal of Public Policy, 10*, 391–416.

Iversen, T. (2007). Economic shocks and varieties of government response. In B. Hancké, M. Rhodes, & M. Thatcher (Eds.), *Beyond varieties of capitalism: Conflict, contradictions, and complementarities in the European economy.* New York: Oxford University Press.

Iversen, T., & Soskice, D. (2006). Electoral institutions and the politics of coalitions: Why some democracies redistribute more than others. *American Political Science Review, 100*(2), 165–181.

Iversen, T., & Soskice, D. (2009). Distribution and redistribution: The shadow of the nineteenth century. *World Politics, 61*(3), 438–486.

Iversen, T., & Stevens, J. (2008). Partisan politics, the welfare state, and three worlds of human capital formation. *Comparative Political Studies, 41*(4–5), 600–637.

Jackson, G. (2001). The origins of nonliberal corporate governance in Germany and Japan. In W. Streeck & K. Yamamura (Eds.), *The origins of nonliberal capitalism: Germany and Japan in comparison.* Ithaca, NY: Cornell University Press.

James, P. (2003). *The German electoral system*. Burlington: Ashgate Publishing Company.
Judt, T. (2005). *Postwar: A history of Europe since 1945*. New York: The Penguin Press.
Katzenstein, P. J. (1985). *Small states in world markets: Industrial policy in Europe*. Ithaca, NY: Cornell University Press.
King, D., & Wood, S. (1999). The political economy of neoliberalism: Britain and the United States in the 1980s. In H. Kitschelt, P. Lange, G. Marks, & J. Stephens (Eds.), *Continuity and change in contemporary capitalism*. Cambridge: Cambridge University Press.
Kitschelt, H. (1994). *The transformation of European social democracy*. Cambridge: Cambridge University Press.
Kitschelt, H., Lange, P., Marks, G., & Stephens, J. D. (Eds.). (1999). *Continuity and change in contemporary capitalism*. New York: Cambridge University Press.
Korpi, W. (1983). *The democratic class struggle*. London: Routledge & Kegan Paul.
Korpi, W. (2006). Power resources and employer-centered approaches in explanations of welfare states and varieties of capitalism: Protagonists, consenters, and antagonists. *World Politics, 58*(2), 167–206.
Lijphart, A. (1984). *Democracies: Patterns of majoritarian and consensus democracies in twenty-one countries*. New Haven, CT: Yale University Press.
Lijphart, A. (1994). *Electoral systems and party systems: A study of twenty-seven democracies, 1945–1990*. New York: Oxford University Press.
Lijphart, A. (1999). *Patterns of democracy: Government forms and performance in thirty-six countries*. New Haven, CT: Yale University Press.
Lijphart, A., & Crepaz, M. M. L. (1991). Corporatism and consensus democracy in eighteen countries: Conceptual and empirical linkages. *British Journal of Political Science, 21*(2), 235–246.
Mannin, M. L. (2010). *British government and politics: Balancing Europeanization and independence*. Lanham, MD: Rowman & Littlefield.
Manow, P. (2001a). New coalitions of welfare state reform. In P. Pierson (Ed.), *The new politics of the welfare state*. New York: Oxford University Press.
Manow, P. (2001b). *The political construction of a coordinated political economy*. Paper presented at the Business Interests and the Varieties of Capitalism: Historical Origins and Future Possibilities Meeting.
Manow, P. (2001c). Welfare state building and coordinated capitalism in Japan and Germany. In W. Streeck & K. Yamamura (Eds.), *The origins of nonliberal capitalism: Germany and Japan in comparison*. Ithaca, NY: Cornell University Press.
Manow, P. (2009). Electoral rules, class coalitions and welfare state regimes, or how to explain Esping-Andersen with Stein Rokkan. *Socio-Economic Review, 7*, 101–121.

Martin, C. J., & Swank, D. (2008). The political origins of coordinated capitalism: Business organizations, party systems, and state structure in the age of innocence. *American Political Science Review, 102*(2), 181–198.

Martin, C. J., & Thelen, K. (2007). The state and coordinated capitalism: Contributions of the public sector to social solidarity in postindustrial societies. *World Politics, 60*, 1–36.

North, D. C. (1990). *Institutions, institutional change, and economic performance.* Cambridge: Cambridge University Press.

Norton, B. F. (2007). *Politics in Britain.* Washington, DC: CQ Press.

Roberts, G. (2006). *German electoral politics.* Manchester: Manchester University Press.

Roe, M. J. (2003). *Political determinants of corporate governance.* Oxford: Oxford University Press.

Sartori, G. (1976). *Parties and party systems: A framework for analysis.* Cambridge, England and New York: Cambridge University Press.

Schmidt, V. A. (2007). *Changes in comparative political economy: Taking labor out, bringing the state back in, putting the firm front and center.* Paper presented at the European Studies Association Meeting.

Schmidt, V. A. (2009). Putting the political back into political economy by bringing the state back in yet again. *World Politcs, 61*(3), 516–546.

Schmitter, P. (1979). Still the century of corporatism? In P. Schmitter & G. Lehmbruch (Eds.), *Trends toward corporatist intermediation.* London: Sage Publications.

Soskice, D. (1999). Divergent production regimes: Coordinated and uncoordinated market economies in the 1980s and 1990s. In H. Kitschelt, P. Lange, G. Marks, & J. D. Stephens (Eds.), *Continuity and change in contemporary captialism* (pp. 101–134). New York: Cambridge University Press.

Soskice, D. (2007a). Macroeconomics and varieties of capitalism. In B. Hancké, M. Rhodes, & M. Thatcher (Eds.), *Beyond varieties of capitalism: Conflict, contradictions, and complementarities in the European economy.* New York: Oxford University Press.

Soskice, D. (2007b). Macroeconomics and varieties of capitalism. In B. Hancké, M. Rhodes, & M. Thatcher (Eds.), *Beyond varieties of capitalim: Conflict, contradictions, and complementarities in the European economy.* New York: Oxford University Press.

Streeck, W. (2001). Introduction: Explorations into the origins of nonliberal capitalism in Germany and Japan. In W. Streeck & Y. Kozo (Eds.), *The origins of nonliberal capitalism in Germany and Japan.* Ithaca, NY: Cornell University Press.

Streeck, W., & Yamamura, K. (Eds.). (2001). *The origins of nonliberal capitalism: Germany and Japan in comparison.* Ithaca, NY: Cornell University Press.

Swank, D. (2001). Political institutions and welfare state restructuring: The impact of institutions on social policy change in developed democracies. In P. Pierson (Ed.), *The new politics of the welfare state*. New York: Oxford University Press.
Swank, D. (2002). *Global capital, political instiutions, and policy change in developed welfare states*. New York: Cambridge University Press.
Thelen, K. (2001). Varieties of labor politics in the developed democracies. In P. A. Hall & D. Soskice (Eds.), *The varieties of capitalism: The institutional foundations of comparative advantage*. New York: Oxford University Press.
Tsebelis, G. (1995). Decision making in political systems: Veto players in presidentialism, parliamentarism, multicameralism and multipartyism. *British Journal of Political Science, 25*(3), 289–325.
Van Kersbergen, K. (1999). Contemporary Christian Democracy and the demise of the politcs of mediation. In H. Kitschelt, P. Lange, G. Marks, & J. Stephens (Eds.), *Contintuity and change in contemporary capitalism*. Cambridge: Cambridge University Press.
Vitols, S. (2001). The origins of bank-based and market-based systems: Germany, Japan, and the United States. In W. Streeck & K. Yamamura (Eds.), *The origins of nonoliberal capitalism: Germany and Japan in comparison*. Ithaca, NY: Cornell University Press.
Wood, S. (2001). Business, government, and patterns of labor market policy in Britain and the Federal Republic of Germany. In P. Hall & D. Soskice (Eds.), *Varieties of capitalism*. New York: Oxford University Press.

CHAPTER 6

The Economic Effects of Electoral Reform: New Zealand

As the previous chapters suggest, and the quantitative analysis supports, political institutions matter in regard to the type of capitalist economies present in advanced industrial democracies. Specifically, countries with majoritarian political institutions are associated with LMEs, while countries with more consensus-oriented political institutions are associated with CMEs.

The logic posits that majoritarian political institutions lead to greater competition between economic and political actors. Such competition, in turn, is transferred to the structure of the political economy. On the other hand, consensus-oriented institutions create greater cooperation between relevant actors. Such relationships subsequently lead to greater cooperation in economic arenas.

In order to test the effects of political institutions on capitalist variation, I examine the effects of electoral reform on the New Zealand economy during the 1980s and 1990s. In an attempt to achieve a controlled comparison, the New Zealand case is subjected to a "before-after" analysis. That is, "instead of trying to find two different cases that are comparable in all ways but one, the investigator may be able to achieve 'control' by dividing a single longitudinal case into two sub-cases" (George & Bennett, 2005, p. 166).

Such an approach is beneficial in exploring causal mechanisms. The premise of this design is that the dependent variables—in this case levels of market coordination, industrial relations, corporate governance,

M.P. Arsenault, *The Effects of Political Institutions on Varieties of Capitalism*, DOI 10.1007/978-3-319-50892-4_6

inter-firm relations, and vocational training and education—are examined and measured both prior to, and after, changes in the proposed causal variables, the assumption being that the dependent variables should change in value following the application of the stimulus, here changes in electoral system.

According to the quantitative analysis of Chap. 4, variation in electoral systems appears to be the strongest indicator of VOC. That is, SMDs, or plurality systems, are strongly associated with LMEs, while PR systems are strongly associated with CMEs. Additionally, Chap. 5 suggested that the strength of the relationship between electoral systems and VOC stems from the ability of electoral system to constrain the abilities of competing interests to participate in the political process, and either promote or reject economic reforms.

Based on the strength of the electoral system variable, the following case study seeks to explore the mechanisms linking electoral system with VOC. Specifically, I examine the ways in which electoral systems and their associated political institutions constrain economic policy. As Lijphart points out:

> One of the best-known generalizations about electoral systems is that they tend to be very stable and to resist change. In particular, as Dieter Nohlen has emphasized, 'fundamental changes are rare and arise only in extraordinary historical circumstances'. The most fundamental change that Nohlen has in mind is the shift from plurality to PR or vice versa. (1994, p. 54)

The case of New Zealand in the 1990s offers an example of Nohlen's "fundamental change," that is a move from an SMD to an MMP electoral system based largely on the German electoral model.[1] As Vowles et al. point out, New Zealand proves to be a very rare natural experiment.[2] The authors report that only 14 peaceful electoral changes have occurred between 1885 and 1985 (Vowles, Aimer, Banducci, & Karp, 1998a). Building upon this "controlled political experiment" I expect that the transition to an MMP system will likely affect neoliberal policies implemented by the Labour and National governments of the 1980s (Nagel, 1994, p. 529).

Chapter Outline

This chapter begins with an examination of the neoliberal reforms adopted by New Zealand in the early 1980s. I identify the causes of the economic change, the relevant actors and interests pushing for neoliberal reform, as well as the actors and interests affected—positively and negatively—by such changes.

I then discuss the causes of the institutional change from an SMD electoral system to the current MMP system. Specifically, I highlight the disillusionment of the New Zealand electorate with the perceived lack of democratic input into the policy process, especially in regard to the neoliberalization of the economy.

Next, I illustrate and discuss the political institutional changes which accompanied the switch to the MMP system. Namely I illustrate the accompanying increase in the number of political parties,[3] changes to the coalition structures of government, and the increasing number of constitutional constraints of the New Zealand system.

Finally, I illustrate and discuss changes to the economic structures following the transformation of political institutions. Specifically, I look at changes in overall levels of market coordination, corporate governance, industrial relations, vocational training and education, and inter-firm relations.

Economic and Political Reform in New Zealand

At the turn of the twentieth century, New Zealand ushered in one of the most comprehensive welfare state systems in the world. Throughout the first half of the twentieth century, the country was characterized by far-reaching labor unions, social democratic political parties, and a "cradle to the grave" welfare state. In the 1950s and 1960s, New Zealand—like other OECD countries—sought to expand the welfare state system on the back of rapid post-war economic growth. However, by the late 1960s it became apparent that the large-scale social expenditures were growing unsustainable (Castles, Gerritsen, & Vowles, 1996b, pp. 1–8).

Like many OECD countries, New Zealand faced economic crises in the late 1970s and early 1980s (Castles et al., 1996b; Vowles et al., 1998a). High rates of unemployment, inflation, and increasing levels of national debt placed significant pressure on the New Zealand government to address growing economic difficulties (Boston, Levine, McLeay, & Roberts, 1996). Pressures emerging from a changing global economy, that is, globalization and increasing international competition, made New Zealand's traditional protectionist and interventionist policies increasingly untenable (Easton & Gerritsen, 1996, p. 22).

In part, the difficulties stemmed from New Zealand's traditional heavy reliance on primary product exports, with the majority of such exports destined for the British market. With the decline of Britain in the post-war years, increasing European interdependence, and the great distance between New Zealand and European markets, the reliance of primary product exports to fund social expenditures grew unsustainable (Huber & Stephens, 2001, p. 287).

The 1975–1984 National government, led by PM Robert Muldoon, was the first to recognize and take steps to address the growing economic crisis. However, Muldoon's right-leaning National party attempted to maintain the expansive New Zealand welfare state and the existing economic structures through interventionist policies despite international and domestic pressures to adopt neoliberal reforms (Castles et al., 1996a).[4]

In 1984, in the face of a growing economic crisis, a loss of support from the business constituency, and a backlash against the authoritarian nature of the Muldoon government, the National government was voted from power and replaced by Labour (Aimer & Miller, 2002; Vowles, 1995). By 1985, Labour had undertaken extensive neoliberal reforms.[5] "David Henderson (1995), an experienced OECD observer, has called [these reforms] 'one of the most notable episodes of liberalization that history has to offer'" (L. Evans, Grimes, Wilkinson, & Teece, 1996, p. 1856). Huber and Stephens describe the new regime well, and it proves useful to cite their description at length:

> Outside of industrial relations and social policy, the government introduced neoliberal marketizing reforms with breakneck speed: the currency was floated; state-owned enterprises were ordered to behave like private enterprises and then many were privatized; tariffs were progressively reduced; import licensing was eliminated; subsidies to industry and agriculture were progressively eliminated; where feasible, government departments were corporatized and in some cases privatized; the financial and banking system was deregulated; the Reserve Bank was made more independent and ordered to focus on price stability as its overriding goal… These radical and rapid changes moved the New Zealand economy in 1984 from the most regulated economy among OECD countries to one of the least regulated at the end of Labour's second term in 1990. (2001, p. 293)

At first, Labour's reforms appeared to improve the New Zealand economy and subsequently ushered in a return of a Labour government in the 1987 election (Castles et al., 1996a). However, the "honeymoon" period of neoliberalism was short-lived (L. Evans et al., 1996). Labour's neoliberal reforms led to significant stresses on the New Zealand citizenry and proved highly unpopular with the public at large, especially on the part of the traditional Labour electorate who viewed the reforms as anathema to the conventional policy positions of Labour, and significantly different from Labour's pre-election policy platform (Bray & Nielson, 1996; Vowles, 1995). In part, the neoliberal policies led to a fractionalization of the traditional left, leading to the emergence of the more left-leaning New Labour Party in 1987.

> The fact is that in New Zealand, Labour's austerity policy and efforts were so severe that not only a more leftist New Labour Party split off after the 1987 election and won 5% of the popular vote in 1990, but also allowed the conservatives to leapfrog Labour in the 1990 campaign. (Kitschelt, 1994, p. 292)

Such a three-way race in an SMD or an FPP system will ultimately punish the smaller party, as well as the party from whom voters were taken. This will likely allow a party with less than a majority of popular votes to control parliament, and consequently reduce "the proportionality of election outcomes" (Vowles, 1995, p. 100). In this case, Labour was defeated in the 1990 election and replaced by a National government (Boston, et al., 1996, p. 9; Palmer & Palmer, 1997).[6] National then went on to control New Zealand politics for the next nine years continuing the neoliberalization program at an even more rapid rate.[7] "The Bolger National government continued the process of state restructuring, by introducing increased targeting and means-testing of welfare spending, ending centralised wage bargaining and reorganising the health administration" (Mulgan, 1997, p. 240). Like Labour in 1987, National's continued attacks on social policies diverged significantly from the pre-election policy platforms which led to increasing disillusionment on the part of the National constituency (Vowles, 1995, p. 101).

As Aimer and Miller point out, "The 1990s were the most electorally unsettled decade for more than fifty years" (Aimer & Miller, 2002, p. 1). To a great extent, the political instability was largely the result of the radical economic reforms of the 1980s (Aimer & Miller, 2002; Easton & Gerritsen, 1996, p. 2). Support for "constitutionally unconstrained government ebbed dramatically, as both major parties in turn, first Labour and then National, imposed major structural reforms on the state and the economy in open defiance of democratic consultation" (Mulgan, 1997, p. 64). Specifically, as Boston et al. point out, such disillusionment was largely the result of "the way in which economic dislocation fell more heavily on some groups than on others" (1996, p. 5).

Origins of Electoral Reform

In 1984, the Labour Party—in response to being defeated by National in 1978 and 1981, despite winning a plurality of votes—called for the creation of a commission to examine the FPP system, and consider moves toward a PR electoral system (Nagel, 1994).[8] The Royal Commission on the Electoral System (RCES) found that "New Zealand's system ranked 'near the bottom on every measure' of proportionality" (Boston et al., 1996, p. 16). According the Royal Commission an MMP system would address the perceived democratic deficit. The Commission "argued for a change to MMP on three grounds: the MMP would be fairer, provide better representation, and allow for wider participation in New Zealand politics" (Vowles et al., 1998b, p. 192).

In 1992, agreements between Labour and National led to a nonbinding referendum that placed the decision to retain or change the FPP system directly in the hands of the New Zealand public. Voters favored a reform of the FPP electoral system 84.7 percent to 15.3 percent (Boston et al., 1996, p. 21). The binding referendum of 1993 was much closer, but still ushered in the change to MMP rules by a vote of 53.9 percent to 46.1 percent (Boston et al., 1996, p. 23). As such, the stage had been set for the first MMP election in 1996.

In short, the evidence suggests that electoral reform was the result of public disillusionment with the majoritarian rule of existing Labour and National parties, and particularly the perceived undemocratic neoliberalization reforms of the 1980s and 1990s. Like the British system, the majoritarian structures of New Zealand's political regime allowed for radical policy change. As Vowles points out, "governments have been more able to put through unpalatable policies in the teeth of public opposition" (1995, p. 97). As expected, changes to the New Zealand electoral system were accompanied by considerable changes to other existing political institutions.

The Effects of Electoral Reform on Political Institutions

As Mulgan writes, prior to the transition to MMP, "The New Zealand system was more Westminster than Westminster itself" (1997, p. 63). From 1938 to 1993, New Zealand politics were dominated by two large political parties—National and Labour—and parliaments were governed by single-party majorities (Boston et al., 1996; Palmer & Palmer, 1997). The transition from an FPP system to an MMP system ushered in significant changes to other political institutions. Most notably, we see an increase in the number of political parties in legislature, a move away from majoritarian governments and the rise of governing coalitions, evolving ideological control of the state, and increasing numbers of constitutional veto points. The following sections provide empirical evidence of the changes to political institutions that accompanied the move to an MMP electoral system.

Number of Political Parties

The most obvious institutional result of the change to an MMP system is the increase in the number of political parties gaining seats in the New Zealand legislature. As Duverger pointed out, SMD systems are characterized by two-party systems, while PR systems are characterized multiple political parties (1954). As expected, the adoption of an MMP system led to the addition of a number of new political parties to the New Zealand legislature.

However, in the case of New Zealand, the potential move toward MMP affected the party system prior to ratification of the national referendum of 1993. In the 1990 election the New Zealand citizenry was growing increasingly disillusioned with the political process, especially the perceived "'elective dictatorship' of one party governments" (Palmer & Palmer, 1997, p. 25).

Nearly 14 percent of the electorate voted for parties other than Labour or National, with the Green Party garnering 6.9 percent, New Labour garnering 5.3 percent, and the Democrat party earning 1.7 percent of the popular vote (Palmer & Palmer, 1997, p. 25). Due to the existing FPP system, only one MP from the emerging parties (New Labour) won a seat in the legislature (Aimer & Miller, 2002, p. 2). Similar results occurred in the 1993 election, with the left-leaning Alliance garnering 18.3 percent of the vote, and the right-center New Zealand First taking 8.4 percent. Still, under FPP, both Alliance and New Zealand First earned only two seats in legislature, thus remaining largely politically ineffectual (Palmer & Palmer, 1997, p. 32).

The 1996 election, the first under the new MMP rules, ushered in changes to the New Zealand party system. Ironically, the 1996 election did not drastically change the vote shares for parties, nor did it significantly increase the number of parties. Only ACT New Zealand became a new party by meeting the 5 percent popular vote threshold required for representation.[9] "The greatest impact of MMP, however, was not the small increase in the number of elected parties, but the proportional allocation of parliamentary seats" (Aimer & Miller, 2002, p. 6). Table 6.1 illustrates the increased proportionality of seat allocation from 1993 to 1996.

The number of political parties gaining legislative representation continued to increase after the 1996 MMP election, reaching a high of eight parties in 2004.[10] Figure 6.1 illustrates a significant increase in the number of political parties garnering a minimum of one seat in the New Zealand legislature between 1970 and 2011. Of note is the increasing number of political parties in the lead-up to the first MMP election in 1996, and the continued increase up to the most current election in 2011.

Table 6.1 Disproportionality of seat allocation in New Zealand: 1993 and 1996 elections

Party	*Vote %*	*Total seats*	*Percentage of seats*
1993 election			
National	35.0	50	50.5
Labour	34.7	45	45.5
Alliance	18.2	2	2
NZ First	8.4	2	2
Other	3.7	0	0
1996 election			
National	33.8	44	36.7
Labour	28.2	37	30.8
NZ First	13.4	17	14.2
Alliance	10.1	13	10.8
ACT	6.1	8	6.7
Christian	4.3	0	0
United	0.9	1	0.08
Other	3.2	0	0

Note: Data drawn from Palmer and Palmer (1997, p. 32) and Vowles (1998, p. 29)

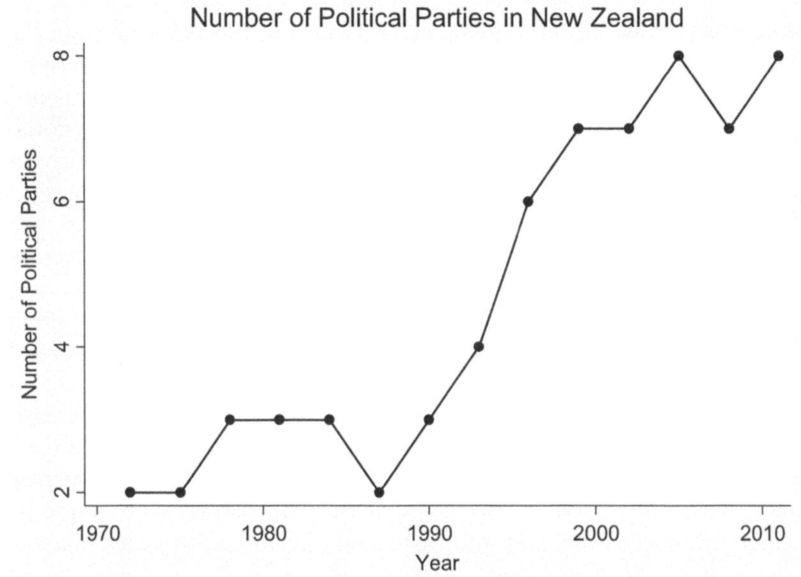

Fig. 6.1 Change in the number of political parties in New Zealand. *Note*: Data from Palmer and Palmer (1997), and http://www.elections.org.nz

However, as Vowles points out, "MMP has shaped the social groundings of the New Zealand party much less than many expected" (Vowles, 1998, pp. 45–46). Many hypothesized that increasing numbers of political parties would lead to increasing levels of social differentiation in regard to party choice. However, this was not the case. The change to MMP did not substantively change the coalition structure of government. Rather, a "bifurcation" between potential coalition partners emerged, and subsequently led to maintenance of a centripetal party system (Kitschelt, 1994; Sartori, 1976).

Coalition Governments

Under the FPP system, "government was almost always determined by the electoral cycle" (Palmer & Palmer, 2004, p. 39). That is, the winning party stayed in power until (at least) the next election held every three years. As such, between 1930 and the 1994 election, New Zealand government was characterized by single-party majorities (Boston et al., 1996, p. 31; Vowles et al., 1998c, p. 7). However, the 1996 election, the first under MMP, brought significant changes to the structure governing coalitions. Under the new MMP system, the era of "manufactured majorities" was over. "Now there almost always has to be some sort of negotiation between the parties after an election about which parties will form or support a government" (Palmer & Palmer, 2004, p. 39).[11]

For example, in 1993, the National party won 35 percent of the vote and still won a parliamentary majority. However, in 1996, the first election under MMP electoral rules, National won 34 percent of the vote, but was short of the 16 seats necessary to form a single-party majority government (Aimer & Miller, 2002; Huber & Stephens, 2001). Table 6.2 illustrates the changing governing coalition structures in New Zealand.

Interestingly, as Aimer (1998) points out, the parties gaining legislative seats in the 1996 election did not necessarily create the "centrifugal" structures expected to emerge under MMP. Rather, a two-block structure emerged (Sartori, 1976). "This bloc structure then largely determines the configuration of formal and informal coalitions in which parties share or support others in government" (Aimer, 1998, p. 55). In the New Zealand case, this was largely the result of voters not switching their votes from

Table 6.2 Changes in government type in New Zealand: 1972–2011

Election year	*Government type*	*Governing party/coalition*
1972	Single-party majority	Labour
1975	Single-party majority	National
1978	Single-party majority	National
1981	Single-party majority	National
1984	Single-party majority	Labour
1987	Single-party majority	Labour
1990	Single-party majority	National
1993	Single-party majority	National
1996	Majority coalition	National, NZ first
1999	Minority coalition	Labour, alliance
2002	Minority coalition	Labour, progressive
2005	Minority coalition	Labour, progressive
2008	Minority coalition	National, ACT
2011	Majority coalition	National, ACT, united

Note: Data drawn from Palmer and Palmer (1997, 2004), and Elections New Zealand, http://www.elections.org.nz

one bloc to another, but rather from one party to another party within the same bloc (Aimer, 1998). "Going by the early experience with MMP in New Zealand, it certainly seems difficult for a minor coalition partner to retain its separate identity and, therefore, its united nerve to continue in coalition till the next election" (Palmer & Palmer, 2004, p. 43). As such, in the case of New Zealand, the consensus predicted by the change in electoral rules did not emerge. Rather, the coalitions that formed were relatively stable and remained largely divided along the left–right continuum that pre-dated electoral system reform.

Constitutional Structures

Huber and Stephens contend that prior to the adoption of the MMP electoral system, New Zealand's constitutional structures possessed no veto points (2001, p. 298). It is argued by Huber and Stephens (2001), Palmer and Palmer (1997), Evans et al. (1996), and the majority of authors in Castles et al.'s (1996b) edited volume that the lack of constitutional veto points proved instrumental to the ability of first Labour, and then National, to implement the radical economic reforms in the 1980s.

"New Zealand's constitution under FPP offered the most streamlined executive decision-making machine in the democratic world—once elected to government a political party could do what it liked for the next three years" (Palmer & Palmer, 1997, p. 3). This is most readily illustrated by Labour's "blitzkrieg" policy process of the mid-1980s in which the Labour government made a radical departure from existing policy with little or no consultation with other parties, parliament, constituency, or organized labor (Easton & Gerritsen, 1996). In describing Labour's policy strategy, Kelsey writes, "The major decisions would already have been taken; any consultation was limited to details" (Kelsey, 1997).

With the advent of MMP a number of additional constitutional constraints have been added to the New Zealand system, the most obvious being the increasingly likely chance of a vote of no confidence. Under the FPP system, governments were largely characterized by single-party majorities. The party receiving a majority of votes maintained a majority of seats in parliament and subsequently was unlikely to ever face a vote of no confidence. However, under MMP, the ruling party faces pressures from opposition, or coalition parties to either adopt, or halt, specific policies (Palmer & Palmer, 2004, pp. 373–374).

I contend, like Huber and Stephens (2001), Castles et al. (1996b), Palmer and Palmer (1997), and Kelsey (1997), that the lack of constitutional veto points was conducive to the radical neoliberal policy reforms adopted first by Labour, and continued by National. A system characterized by additional constitutional veto points should have created a system of increased checks and balances which, in turn, would force Labour and National to be more consultative with each other, their constituency, and the emerging political parties, which would have led to a milder, more cooperative policy outcome.[12] Many believed that the adoption of MMP electoral system would lead to a less adversarial, more consensually oriented political environment (Boston et al., 1996). However, to a great extent, increased consultation has not been the case (Palmer & Palmer, 2004, p. 376). The adversarial nature of New Zealand politics has largely remained the norm. The lack of consultation is, to a great extent, the result of the institutional legacies of the longstanding majoritarian system.

The New Zealand case falls into Sartori's "moderate pluralist" category (1976). That is, "Instead of only two parties, we generally find bipolar alignments of alternative coalitions" (Sartori, 1976, p. 179). The bipolar coalitions remain divided along the left–right continuum without a strong center party occupying the middle of the ideological spectrum. The competing parties remain relatively close along the ideological spectrum and subsequently the system remains centripetal, that is, the bipolar coalitions vie for control of the ideological center. As such, the potential for alternation between a center-right or center-left coalition remains the norm regardless of the proportional electoral system. Under such conditions, voter choice—at least in the present—remains largely relegated to the two largest parties: Labour and National. Such outcomes have been well documented by Aimer, who finds that under New Zealand's MMP rules, voters largely changed their vote within coalitions rather than between parties of the left and right (1998).

The Effects of Electoral Reform on Economic Institutions

As stated previously, New Zealand implemented radical neoliberal reforms, the likes of which were unprecedented in other OECD countries (Castles et al., 1996b). Only the United Kingdom, under the

Thatcher government, adopted more far-reaching policy actions (Huber & Stephens, 2001). The question remains to what extent did the electoral changes of 1996 affect the radical moves to a more liberal market economy. The following analysis will be temporally divided between two time frames: pre- and post-MMP reforms. The following section examines changes to the New Zealand political economy in four major areas—market coordination, labor coordination, business organization, and the degree of state intervention—as measured by Casey's (2009) comparative capitalism indices.

Market Coordination

Casey's (2009) comparative capitalism index seeks to differentiate various types of capitalist economies. The scaled index, coded 0–1, is derived from three sub-indices measuring labor coordination, business coordination, and state intervention. Higher scores indicate greater levels of coordinated capitalism, while lower scores indicate more liberal capitalist systems. Casey points out that "Over time, there has been a general movement toward liberalization, with some states, such as New Zealand, liberalizing substantially" (2009, p. 255).

Table 6.2 illustrates the significant changes to the New Zealand economy. As expected, the New Zealand economy increased its level of market coordination between 1975 and 1990, largely as a result of implementation and legacies of the interventionist policies of the Muldoon-led National government. Over this period New Zealand maintained a significantly higher degree of coordination than the OECD average. However, in opposition to the proposed causal logic, between 1990 and 1994 the New Zealand economy underwent a precipitous decline and continued to become increasingly liberal following the 1996 election and continuing to decline through 2005.

The figure suggests that the adoption of MMP electoral rules did not lead to a retrenchment of the neoliberal reforms. In fact, Fig. 6.2 illustrates an increase in market liberalization following the 1996 MMP election. The following sections attempt to disaggregate the capitalism measure into its constituent elements—labor organization, business organization, and state intervention—in order to shed greater light on the changes to the New Zealand economy.

Fig. 6.2 Comparative capitalism index in New Zealand: 1970–2005. *Note*: Data drawn from Casey (2009)

Changes in Labor Coordination

Casey offers a measure designed to capture the major labor distinctions between CMEs and LMEs (2009). Casey has developed a scaled variable, coded 0–1, consisting of measures of trade union density, coverage of collective bargaining agreements, the centralization and coordination of wages, and levels of educational attainment. As such, Casey's measure approximates an aggregate of the industrial relations, vocational training and education, and "employees" categories proposed by Hall and Soskice (2001, p. 7). Changes in the organization of labor are illustrated in Fig. 6.3.

Prior to 1989, New Zealand maintained extremely high scores of labor power in relation to the OECD average. This is likely a carryover of the long-standing and encompassing New Zealand welfare state, and the tenure of the Muldoon administration.

Additionally, in the sequencing of New Zealand liberalization, labor market reform came long after the liberalization of financial and goods

Fig. 6.3 Labor coordination in New Zealand: 1970–2005. *Note*: Data from Casey (2009)

markets and the capital account. To a large extent, this was because, politically, "a Labour government could not realistically deregulate the labor market or reduce welfare spending as readily as a National government" (L. Evans et al., 1996, pp. 1870–1871). However, between 1989 and 1995, the power of labor declined precipitously under the National government, especially with the implementation of the Employment Contract Act (ECA) in 1991. This act "replaced centralized bargaining structures by decentralized enterprise bargaining, bringing the labor market institutions closer to the U.S. model then the European model hitherto adopted" (L. Evans et al., 1996, p. 1878). Labor organization increased slightly between 1996 and 2000, before again trending steeply downward from 2000 to 2005 largely as a result of the continuing decline of union membership.

As stated previously, New Zealand maintained an extensive welfare state system during the post-war era. In regard to labor, between the 1930s and 1970s, labor market relations were characterized by a high degree of centralization with a system of compulsory union membership and a system of "centralized wage orders ... determined by an Arbitration Court" (L. Evans et al., 1996, p. 1878). Under the National government legislation was passed severely curtailing the power of unions, namely, the abandonment of compulsory union membership, and the dissolution of centralized wage bargaining. When reforms became an inevitable necessity, labor was in a very weak position to halt the neoliberal reform.

With Labour's victory in the 1984 snap election, the power of unions was even further eroded, and labor markets opened up significantly. As Kelsey writes, "Under the Labour government, compulsory arbitration was withdrawn, unions were required to consolidate to secure recognition, and bargaining shifted progressively from industry to enterprise agreements" (Kelsey, 1997, p. 3).[13] The result was that "Peak union organizations ... had relatively little power over affiliates, especially in terms of central funding and the right to strike" (Bray & Nielson, 1996, p. 70).

One likely explanation of Labour's radical move toward neoliberal policies stems from the governing party in New Zealand's ability to act without the consent of interest groups concerned, in this case, organized labor (Bray & Nielson, 1996). In part, this is a result of New Zealand's "less formal constitution with fewer checks and balances to hinder the implementation of governmental policies" (Easton & Gerritsen, 1996, p. 34). This is the opposite of Germany's courts consistently upholding the constitutionally protected codetermination laws.

Parliament has been extremely powerful and relatively unconstrained in New Zealand. There is no constraining upper House; the nonfederal system allowed for centralized control over regional and local governments; legislation passed by parliament is not subject to judicial review. "The only major constitutional check on government was the requirement that it must face an election in no more than three years' time" (Mulgan, 1997, p. 63).

Additionally, New Zealand's two-party system made a need for coalition building a non-issue. Had a strong, politically relevant party representing organized labor existed (like the AUP in Australia)[14] it is likely that Labour—or whatever center-left party may have been in place—would have been more receptive to the whims of organized labor than under the two-party system. Instead, "In ... New Zealand, economic difficulties meant that influence of capital was heightened and Labour governments were more prone to divorce themselves from their traditional constituents among organised labour" (Bray & Nielson, 1996, p. 69).

Changes in Business Organization

The proposed hypotheses would suggest that New Zealand business would be more constrained under the new MMP rules, and indicate a more coordinated production regime. In order to examine the effects of electoral reform on business organization, I rely on Casey's measure of business organization. Casey offers a scaled measure, coded 0–1, of overall business organization. The variable is designed to measure corporate finance, corporate governance, and inter-firm relations (2009, p. 265). Specifically, the variable captures the level of stock market capitalization and the percentage of widely held firms.[15]

As such, Casey's business measure largely captures the structure of corporate governance types—shareholder versus stakeholder—used by Hall and Soskice (2001) and others differentiating liberal market and coordinated market production regime in the VOC.[16]

Figure 6.4 illustrates the degree of business organization in New Zealand as compared to the OECD average. Interestingly, the New Zealand business measure remained quite high throughout the time frame under investigation, and, as expected, actually increased between 1980 and 1990, and remained relatively stable through 2005.

As stated above, both Labour and National neither expected nor wanted the radical changes to the electoral system when the RCES was first formed. However, as it became evident that the change from SMD to MMP was inevitable, many MPs began to accept the proposed changes. Labour prime minister David Lange "quipped that the only way the major parties could stop MMP would be to endorse it" (Nagel, 1994, p. 526).

Still, with the politicians essentially accepting the inevitable, organized business maintained a strong opposition to the potential shift to MMP.

> Into the breach vacated by demoralized politicians stepped leaders of big business. Their pro-FPP Campaign For Better Government (CBG), consisting of the Business Round Table (an organization consisting of over 40 CEOs of New Zealand's largest firms), the Employers Foundation, and the organization New Zealand Federated Farmers, launched a lavishly funded, sophisticated advertising blitz against MMP. (Nagel, 1994, p. 526; Vowles, 1995, p. 106)

Fig. 6.4 Business coordination in New Zealand: 1970–2005. *Note*: Data from Casey (2009)

It is possible that such findings support the work of Martin and Swank (2008) that electoral systems, and subsequently party systems, shape the type of peak employer associations. They find that PR and multi-party systems will lead to corporatist peak associations while two-party systems will lead to pluralist associations. The logic contends that that in PR/multi-party systems, parties will emerge (here dominantly ACT New Zealand) that support business interests. This results in cooperation between like-minded groups, and the formation of coalitions that support business interests.

Changes in State Intervention

CMEs are characterized by a great deal of state intervention in the market, while LMEs maintain a "hands-off" approach to the market (Hall & Soskice, 2001). Throughout the majority of New Zealand's history, the state—under both Labour and National regimes—maintained very strong interventionist policies. However, "Rolling back the state is a fundamental tenet of any structural adjustment programme" (Kelsey, 1997). Beginning in the early 1980s the New Zealand state began to dramatically distance itself from market intervention and deregulated industry (Ratnayake, 1999). For example, Evan et al. find a "massive reduction in direct government assistance to industry from 16.2 percent of government (non-debt) expenditure to 4.0 percent in 1993/1994" (L. Evans et al., 1996, p. 1884).

I examine Casey's (2009) measure of state organization to judge the degree of intervention in the market. The measure is scaled 0–1 with high scores representing greater degrees of intervention. The variable measures the size of government, the degree of economic regulation, levels of employment protection legislation, levels of unemployment benefits, and the degree of active labor market policies (Casey, 2009, p. 263). Figure 6.5 indicates the precipitous decline in state intervention between 1990 and 2000, with a small increase between 2000 and 2005.

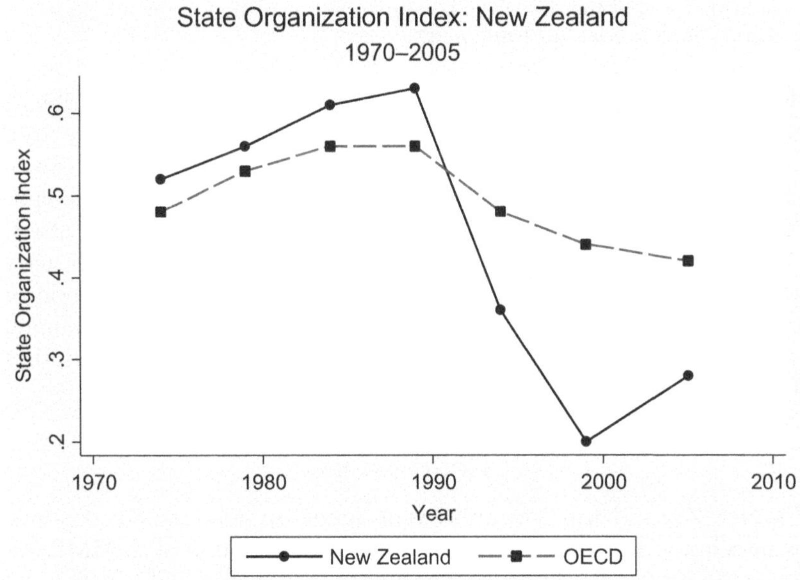

Fig. 6.5 State intervention in New Zealand: 1970–2005. *Note*: Data from Casey (2009)

Beginning in 1984, the Labour government adopted a much more laissez-faire relationship in economic matters, specifically in regard to participating in negotiations between labor and business. Such moves were largely the result of relatively autonomous technocrats influenced by the economic policies of the United States and Britain (Kelsey, 1997). Additionally, "immediately after the election in 1984, the Labour Government announced a programme for gradual reduction of tariffs and removal of quantitative restrictions on imports" (Ratnayake, 1999, p. 1042). The purpose here, coupled with anti-trust measures, was to increase domestic competition between firms "while avoiding industry-specific regulation" (L. Evans et al., 1996, p. 1863).

Bray and Nielson describe the withdrawal of the New Zealand state eloquently:

> In industrial relations policy, National moved quickly to finish what Labour, under Roger Douglas's influence had started. The passing of the *Employment Contracts Act* in May 1990 heralded in the final step in the establishment of the New Right paradigm in practice and probably represents the most radical withdrawal of the state from labour market regulation in the developed world. (Bray & Nielson, 1996, p. 82)

Overall, the purpose of the reforms was to achieve "wherever possible, a competitive environment in which markets can operate relatively free from subsequent intervention by government" (L. Evans et al., 1996, p. 1863). The economic deregulation was joined with parallel moves to deregulate business coupled with the ultimate goal of privatizing of state assets. The stated purpose of privatization was to increase economic efficiency (Kelsey, 1997, p. 116). This was represented by the implementation of policies based on the British model which led to a significant streamlining of public sector employment, and a selling-off of state-owned enterprises (L. Evans et al., 1996, p. 1873).

Conclusion

The New Zealand economy underwent significant political and economic changes in the 1980s and 1990s. Politically, the adoption of an MMP system led to increased numbers of effective political parties in legislature, an increased likelihood of coalition government, and subsequent weakening of the executive. New Zealand has moved away from its label as "more

Westminster than Westminster" and, institutionally, has become a more consensual political regime (Mulgan, 1997, p. 63). Economically, New Zealand has adopted radical neoliberal economic reforms in the face of changing domestic and international economic circumstances (Allen & Ng, 2000; Casey, 2009; Castles et al., 1996c; Kelsey, 1997).

The proposed hypothesis suggested that following the adoption of MMP rules, and subsequent emergence of a more consensually oriented political regime, New Zealand would have shown an increased degree of market coordination. However, contrary to the proposed hypothesis, the New Zealand economy became increasingly liberal following the adoption of MMP electoral rules. Figure 6.6 illustrates considerable declines in all but one measure of economic organization, that being business organization. The concluding section offers some explanations for the unexpected trends in the New Zealand economy following the implementation of the MMP electoral system.

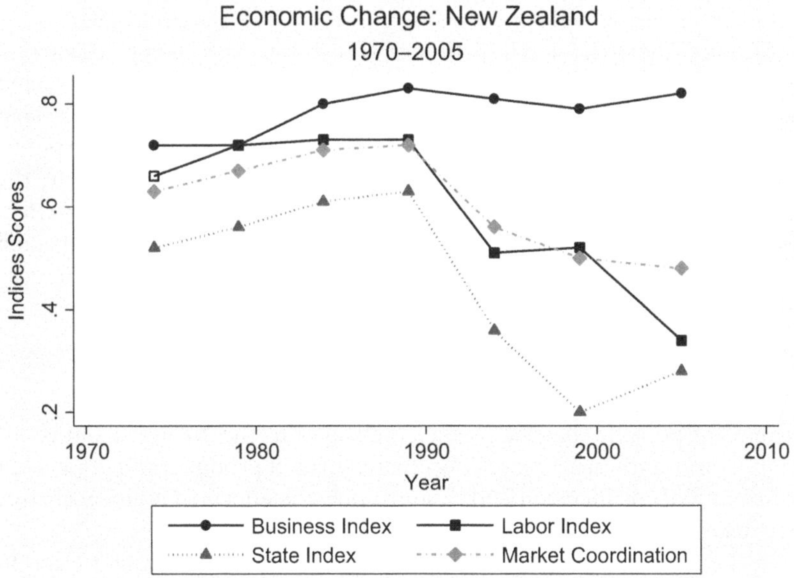

Fig. 6.6 Economic change in New Zealand: 1970–2005. *Note*: Data from Casey (2009)

In general, the New Zealand political economy did not retrench the neoliberal reforms following the adaptation of the new MMP system. The lack of economic institutional change likely stems from three major issues. First, changes to the electoral system did not affect the structure of New Zealand politics to a great degree. Second, due to the limited time horizon under investigation, the causal chain between changes in political institutions and economic institutions has yet to unfold. Third, the pressures from globalization may have proved too great to allow for an abandonment of neoliberal policies in the face of public discontent.

A Lack of Substantive Political Change

Both the left-leaning Labour Party and the right-leaning National Party were able to implement major neoliberal policies in the 1980s in the face of public protest. The ability of the government to implement such policies was largely the result of the majoritarian political system, and the subsequent path dependence of the Westminster tradition. Although the economic measures were unpopular, New Zealand did not retrench the neoliberal reforms following the move to the MMP system in 1996.

In part, the lack of retrenchment was due to the lasting legacies of the British-modeled Westminster institutions that governed New Zealand politics from approximately 1893 to 1996 (Mulgan, 1997, p. 233). That is, the switch to the MMP system did not fundamentally change the political structure of the New Zealand government. As stated previously, the changes in electoral rules, and subsequent increase in the number of effective political parties, did not create the centrifugal structures expected under the MMP system, but rather maintained a "high premium on centripetal competition and pivoting" (Kitschelt, 1994, p. 291).

Short-Term Time Horizons

It remains possible that the predicted changes to the New Zealand economy—a move toward a more coordinated market production regime—has yet to unfold. As Pierson (2004) points out, the effects of political change may take significant time to appear.

It has been approximately 15 years since New Zealand's first election using MMP rules. Social processes can take significant time to unfold, and subsequently causal processes can be extremely slow moving and take a good deal of time to emerge. In regard to causal chains, "in many cases the story runs more like the following '*x* triggers sequence *a*, *b*, *c* which yields *y*.' If *a*, *b*, and *c* take some time to work themselves out, there is likely to be a substantial lag between *x* and *y*" (Pierson, 2003, p. 187).

In other words, if the time horizon under investigation is too limited in scope, a misreading of causal relationships may occur. In analyzing slow-moving outcomes—here changes in economic structures—researchers must remain cognizant that there are times "where meaningful change in the dependent variable occurs only over the long run" (Pierson, 2003, p. 189). It remains to be seen if, with an expanded time horizon, the changes to electoral system will have the expected effects on levels of market coordination in New Zealand.

Small States in the Global Economy

As stated previously, by the 1980s New Zealand had become too dependent on world markets to maintain its "domestic defense" protectionist policies (Castles et al., 1996b; McCraw, 1993). As Casey points out:

> A small state like Belgium [or in this case, New Zealand], given its limited market resources, by necessity is more exposed to the world economy than a large, continental economy like the United States. For many states the choice of being open or not is effectively removed. (2002, p. 21)

Katzenstein has examined the role of political parties and electoral systems on the emergence of the unique economic structures of the small European states, specifically how the small states of Europe have realigned "their domestic economies with world markets" (1985, p. 21). He contends that the corporatist structures of small European states are the result of the multi-party systems and PR electoral systems distinct to these countries.

Katzenstein argues that the unique political structures of these states lead to the emergence of minority governments which in turn play a strong role on the unique policy process of his selected cases. Minority governments ensure conciliation, compromise, and cooperation between actors because parties are unlikely to win an outright majority. In a government characterized by minority rule, "according Nils Stjernquist, 'the aim of an opposition in a system of this kind would be to influence policy-making process. The means available to the opposition would be compromise, its tactics, bargaining'" (Katzenstein, 1985, p. 101).

In expanding Katzenstein's argument, since New Zealand adopted many of the political institutions of its small European cousins, that is, multiple political parties, PR systems, and the presence of minority governments, it should have adopted more consensual, incremental, and less extreme economic policy reforms. Obviously, this was not the case.

Although facing many of the same pressures of European small states, the New Zealand case ultimately led to a very different outcome. Whereas the small states tended to adopt corporatist/coordinated economic policies, not only did New Zealand adopt radical neoliberal policies, it also maintained these policies after the implementation of the MMP electoral system. The major differences between Katzenstein's small states and New Zealand lie in the structure of political institutions. Katzenstein focused on the small *corporatist* European countries which were highly unlike the Westminster system of New Zealand.

As such, it appears that the moves to a highly deregulated political economy were largely the result of the political institutions that characterized the New Zealand system. Although the MMP system did "slow the pace of neoliberal reform," the system did not facilitate or allow a return of the pre-1980s interventionist economy (Huber & Stephens, 2001, p. 299).

In short, like the case of the United Kingdom first under Margaret Thatcher, then John Major, and continued under Tony Blair, the Westminster majoritarian regime allowed for much more drastic neoliberal reforms than those found under Germany and many other continental European states. In the case of New Zealand, the legacies of majoritarian institutions lasted beyond the institutional reforms of 1996. Unlike the German case, institutional checks did not exist at the time of neoliberal implementation, thus allowing for the radical policy changes to occur.

The above research findings call into question the applicability of the theory that consensus-oriented political institutions will lead to greater coordination in capitalist systems. In the case of New Zealand, it appears that changes in the political system did not affect the neoliberal path adopted by the Labour government of the 1980s and continued under National in the 1990s. This is not to say that the theory is in and of itself incorrect. The theory may illustrate that political institutions can help explain the origins of LMEs and CMEs during early industrialization (Martin & Swank, 2008). Yet the argument seemingly fails to predict change in contemporary capitalist economies. As such, much work remains to be done explaining the strong correlation between political institutions and VOC. In part, such difficulty lies in available data. Electoral change remains a rare phenomenon, especially among comparable OECD states (Lijphart, 1994). With limited variation among independent variables generalizable, statistical tests remain difficult. For the time being, it may behoove scholars to continue additional qualitative studies in pursuit of theory building, while working along the vein of Casey (2009) to develop more robust and encompassing measures of capitalist variation.

Notes

1. It can be argued that because the New Zealand case possesses an SMD vote, the electoral system is not necessarily proportional. However, building on James's (2003) discussion of the German system (the model for New Zealand MMP) I contend that the New Zealand case remains a PR system. James writes, "Because the German electoral system is fundamentally a proportional one, it is the voter's second vote that establishes the strength of parties in parliament, and therefore decides who will become Federal Chancellor" (2003, p. 21). Similarly, the second vote in the New Zealand MMP system decides the strength of party power in parliament, and ultimately leads to the selection of prime minister (Mulgan, 1997, p. 100).
2. In the 1990s, both Italy and Japan made moves toward MMP systems. However, as Vowles et al. point out, neither Italy nor Japan's electoral reform substantively affected the proportionality of the electoral systems, leaving New Zealand a unique case (Vowles et al., 1998a).
3. New Zealand has long been dominated by two political parties: Labour and National. Labour traditionally has been strongly supported by trade unions, and is associated with "advancing socialist principles." The National Party, on the other hand, is "rooted in the farming and business communities" and is "interested in promoting free enterprise and protecting individual freedom" (McCraw, 1993, p. 8).
4. Easton and Gerritsen (1996), Kelsey (1997), and Huber and Stephens (2001) contend that the right-leaning National party's maintenance of the existing economic structures stemmed from the party's long-term support from the landholding agrarian class—who benefited from the existing protectionist policies—the uneducated, and the elderly, both reliant on the expansive welfare

state benefits. National's reliance on such a constituency for electoral support made the adaptation of neoliberal reforms politically difficult.

5. It may seem counterintuitive that the most extreme economic reforms would be implemented by a Labour government. The public had grown disillusioned with National's handling of the economy. As such, Labour was, at least in part, reacting to the long-term policy failures of the right-leaning National government. As such, Labour made a radical policy change of its own drastically different from policy programs traditionally associated with the labor movement. "The logic of two-party competition disposed the two parties habitually in opposition to adopt alternative policies, and tradition therefore gave way to opportunity and a contingent policy response" (Castles et al., 1996a, p. 216).
6. Of particular interest and note, this fractionalization of the Labour Party parallels a similar phenomenon in the British system where Labour split with the emergence of the Liberal/Social Democratic Party in 1983 and 1987. In both cases the major Labour Party was defeated as a result of the disproportionality of the SMD electoral system, and the subsequent majoritarian nature of parliamentary control.
7. Building on the work of Castles et al. (1996a), it is likely that the change in voter preference from Labour to National was more of a rejection of Labour policies than support for the National party. Nadeau and Lewis-Beck examine the effects of economics on voting preferences (2001). Voter preferences change with changes in economic conditions. The two-party nature of the New Zealand electoral system limited voter choice to either an acceptance or rejection of one party in favor of the other rather than a preexisting coalition policy platform that would likely emerge in a more proportional electoral system.
8. Interestingly, Labour did not intend to radically alter the existing FPP system (Vowles, 1995). The purpose of the RCES was to "propose modest reforms that would not disturb the Labour-National duopoly" (Nagel, 1994, p. 526). However, the RCES, under Sir Geoffrey Palmer, proposed the radical change to an MMP system which was soon furthered by a large grassroots organization. In 1990, although campaigning on a message that elec-

toral reform would be decided through referendum, National attempted to close the Pandora's box of institutional reform through unsuccessful and "not so subtle maneuvers" (Nagel, 1994, p. 526). This illustrates the degree to which self-preservation was on the minds of the two major political parties.

9. The increase in the number of effective political parties in 1993 was the result of the fractionalization of both Labour and National into a number of "niche parties" in the run-up to the 1996 election (Aimer & Miller, 2002).
10. An increase in the number of political parties did occur between 1972 and 1976. Specifically, we see the rise of the Social Credit Political League. This represents the growing disillusionment of the New Zealand electorate with the dominant two-party system, and Labour and National specifically, and the subsequent strength of FPP in maintaining a two-party system (Aimer, 1998; Kelsey, 1997, p. 25).
11. Interestingly, the Campaign for Better Government (CBG), consisting of a number of groups representing business interests, argued that the addition of smaller parties in coalition formation would ultimately prove undemocratic in that "Minor parties holding the balance of power would … undemocratically dictate policies to larger parties as a price of their support" (Vowles, 1995, p. 110). This illustrates the emphasis that business interests placed on the maintenance of SMD rules in face of a potential threat from a move to PR electoral rules.
12. Easton and Gerritsen, in their comparison of economic reform in Australia and New Zealand, compellingly argue that Australian economic reforms were much less extreme due to the presence of a federated system, a bicameral legislature, and formal constitution (1996, p. 34).
13. To an extent, Labour's abandonment of the traditional labor constituency led both the New Zealand Federation of Labour and its successor, the New Zealand Council of Trade Unions, to strongly back the proposed reforms to anMMP system. However, due to the weakening structure of labor and declining labor membership, the ability of such organizations to effect change was quite limited (Vowles, 1995, p. 105).
14. For a more in-depth comparison of Australian and New Zealand labor parties and politics, see Castles and Shirley (1996).

15. Casey's OECD measure includes the degree to which firms are able to operate independently from shareholders, but regrettably, the component variable, derived from the AMADEUS database, is limited to European countries and is not available for New Zealand.
16. I recognize that Casey's measure fails to capture other notable aspects that traditionally differentiate business relationships between varieties of capitalism, namely, inter-firm relationships. Nevertheless, the measure does serve as a proxy measure on which to build a theoretical discussion of changes to business organization during the New Zealand liberalization period.

References

Aimer, P. (1998). Old and new party choices. In J. Vowles, P. Aimer, S. Banducci, & J. Karp (Eds.), *Voters' victory?: New Zealand's first election under proportional representation*. Auckland: Auckland University Press.

Aimer, P., & Miller, R. (2002). New Zealand politics in the 1990s. In P. Aimer, J. Vowles, S. Banducci, & J. Karp (Eds.), *Proportional representation on trial: New Zealand's second MMP election and after*. Auckland: Auckland University Press.

Allen, M., & Ng, S. H. (2000). Self-interest, economic beliefs, and political preference in New Zealand. *Political Psychology, 21*(2), 323–345.

Boston, J., Levine, S., McLeay, E., & Roberts, N. (1996). *New Zealand under MMP: A new politics?* Auckland: Auckland University Press.

Bray, M., & Nielson, D. (1996). Industrial relations reform and the relative autonomy of the state. In F. Castles, R. Gerritsen, & J. Vowles (Eds.), *The great experiment: Labour parties and public policy transformation in Australia and New Zealand*. St. Leonards, Australia: Allen and Unwin.

Casey, T. (2002). *The social context of economic change in Britain: Between policy and performance*. Manchester: Manchester University Press.

Casey, T. (2009). Mapping stability and change in advanced capitalisms. *Comparative European Politics, 7*(2), 255–278.

Castles, F., Gerritsen, R., & Vowles, J. (1996a). Introduction: Setting the scene for economic and political change. In F. Castiles, R. Gerritsen, & J. Vowles (Eds.), *The great experiment: Labour parties and public policy transformation in Australia and New Zealand*. St. Leonards, Australia: Allen and Unwin.

Castles, F., Gerritsen, R., & Vowles, J. (1996b). Conclusion: The great experiment in perspective. In F. Castles, R. Gerritsen, & J. Vowles (Eds.), *The great experiment: Labour parties and public policy transformation in Australia and New Zealand*. St. Leonards, Australia: Allen and Unwin.

Castles, F., Gerritsen, R., & Vowles, J. (Eds.). (1996c). *The great experiment: Labour parties and public policy transformations in Australia and New Zealand.* St. Leonards, Australia: Allen and Unwin.

Castles, F., & Shirley, I. (1996). Labour and social policy: Gravediggers or refurbishers of the welfare state. In F. Castles, R. Gerritsen, & J. Vowles (Eds.), *The great experiment: Labour parties and public policy transformation in Australia and New Zealand.* St. Leonards, Australia: Allen and Unwin.

Duverger, M. (1954). *Political parties.* New York: Science Editions.

Easton, B., & Gerritsen, R. (1996). Economic reform: Parallels and divergences. In F. Castles, R. Gerritsen, & J. Vowles (Eds.), *The great experiment: Labour parties and public policy transformation in Australia and New Zealand.* St. Leonards, Australia: Allen and Unwin.

Evans, L., Grimes, A., Wilkinson, B., & Teece, D. (1996). Economic refom in New Zealand 1984–95: The pursuit of efficiency. *Journal of Economic Literature, 34*(December), 1856–1902.

George, A., & Bennett, A. (2005). *Case studies and theory development in the social sciences.* Cambridge, MA: The MIT Press.

Hall, P. A., & Soskice, D. W. (2001). *Varieties of capitalism: The institutional foundations of comparative advantage.* Oxford, England and New York: Oxford University Press.

Huber, E., & Stephens, J. (2001). *Development and crisis of the welfare state: Parties and policies in global markets.* Chicago: University of Chicago Press.

James, P. (2003). *The German electoral system.* Burlington: Ashgate Publishing Company.

Katzenstein, P. J. (1985). *Small states in world markets: Industrial policy in Europe.* Ithaca, NY: Cornell University Press.

Kelsey, J. (1997). *The New Zealand experiment: A world model for structural adjustment?* Auckland: Auckland University Press.

Kitschelt, H. (1994). *The transformation of European social democracy.* Cambridge: Cambridge University Press.

Lijphart, A. (1994). *Electoral systems and party systems: A study of twenty-seven democracies, 1945–1990.* New York: Oxford University Press.

Martin, C. J., & Swank, D. (2008). The political origins of coordinated capitalism: Business organizations, party systems, and state structure in the age of innocence. *American Political Science Review, 102*(2), 181–198.

McCraw, D. J. (1993). New Zealand's foreign policy under National and Labour governments: Variations on the "small state" theme. *Pacific Affairs*, 7–25.

Mulgan, R. (1997). *Politics in New Zealand.* Auckland: Auckland University Press.

Nadeau, R., & Lewis-Beck, M. (2001). National economic voting in the US presidential elections. *Journal of Politics, 63*, 159–181.

Nagel, J. H. (1994). What political scientists can learn from the 1993 electoral reform in New Zealand. *PS: Political Science and Politics, 27*, 525–529.

Palmer, G., & Palmer, M. (1997). *Bridled power: New Zealand and government under MMP*. Oxford: Oxford University Press.

Palmer, G., & Palmer, M. (2004). *Bridled power: New Zealand's constitution and government*. Oxford: Oxford University Press.

Pierson, P. (2003). Big, slow-moving, and ... invisible. In J. Mahoney & D. Reuschemeyer (Eds.), *Comparative historical analysis in the social sciences* (pp. 177–207). Cambridge: Cambridge University Press.

Pierson, P. (2004). *Politics in time: History, institutions, and social analysis*. Princeton: Princeton University Press.

Ratnayake, R. (1999). Industry concentration and competition: New Zealand experience. *International Journal of Industrial Organization, 17*, 1041–1057.

Sartori, G. (1976). *Parties and party systems: A framework for analysis*. Cambridge, England and New York: Cambridge University Press.

Vowles, J. (1995). The politics of electoral reform in New Zealand. *International Political Science Review, 15*, 95–115.

Vowles, J. (1998). A new post-MMP party system? In J. Vowles, P. Aimer, S. Banducci, & J. Karp (Eds.), *Voters' victory?: New Zealand's first election under proportional representation*. Auckland: Auckland University Press.

Vowles, J., Aimer, P., Banducci, S., & Karp, J. (1998a). Expectations of change. In J. Vowles, P. Aimer, S. Banducci, & J. Karp (Eds.), *Voters' victory?: New Zealand's first election under proportional representation* (pp. 1–27). Auckland: Auckland University Press.

Vowles, J., Aimer, P., Banducci, S., & Karp, J. (1998b). Voter rationality and the advent of MMP. In J. Vowles, P. Aimer, S. Banducci, & J. Karp (Eds.), *Voters' victory?: New Zealand's first election under proportional representation*. Auckland: Auckland University Press.

Vowles, J., Aimer, P., Banducci, S., & Karp, J. (Eds.). (1998c). *Voters' victory?: New Zealand's first election under proportional representation*. Auckland: Auckland University Press.

CHAPTER 7

Conclusion

Although a general consensus exists regarding the existence of capitalist variation, a pressing issue for comparative political economists "has been how to explain the absence of convergence upon a common form of industrial policy, and the continued distinctiveness of national capitalisms" (Howell, 2007, p. 241). Since the early 2000s, the VOC framework has been one of dominant explanatory models in the comparative capitalism sub-discipline.

The VOC framework contends that capitalist production regimes can be classified into CMEs and LMEs. The CME production regimes are typified by cooperation, that is, cooperation between industry-specific firms (especially on issues like wage determination), cooperation between the labor force and the firms, and cooperation between the companies and capital holders (Soskice, 1999, p. 106).

Where the CME production regime is characterized by cooperation, the LME regime is typified by strong competition. Under an LME regime, the economic actors have only a limited ability to coordinate their actions. LME production regimes include short-term financial timeframes, "deregulated labor markets," an emphasis on general skills in the workforce, and fierce competition between firms (Soskice, 1999, p. 110).

The VOC literature contends that the key causal difference between production regimes is the "strategic interaction central to the behavior

M.P. Arsenault, *The Effects of Political Institutions on Varieties of Capitalism*, DOI 10.1007/978-3-319-50892-4_7

of economic actors," particularly the coordination capacity between firms (Hall & Soskice, 2001, p. 5). In other words, firms will pursue production policies shaped by the existing economic institutional structures, particularly: financial, industrial relations, education, and inter-company relations systems. Where interactions within the above arenas are governed by institutions favoring competition and other neoclassical economic principles, an LME production regime will emerge. In cases where the above arenas are governed by institutions promoting cooperation, collaboration, exchange of information, sanctions for defection, and so on, we will find the emergence of CME production regimes.

Although the VOC has made significant contributions to the understanding capitalist economies, I, and others, remain skeptical of the causal logic (Hancké, 2009b). I contend that a greater emphasis on the role of politics and political institutions is imperative to understanding variation in capitalist economies. For example, a strong correlation exists between political regime and the LME and CME dichotomies posed by the VOC framework (Gourevitch, 2003; Roe, 2003). However, debate continues regarding the connection between political institutions and VOC. The purpose of this book was to open the proverbial "black box" and identify the causal mechanisms linking political institutions and variation in capitalist systems.

I find that the behavior of firms and other economic actors does not occur in a political vacuum. Rather, the ability of actors to cooperate or compete, and the subsequent strategies of firms, are shaped and constrained by the institutions structuring the political environment in which economic players operate. This research book, building on a strong emerging research program, has illustrated that the institutions composing majoritarian and consensus political regimes are instrumental in constraining the choice sets of political and economic actors, specifically in regard to cooperation and competition. Such constraints subsequently shape the behavior of economic actors in advanced industrial societies.

Additionally, I find that once such political regimes are in place it is difficult for an economy to diverge from its given capitalist type, even in the face of international pressures to modify existent structures. The most important variables shaping variation in capitalist economies are partisanship and policy legacies, electoral system, the number of effective political parties, and the number of constitutional constraints.

Chapter Outline

This chapter begins by synthesizing the empirical findings regarding the effects of political institutions on VOC and evaluates the merits of this book in reference to answering the proposed research questions. I also illustrate how such findings fit with existing theories in the VOC literature.

Next, I discuss the theoretical contributions and implications of this research book. I frame the book within the comparative capitalism literature in general, and the continuing research program examining the relationship between political institutions and VOC (Martin & Swank, 2008). Specifically, I reference the ways that this book has built upon and lent credence to recent VOC studies.

Then, I discuss some difficulties common to studies of comparative capitalism in general and this book specifically. I draw explicit attention to the limited availability of comparable data capturing the major aspects of the VOC framework. Second, I draw attention to the potentially problematic aggregate measure of constitutional constraints applied in the quantitative chapter, and suggest an alternative strategy for further research.

Furthermore, I suggest a path ahead for continued research toward developing a better understanding of the relationship between political institutions and capitalist variation. I illustrate the necessity of engaging in a concentrated effort to develop comparable comparative capitalism data, the need to place greater emphasis on the role of institutional veto players, and suggest how this book may lend clarity to the current European economic crisis.

Synthesis of Empirical Findings

The quantitative inquiries of this book sought to answer three questions. First, what political institutions are related to variation in capitalist systems? Second, what political institutions serve as the strongest indicators of CMEs and LMEs? Third, what are the effects of specific political institutions on the arenas that typically characterize CMEs and LMEs?

In answering the first and second questions, quantitative findings illustrate that partisanship and policy legacies, the number of political parties, and electoral rules are significant indicators of LMEs and CMEs.

Partisan control of government and the subsequent policy legacies matter in regard to the development and variation of capitalist economies. Long-term control of government by parties of the right leads to the pursuit of policies favorable to the interests of business and capital holders, and is associated with LMEs. Long-term control of government by parties of the left tends to favor the interests of labor and others lower on the socioeconomic scale, and is associated with CMEs. Such findings thus support the work of Esping-Andersen (1990), Hicks and Swank (1992), Brady and Leicht (2007), and Huber and Stephens (2001).

The number of political parties matters in shaping variation in capitalist systems. Two-party systems are associated with LMEs, while multi-party systems are associated with CMEs. The number of political parties affects variation in capitalist economies in that higher numbers of political parties increase the number of relevant actors, and subsequently the number of interaction streams in the political process (Sartori, 1976). Higher numbers of interaction streams create an environment in which cooperation and coordination are necessary to implement policy. On the other hand, in two-party systems, generally characterized by majority rule, the ruling party is able to enact their desired policy with little or no input from the opposition.

Additionally, my findings support much of the comparative capitalism literature in that electoral systems play a decisive role in shaping the structure of the political and economic regimes of various states (Cusack, Iverson, & Soskice, 2007; Katzenstein, 1985; Martin & Swank, 2008). According to the quantitative model applied in this book, electoral rules are the most robust indicator of variation in capitalist economies. Single-member district electoral systems are strongly associated with LMEs, while proportional representation electoral systems are strongly associated with CMEs. The strength of the variable lies in the influence of electoral systems on the number of effective political parties (Duverger, 1954), the strength of the executive (Lijphart, 1999), and the structuring of governing cabinets (Manow, 2001). As such, it is the electoral system that proves instrumental in creating an environment of coordination and cooperation, through a PR electoral system, multiple political parties, peak associations, and coalition governments, or an environment of competition driven by SMD electoral rules, a two-party system, pluralistic interest associations, and majoritarian governance.

In answering the third question, across all four economic arenas under investigation—corporate governance, industrial relations, vocational training and education, and inter-firm relations—the role of politics and political institutions matters. However, the degree to which political institutions affect the different arenas varies. Although this book has illustrated a strong relationship between various political institutions and the economic arenas composing the liberal and coordinated market economies, the causal mechanisms linking specific political institutions and corporate governance, industrial relations, vocational training and education, and inter-firm relations remain unclear and require further investigation.

Nevertheless, electoral systems proved especially strong across the board. In part, the strength of the electoral systems variable stems from the ability of electoral rules to shape peak associations and policy stability. In turn, peak associations and policy stability appear to be important mechanisms shaping the economic arenas of VOC. This is especially relevant in the corporate governance, industrial relations, and inter-firm relations arenas.

In corporate governance, electoral system shapes policy stability. In PR systems policy remains relatively stable. This leads to investors making credible commitments to longer-term investments. In SMD systems, where policy can change rapidly, investors are less likely to make credible commitments, instead favoring short-term returns on capital.

In the industrial relations and inter-firm relations arenas electoral systems prove instrumental in the shaping of peak associations. In PR systems, we are more likely to find large, centralized labor and employer associations which in turn foment greater cooperation between labor and employer groups. On the other hand, in SMD systems, we are likely to find much more pluralistic and decentralized employer and labor associations which in turn create a much more adversarial environment.

The qualitative inquiries of this book sought to answer three questions. First, do the proposed causal relationships between political institutions and VOC exist in real-world cases? Second, do the political institutions affect the economic component arenas? Third, what alternative or intervening variables become apparent through the qualitative research?

It goes without saying that the changes to the global economy, beginning in the 1970s, proved instrumental in shaping structures of capitalist economies. Without question, the advanced industrial economies have become increasingly liberal (Casey, 2009). However, a total convergence toward a one best neoliberal conception of capitalism has not occurred. Rather, we see a continued "bifurcation" between CME and LME frameworks (Soskice, 1999). The continental European states retain the characteristics of a CME, while the Anglo-Saxon countries most closely represent an LME. This confirms much of what the comparative capitalism literature which suggests, that is, there are a number of ways by which countries adapt to changing global markets (Martin & Thelen, 2007), and these strategies are largely governed by political regime.

This study suggests that the abilities for a given state to either adopt neoliberal reforms, or maintain coordinated economic structures largely depends on the political institutions composing a given political regime. States with majoritarian systems—or in the case of New Zealand, a legacy of majoritarian systems—were able to implement significant neoliberal changes when compared to states with consensus political systems.

The most recognizable intervening variable to be revealed in the qualitative case studies lies in the role of constitutional constraints, or institutional veto players, in shaping the choice sets of economic actors. The necessity of including such measures is discussed in greater depth in the "path ahead" section.

Theoretical Implications

This book has contributed to the growing research program calling into question the causal underpinnings of the VOC framework. Whereas the VOC approach focuses largely on the strategic behavior of the firm, this book contributes to a camp of scholars who "look for the sources of diversity elsewhere—in politics, history, or culture rather than in the microstructure of markets" (Hancké, 2009a, p. 8).

By concentrating on the role of politics, this book has answered Deeg and Jackson's call for greater focus on the ways in which political institutions, and other "formal rule-making systems" shape the processes by which VOC are structured (2007, p. 169). Similarly, I have continued the work of Amable and Palombarini, who called for greater emphasis on the ways that states and political institutions constrain the behavior of actors operating within the political economy, and the ability of those controlling the state to autonomously institute changes to the institutional structure (2009, pp. 126–129).

By concentrating on political institutions, I have built upon and lent credence to a number of comparative capitalism studies. For example, I confirm Birchfield and Crepaz's findings that majoritarian systems, characterized by a unicameral government, single-member districts, two-party systems, and single-party majority governments, are conducive to a system of adversarial politics and strong competition between actors.

On the other hand, I find that consensus systems—PR rule, multi-party legislatures, multi-party governments, and bicameral legislatures—tend to promote compromise and negotiation (1998, p. 179). However, I move beyond Birchfield and Crepaz by illustrating how the propensity for a particular political regime to shape competition or cooperation can shape variation in capitalist systems.

Similarly, I confirm the work of Iversen and Soskice (2006) and Cusack et al. (2007) that electoral system and party system variables shape class coalitions and can affect economic outcomes. Specifically, I find that majoritarian systems tend to favor the interests of the center-right, while consensus systems tend to favor the interests of the center-left.

Furthermore, my findings suggest, like Martin and Swank's (2008), that party systems matter in regard to the development of peak associations. Specifically I find that proportional representation and multi-party systems are conducive to the development of strong peak labor and businesses organizations, while single-member district electoral rules and two-party systems are conducive to more pluralist associations.

Also, I confirm the findings of Korpi (2006), Esping-Andersen (1990), and Brady and Leicht (2007) that partisanship and policy legacies matter in shaping the structures of differing capitalist systems. Specifically, I find that majoritarian institutions favor the right while consensus systems favor the left. Where the political right maintains long-term control of cabinets, we are likely to see policies favoring the interests of capital holders and business, while long-term cabinet tenure of left-leaning parties are conducive to policies favoring labor and those lower on the socioeconomic scale.

Lastly, this book has laid a significant groundwork for further efforts to examine the role that political institutions play in constraining the adjustment paths of European Union countries in the face of pressures to adopt severe austerity measures in light of the current economic crisis. As in the 1980s, much of Europe is facing significant pressures to adopt neoliberal economic policies. However, as can be seen by the social backlash of Greece, Spain, and others, the degree to which domestic economies will adopt such proposed changes remains to be seen. As such, this book lends credence to the findings of Hooghe and Marks (1999) and Swank (2001, 2002) that domestic institutions may allow for the continued domestic "variety of capitalism" despite international pressures to adopt neoliberal policies.

The Path Ahead and Suggestions for Further Research

First, a major difficulty in conducting temporal studies of variation in capitalist systems lies in the general scarcity of comparable quantitative data capturing specific aspects of varieties of capitalist systems over a significant period of time. The work of Terrence Casey (2009) that developed an encompassing set of relevant and comparable data capturing the most important aspects of capitalist variation is a welcome step in the right direction. Scholars operating within the comparative capitalism field should make a more concerted effort to build upon Casey's efforts. More refined measures will allow for more broad and generalizable quantitative investigations, lend greater validity and reliability to empirical findings, and thus contribute significantly to the current research program addressing comparative capitalism generally, and political institutions and VOC specifically.

Second, the role of constitutional constraints, specifically institutional veto players, on capitalist variation deserves further investigation. Although the quantitative evidence suggested that constitutional constraints were largely insignificant, the qualitative case studies indicate that such constraints play a key role in shaping the structure of a capitalist economy. In order to plumb deeper into the effects of institutional veto players it will behoove future quantitative inquiries to disaggregate the additive index created in this book into its constituent elements, namely, federalism, presidentialism, bicameralism, the use of referenda, and the degree of judicial review. By adding dichotomous variables capturing individual institutional veto points into the model, greater empirical leverage will be gained in identifying the strength and direction of relationship, as well as the relevant causal mechanisms linking specific constitutional constraints and VOC.

Conclusion

Capitalism has risen to become the dominant economic system for all advanced industrial societies. However, it would be a tremendous oversimplification to assume that all capitalist economies are the same. Rather, significant variation exists between the capitalist structures of different states. As such, it is imperative to understand the underpinnings of different capitalist economies.

This book has contributed to the comparative capitalism literature in three major ways. First, this book confirms the existence of a liberal and CME dichotomy. Second, this book confirms the strong correlation between majoritarian systems and LMEs, and consensus political systems and CMEs. Third, and most importantly, this book has soundly illustrated that the role specific political institutions play on shaping the capitalist economies of advanced industrial societies should not understated.

This study has illustrated the necessity of augmenting the VOC framework with a more refined and encompassing discussion regarding the function of political institutions on capitalist divergence. Specifically, this book calls for a greater emphasis on the ways that political institutions constrain the incentive structures of relevant economic actors to cooperate or compete, thus shaping the structures of divergent capitalist systems.

References

Amable, B., & Palombarini, S. (2009). A neorealist approach to institutional change and the diversity of capitalism. *Socioeconomic Review, 7*(1), 123–143.

Birchfield, V., & Crepaz, M. (1998). The impact of constitutional structures and collective and competitive veto points on income inequality in industrialized democracies. *European Journal of Political Research, 34*, 175–200.

Brady, D., & Leicht, K. (2007). *Party to inequality: Right party power and income inequality in affluent western democracies.* Luxembourg Income Study Working Paper Series.

Casey, T. (2009). Mapping stability and change in advanced capitalisms. *Comparative European Politics, 7*(2), 255–278.

Cusack, T. R., Iverson, T., & Soskice, D. (2007). Economic interests and the origin of electoral systems. *American Political Science Review, 101*(3), 373–391.

Deeg, R., & Jackson, G. (2007). Towards a more dynamic theory of capitalist variety. *Socioeconomic Review, 5*(1), 149–179.

Duverger, M. (1954). *Political parties.* New York: Science Editions.

Esping-Andersen, G. (1990). *The three worlds of welfare capitalism.* Princeton: Princeton University Press.

Gourevitch, P. A. (2003). Review: The politics of corporate governance regulation. *The Yale Law Journal, 112*(7), 1829–1880.

Hall, P. A., & Soskice, D. W. (2001). *Varieties of capitalism: The institutional foundations of comparative advantage.* Oxford, England and New York: Oxford University Press.

Hancké, B. (2009a). Introducing the debate. In B. Hancké (Ed.), *Debating varieties of capitalism.* Oxford: Oxford University Press.

Hancké, B. (Ed.). (2009b). *Debating varieties of capitalism: A reader*. Oxford: Oxford University Press.

Hicks, A., & Swank, D. (1992). Politics, institutions, and welfare spending in industralized democracies. *American Political Science Review, 84*, 658–674.

Hooghe, L., & Marks, G. (1999). The making of a polity: The struggle over European integration. In H. Kitschelt, P. Lange, G. Marks, & J. Stephens (Eds.), *Continuity and change in contemporary capitalism*. New York: Cambridge University Press.

Howell, C. (2007). The British variety of capitalism: Institutional change, industrial relations and British politics. *British Politics, 2*, 239–263.

Huber, E., & Stephens, J. (2001). *Development and crisis of the welfare state: Parties and policies in global markets*. Chicago: University of Chicago Press.

Iversen, T., & Soskice, D. (2006). Electoral institutions and the politics of coalitions: Why some democracies redistribute more than others. *American Political Science Review, 100*(2), 165–181.

Katzenstein, P. J. (1985). *Small states in world markets: Industrial policy in Europe*. Ithaca, NY: Cornell University Press.

Korpi, W. (2006). Power resources and employer-centered approaches in explanations of welfare states and varieties of capitalism: Protagonists, consenters, and antagonists. *World Politics, 58*(2), 167–206.

Lijphart, A. (1999). *Patterns of democracy: Government forms and performance in thirty-six countries*. New Haven, CT: Yale University Press.

Manow, P. (2001). New coalitions of welfare state reform. In P. Pierson (Ed.), *The new politics of the welfare state*. New York: Oxford University Press.

Martin, C. J., & Swank, D. (2008). The political origins of coordinated capitalism: Business organizations, party systems, and state structure in the age of innocence. *American Political Science Review, 102*(2), 181–198.

Martin, C. J., & Thelen, K. (2007). The state and coordinated capitalism: Contributions of the public sector to social solidarity in postindustrial societies. *World Politics, 60*, 1–36.

Roe, M. J. (2003). *Political determinants of corporate governance*. Oxford: Oxford University Press.

Sartori, G. (1976). *Parties and party systems: A framework for analysis*. Cambridge, England and New York: Cambridge University Press.

Soskice, D. (1999). Divergent production regimes: Coordinated and uncoordinated market economies in the 1980s and 1990s. In H. Kitschelt, P. Lange, G. Marks, & J. D. Stephens (Eds.), *Continuity and change in contemporary captialism* (pp. 101–134). New York: Cambridge University Press.

Swank, D. (2001). Political institutions and welfare state restructuring: The impact of institutions on social policy change in developed democracies. In P. Pierson (Ed.), *The new politics of the welfare state*. New York: Oxford University Press.

Swank, D. (2002). *Global capital, political instiutions, and policy change in developed welfare states*. New York: Cambridge University Press.

References

Ahlquist, J. (2010). Building strategic capacity: The political underpinnings of coordinated wage bargaining. *American Political Science Review, 104*(1), 171–188.

Aimer, P. (1998). Old and new party choices. In J. Vowles, P. Aimer, S. Banducci, & J. Karp (Eds.), *Voters' victory?: New Zealand's first election under proportional representation*. Auckland: Auckland University Press.

Aimer, P., & Miller, R. (2002). New Zealand politics in the 1990s. In P. Aimer, J. Vowles, S. Banducci, & J. Karp (Eds.), *Proportional representation on trial: New Zealand's second MMP election and after*. Auckland: Auckland University Press.

Allen, J. B., & Scruggs, L. (2004). Political partisanship and welfare state reform in advanced industrial societies. *American Journal of Political Science, 48*(3), 496–512.

Allen, M. (2006). *The varieties of capitalism paradigm: Explaining Germany's comparative advantage?* Hampshire: Palgrave Macmillian.

Allen, M., & Ng, S. H. (2000). Self-interest, economic beliefs, and political preference in New Zealand. *Political Psychology, 21*(2), 323–345.

Amable, B. (2003). *The diversity of modern capitalism*. Oxford and New York: Oxford University Press.

Amable, B., & Palombarini, S. (2009). A neorealist approach to institutional change and the diversity of capitalism. *Socioeconomic Review, 7*(1), 123–143.

Armingeon, K., Gerber, M., Leimgruber, P., & Beyeler, M. (2008). *Comparative political data set 1960–2006*. Institute of Political Science, University of Berne. Retrieved from http://www.ipw.unibe.ch/content/team/klaus_armingeon/comparative_political_data_sets/index_ger.html

M.P. Arsenault, *The Effects of Political Institutions on Varieties of Capitalism*, DOI 10.1007/978-3-319-50892-4

Arsenault, M. P., & Crisher, B. (2008). *Examining variation in production regimes: An analytic framework*. Paper presented at the Souther Political Science Association.

Axelrod, R. (1970). *Conflict of interest: A theory of divergent goals with applications to politics*. Chicago, IL: Markham.

Beck, N., & Katz, J. (1995). What to do (and not to do) with time-series cross-section data. *American Political Science Review, 89*, 634–647.

Beck, T., Clarke, G., Groff, A., Keefer, P., & Walsh, P. (2001). New tools in comparative political economy: The database of political institutions. *The World Bank Economic Review, 15*(1), 165–176.

Bennett, A. (2008). Process-tracing: A Bayesian perspective. In J. Box-Steffensmeier, H. Brady, & D. Collier (Eds.), *Oxford handbook of political methodology* (pp. 702–721). New York: Oxford University Press.

Bering, H. (1999). *Helmut Kohl*. Washington, DC: Regnery Publishing.

Berman, S. (2006). *The primacy of politics: Social democracy and the making of Europe's twentieth century*. New York: Cambridge University Press.

Birchfield, V., & Crepaz, M. (1998). The impact of constitutional structures and collective and competitive veto points on income inequality in industrialized democracies. *European Journal of Political Research, 34*, 175–200.

Boix, C. (1998). *Political parties, growth, and equality: Conservative and social democratic economic strategies in the world economy*. New York: Cambridge University Press.

Boix, C. (2003). *Democracy and redistribution*. New York: Cambridge University Press.

Borsch, A. (2007). Institutional variation and coordination patterns in CMEs: Swiss and German corporate governance strategies. In B. Hancké, M. Rhodes, & M. Thatcher (Eds.), *Beyond varieties of capitalism: Conflict, contradictions, and complementarities in the European economy*. New York: Oxford University Press.

Boston, J., Levine, S., McLeay, E., & Roberts, N. (1996). *New Zealand under MMP: A new politics?* Auckland: Auckland University Press.

Brady, D., & Leicht, K. (2007). *Party to inequality: Right party power and income inequality in affluent western democracies*. Luxembourg Income Study Working Paper Series.

Brady, H. E., & Collier, D. (Eds.). (2004). *Rethinking social inquiry: Diverse tools, shared standards*. Lanham, MD: Rowman & Littlefield.

Braumoeller, B., & Bennett, A. (2006). *Where the model frequently hits the road: Combining statistical, formal, and case study methods*. Paper presented at the American Political Science Association.

Bray, M., & Nielson, D. (1996). Industrial relations reform and the relative autonomy of the state. In F. Castles, R. Gerritsen, & J. Vowles (Eds.), *The great experiment: Labour parties and public policy transformation in Australia and New Zealand*. St. Leonards, Australia: Allen and Unwin.

Campbell, J. L., & Pedersen, O. K. (Eds.). (2001). *The rise of neoliberalism and institutional analysis.* Princeton: Princeton University Press.

Casey, T. (2002). *The social context of economic change in Britain: Between policy and performance.* Manchester: Manchester University Press.

Casey, T. (2009). Mapping stability and change in advanced capitalisms. *Comparative European Politics, 7*(2), 255–278.

Castles, F., Gerritsen, R., & Vowles, J. (1996a). Introduction: Setting the scene for economic and political change. In F. Castiles, R. Gerritsen, & J. Vowles (Eds.), *The great experiment: Labour parties and public policy transformation in Australia and New Zealand.* St. Leonards, Australia: Allen and Unwin.

Castles, F., Gerritsen, R., & Vowles, J. (1996b). Conclusion: The great experiment in perspective. In F. Castles, R. Gerritsen, & J. Vowles (Eds.), *The great experiment: Labour parties and public policy transformation in Australia and New Zealand.* St. Leonards, Australia: Allen and Unwin.

Castles, F., Gerritsen, R., & Vowles, J. (Eds.). (1996c). *The great experiment: Labour parties and public policy transformations in Australia and New Zealand.* St. Leonards, Australia: Allen and Unwin.

Castles, F., & Shirley, I. (1996). Labour and social policy: Gravediggers or refurbishers of the welfare state. In F. Castles, R. Gerritsen, & J. Vowles (Eds.), *The great experiment: Labour parties and public policy transformation in Australia and New Zealand.* St. Leonards, Australia: Allen and Unwin.

Coates, D. (2000). *Models of capitalism: Growth and stagnation in the modern era.* Cambridge: Polity Press.

Coffey, D., & Thornley, C. (2009). *Globalization and varieties of capitalism: New labour, economic policy and the abject state.* Hampshire: Palgrave Macmillan.

Collier, D., & Mahon, J. (1993). Conceptual 'stretching' revisited: Adapting categories in comparative analysis. *American Political Science Review, 87*(4), 845–854.

Crouch, C. (2005). *Capitalist diversity and change: Recombinant governance and institutional entrepreneurs.* New York: Oxford University Press.

Cusack, T. R., Iverson, T., & Soskice, D. (2007). Economic interests and the origin of electoral systems. *American Political Science Review, 101*(3), 373–391.

Deakin, S., Hobbs, R., Konzelmann, S. J., & Wilkinson, F. (2006). Anglo-American corporate governance and the employment relationship: A case to answer? *Socioeconomic Review, 4*(1), 155–174.

Deeg, R., & Jackson, G. (2007). Towards a more dynamic theory of capitalist variety. *Socioeconomic Review, 5*(1), 149–179.

Dowding, K. (1996). *Power.* Minneapolis: University of Minnesota Press.

Downs, A. (1957). *An economic theory of democracy.* New York: Harper Collins.

Duverger, M. (1954). *Political parties.* New York: Science Editions.

Easton, B., & Gerritsen, R. (1996). Economic reform: Parallels and divergences. In F. Castles, R. Gerritsen, & J. Vowles (Eds.), *The great experiment: Labour parties and public policy transformation in Australia and New Zealand.* St. Leonards, Australia: Allen and Unwin.

Eckstein, H. (1975). Case studies in political science. In F. Greenstein & N. Polsby (Eds.), *Handbook of political science* (Vol. 7). Reading, MA: Addison-Wesley.
Esping-Andersen, G. (1990). *The three worlds of welfare capitalism.* Princeton: Princeton University Press.
Esping-Andersen, G. (1999). Politics without class: Postindustrial cleavages in Europe and America. In H. Kitschelt, P. Lange, G. Marks, & J. Stephens (Eds.), *Continuity and change in contemporary capitalism.* New York: Cambridge University Press.
Estevez-Abe, M., Iversen, T., & Soskice, D. (2001). Social protection and the formation of skills: A reinterpretation of the welfare state. In P. A. Hall & D. Soskice (Eds.), *Varieties of capitalism: The institutional foundations of comparative advantage.* Oxford: University of Oxford Press.
Evans, G., & Newnham, J. (Eds.). (1998). *The Penguin dictionary of international relations.* London: Penguin Books.
Evans, L., Grimes, A., Wilkinson, B., & Teece, D. (1996). Economic refom in New Zealand 1984–95: The pursuit of efficiency. *Journal of Economic Literature, 34*(December), 1856–1902.
Fukuyama, F. (2006). *The end of history and the last man.* New York: Free Press.
Gamble, A. (1988). *The free economy and the strong state: The politics of Thatcherism.* Durham: Duke University Press.
George, A., & Bennett, A. (2005). *Case studies and theory development in the social sciences.* Cambridge, MA: The MIT Press.
Gerber, L. G. (1995). Corporatism and state theory: A review essay for historians. *Social Science History, 19*(3), 313–332.
Gersemann, O. (2005). *Cowboy capitalism: European myths, American reality.* Washington, DC: Cato Institute.
Gershenkron, A. (1962). Economic backwardness in historical perspective. In A. Gershenkron (Ed.), *Economic backwardness in historical persepective.* Cambridge: Harvard University Press.
Gourevitch, P. A. (2003). Review: The politics of corporate governance regulation. *The Yale Law Journal, 112*(7), 1829–1880.
Hall, P. A. (1986). *Governing the economy: The politics of state intervention in Britain and France.* New York: Oxford University Press.
Hall, P. A. (1999). The political economy of Europe. In H. Kitschelt, P. Lange, G. Marks, & J. Stephens (Eds.), *Continuity and change in contemporary capitalism.* New York: Cambridge University Press.
Hall, P. A. (2007). The evolution of varieties of capitalism in Europe. In B. Hancké, M. Rhodes, & M. Thatcher (Eds.), *Beyond varieties of capitalism: Conflict, contradictions, and complementarities in the European economy.* New York: Oxford University Press.
Hall, P. A., & Gingerich, D. W. (2004). *Varieties of capitalism and institutionanl complementarites in the macroeconomy: An empirical analysis.* Max-Planck Institute for the Study of Societies, Cologne, Germany.

Hall, P. A., & Soskice, D. W. (2001). *Varieties of capitalism: The institutional foundations of comparative advantage*. Oxford, England and New York: Oxford University Press.

Hancké, B. (2009a). Introducing the debate. In B. Hancké (Ed.), *Debating varieties of capitalism*. Oxford: Oxford University Press.

Hancké, B. (Ed.). (2009b). *Debating varieties of capitalism: A reader*. Oxford: Oxford University Press.

Hancké, B., Rhodes, M., & Thatcher, M. (2007). *Beyond varieties of capitalism: Conflict, contradictions, and complementarities in the European economy*. Oxford: Oxford University Press.

Hancock, M. D., & Krisch, H. (2009). *Politics in Germany*. Washington, DC: CQ Press.

Hassel, A. (2007). What does business want? Labour market reforms in CMEs and its problems. In B. Hancké, M. Rhodes, & M. Thatcher (Eds.), *Beyond varieties of capitalism: Conflict, contradictions, and complemetarities in the European economy*. Oxford: Oxford University Press.

Heilbroner, R. L. (1986). *The worldly philosophers: The lives, times and ideas of the great economic thinkers* (6th ed.). New York: Simon & Schuster, Inc.

Hibbs Jr., D. A. (1977). Political parties and macroeconomic policy. *American Political Science Review, 71*, 1467–1487.

Hibbs Jr., D. A. (1992). Partisan theory after fifteen years. *European Journal of Political Economy, 8*, 361–373.

Hicks, A., & Kenworthy, L. (1998). Cooperation and political economic performance in affluent democratic capitalism. *American Journal of Sociology, 103*(6), 1631–1672.

Hicks, A., & Swank, D. (1992). Politics, institutions, and welfare spending in industralized democracies. *American Political Science Review, 84*, 658–674.

Hirschman, A. O. (1970). *Exit, voice, and loyalty: Responses to decline in firms, organizations, and states*. Cambridge, MA: Harvard University Press.

Hooghe, L., & Marks, G. (1999). The making of a polity: The struggle over European integration. In H. Kitschelt, P. Lange, G. Marks, & J. Stephens (Eds.), *Continuity and change in contemporary capitalism*. New York: Cambridge University Press.

Howell, C. (2003). Varieties of capitalism: And then there was one? *Comparative Politics, 36*(1), 103–124.

Howell, C. (2007). The British variety of capitalism: Institutional change, industrial relations and British politics. *British Politics, 2*, 239–263.

Huber, E., Ragin, C., & Stephens, J. (1993). Social democracy, Christian democracy, constitutional structure, and the welfare state. *American Journal of Sociology, 3*, 711–749.

Huber, E., Ragin, C., Stephens, J., Brady, D., & Beckfield, J. (2004). *Comparative Welfare Data Set*. http://www.nsd.uib.no/macrodataguide/set.html?id=8&sub=1

Huber, E., & Stephens, J. (2000). Partisan governance, women's employment, and the Social democratic service state. *American Sociological Review, 65*, 323–342.

Huber, E., & Stephens, J. (2001). *Development and crisis of the welfare state: Parties and policies in global markets.* Chicago: University of Chicago Press.

Immergut, E. M. (1990). Institutions, veto points, and policy results: A comparative analysis of health care. *Journal of Public Policy, 10*, 391–416.

Iversen, T. (2007). Economic shocks and varieties of government response. In B. Hancké, M. Rhodes, & M. Thatcher (Eds.), *Beyond varieties of capitalism: Conflict, contradictions, and complementarities in the European economy.* New York: Oxford University Press.

Iversen, T., & Soskice, D. (2006). Electoral institutions and the politics of coalitions: Why some democracies redistribute more than others. *American Political Science Review, 100*(2), 165–181.

Iversen, T., & Soskice, D. (2009). Distribution and redistribution: The shadow of the nineteenth century. *World Politics, 61*(3), 438–486.

Iversen, T., & Stevens, J. (2008). Partisan politics, the welfare state, and three worlds of human capital formation. *Comparative Political Studies, 41*(4–5), 600–637.

Jackson, G. (2001). The origins of nonliberal corporate governance in Germany and Japan. In W. Streeck & K. Yamamura (Eds.), *The origins of nonliberal capitalism: Germany and Japan in comparison.* Ithaca, NY: Cornell University Press.

James, P. (2003). *The German electoral system.* Burlington: Ashgate Publishing Company.

Judt, T. (2005). *Postwar: A history of Europe since 1945.* New York: The Penguin Press.

Katzenstein, P. J. (1985). *Small states in world markets: Industrial policy in Europe.* Ithaca, NY: Cornell University Press.

Kelsey, J. (1997). *The New Zealand experiment: A world model for structural adjustment?* Auckland: Auckland University Press.

Kenworthy, L. (2006). Institutional coherence and macroeconomic performance. *Socio-Economic Review, 4*(1), 69–91.

King, D., & Wood, S. (1999). The political economy of neoliberalism: Britain and the United States in the 1980s. In H. Kitschelt, P. Lange, G. Marks, & J. Stephens (Eds.), *Continuity and change in contemporary capitalism.* Cambridge: Cambridge University Press.

King, G., Keohane, R. O., & Verba, S. (1994). *Designing social inquiry: Scientific inference in qualitative research.* Princeton: Princeton University Press.

Kitschelt, H. (1994). *The transformation of European social democracy.* Cambridge: Cambridge University Press.

Kitschelt, H., Lange, P., Marks, G., & Stephens, J. D. (Eds.). (1999). *Continuity and change in contemporary capitalism.* New York: Cambridge University Press.

Knight, J. (1992). *Institutions and social conflict.* Cambridge: Cambridge University Press.

Knight, J., & Sened, I. (Eds.). (1995). *Explaining social institutions.* Ann Arbor: University of Michigan Press.

Korpi, W. (1983). *The democratic class struggle.* London: Routledge & Kegan Paul.

Korpi, W. (2006). Power resources and employer-centered approaches in explanations of welfare states and varieties of capitalism: Protagonists, consenters, and antagonists. *World Politics, 58*(2), 167–206.

Laitin, D. D. (2002). Comparative politics: The state of the subdiscipline. In H. Milner & I. Katznelson (Eds.), *Political science: The state of the discipline.* New York: Norton.

Laitin, D. D., Caporaso, J. A., Collier, D., Rogowski, R., Tarrow, S., King, G., et al. (1995). The qualitative-quantitative disputation: Gary King, Robert O. Keohane, and Sidney Verba's designing social inquiry: Scientific inference in qualitative research. *American Journal of Political Science, 89*(2), 454–456.

Lehmbruch, G. (1979). Consociational democracy, class conflict, and the new corporatism. In P. Schmitter & G. Lehmbruch (Eds.), *Trends toward corporatist intermediation.* London: Sage.

Lijphart, A. (1971). Comparative politics and the comparative method. *The American Political Science Review, 65*(3), 682–693.

Lijphart, A. (1984). *Democracies: Patterns of majoritarian and consensus democracies in twenty-one countries.* New Haven, CT: Yale University Press.

Lijphart, A. (1994). *Electoral systems and party systems: A study of twenty-seven democracies, 1945–1990.* New York: Oxford University Press.

Lijphart, A. (1999). *Patterns of democracy: Government forms and performance in thirty-six countries.* New Haven, CT: Yale University Press.

Lijphart, A., & Crepaz, M. M. L. (1991). Corporatism and consensus democracy in eighteen countries: Conceptual and empirical linkages. *British Journal of Political Science, 21*(2), 235–246.

Lipset, S., & Rokkan, S. (1967a). Cleavage structures, party systems, and voter alignments: An introduction. In S. Lipset & S. Rokkan (Eds.), *Party systems and voter alignments: Cross-national perspectives.* New York: The Free Press.

Lipset, S., & Rokkan, S. (Eds.). (1967b). *Party systems and voter alignments: Cross-national perspectives.* New York: The Free Press.

Mannin, M. L. (2010). *British government and politics: Balancing Europeanization and independence.* Lanham, MD: Rowman & Littlefield.

Manow, P. (2001a). New coalitions of welfare state reform. In P. Pierson (Ed.), *The new politics of the welfare state.* New York: Oxford University Press.

Manow, P. (2001b). *The political construction of a coordinated political economy.* Paper presented at the Business Interests and the Varieties of Capitalism: Historical Origins and Future Possibilities Meeting.

Manow, P. (2001c). Welfare state building and coordinated capitalism in Japan and Germany. In W. Streeck & K. Yamamura (Eds.), *The origins of nonliberal capitalism: Germany and Japan in comparison*. Ithaca, NY: Cornell University Press.

Manow, P. (2009). Electoral rules, class coalitions and welfare state regimes, or how to explain Esping-Andersen with Stein Rokkan. *Socio-Economic Review, 7*, 101–121.

Mares, I. (2001). Firms in the welfare state: When, why, and how does social policy matter to employers? In T. Iversen & D. Soskice (Eds.), *Varieties of capitalism: The institutional foundations of comparative advantage*. New York: Oxford University Press.

Mares, I. (2003). *The politics of social risk: Business and welfare state development*. New York: Cambridge University Press.

Marshall, T. H. (1964). *Class, citizenship, and social development*. Chicago: Chicago University Press.

Martin, C. J., & Swank, D. (2008). The political origins of coordinated capitalism: Business organizations, party systems, and state structure in the age of innocence. *American Political Science Review, 102*(2), 181–198.

Martin, C. J., & Thelen, K. (2007). The state and coordinated capitalism: Contributions of the public sector to social solidarity in postindustrial societies. *World Politics, 60*, 1–36.

McCraw, D. J. (1993). New Zealand's foreign policy under National and Labour governments: Variations on the "small state" theme. *Pacific Affairs*, 7–25.

Molina, O., & Rhodes, M. (2007). The political economy of adjustment in mixed market economies: A study of Spain and Italy. In B. Hancké, M. Rhodes, & M. Thatcher (Eds.), *Beyond varieties of capitalism: Conflict, contradictions, and complementarities in the European economy* (pp. 223–252). New York: Oxford University Press.

Mulgan, R. (1997). *Politics in New Zealand*. Auckland: Auckland University Press.

Nadeau, R., & Lewis-Beck, M. (2001). National economic voting in the US presidential elections. *Journal of Politics, 63*, 159–181.

Nagel, J. H. (1994). What political scientists can learn from the 1993 electoral reform in New Zealand. *PS: Political Science and Politics, 27*, 525–529.

North, D. C. (1981). *Structure and change in economic history* (1st ed.). New York: Norton.

North, D. C. (1990). *Institutions, institutional change, and economic performance*. Cambridge: Cambridge University Press.

Norton, B. F. (2007). *Politics in Britain*. Washington, DC: CQ Press.

Olson, M. (1965). *The logic of collective action: Public goods and the theory of groups*. Cambridge: Harvard University Press.

Orloff, A. S. (1993). Gender and the social rights of citizenship: The comparative analysis of gender relations and welfare states. *American Sociological Review, 58*, 303–328.

Palmer, G., & Palmer, M. (1997). *Bridled power: New Zealand and government under MMP*. Oxford: Oxford University Press.
Palmer, G., & Palmer, M. (2004). *Bridled power: New Zealand's constitution and government*. Oxford: Oxford University Press.
Phelps, E. (2006). Dynamic capitalism. *Wall Street Journal, 10*, A14.
Pierson, P. (1994). *Dismantling the welfare state?* New York: Cambridge University Press.
Pierson, P. (Ed.). (2001). *The new politics of the welfare state*. Oxford: Oxford University Press.
Pierson, P. (2003). Big, slow-moving, and ... invisible. In J. Mahoney & D. Reuschemeyer (Eds.), *Comparative historical analysis in the social sciences* (pp. 177–207). Cambridge: Cambridge University Press.
Pierson, P. (2004). *Politics in time: History, institutions, and social analysis*. Princeton: Princeton University Press.
Pontusson, J. (1995). From comparative public policy to political economy: Putting political institutions in their place and taking interests seriously. *Comparative Political Studies, 28*(1), 117–147.
Przeworski, A., & Tenue, H. (1970). *Logic of comparative social inquiry*. New York: Wily-Interscience.
Quinn, D. P., & Shapiro, R. Y. (1991). Business political power: The case of taxation. *American Political Science Review, 85*(3), 851–874.
Ratnayake, R. (1999). Industry concentration and competition: New Zealand experience. *International Journal of Industrial Organization, 17*, 1041–1057.
Riker, W. H. (1962). *The theory of political coalitions*. New Haven, CT: Yale University Press.
Roberts, G. (2006). *German electoral politics*. Manchester: Manchester University Press.
Roe, M. J. (2003). *Political determinants of corporate governance*. Oxford: Oxford University Press.
Rothstein, B., Samanni, M., & Teorell, J. (2010). Quality of government, political power and the welfare state. *The Quality of Government Institute, University of Gothenburg, 6*, 124.
Sargent, L. T. (1999). *Contemporary political ideologies: A comparative analysis* (11th ed.). New York: Harcourt Brace College Publishers.
Sartori, G. (1970). Concept formation in comparative politics. *American Political Science Review, 64*(4), 1033–1053.
Sartori, G. (1976). *Parties and party systems: A framework for analysis*. Cambridge, England and New York: Cambridge University Press.
Schmidt, V. A. (2007). *Changes in comparative political economy: Taking labor out, bringing the state back in, putting the firm front and center*. Paper presented at the European Studies Association Meeting.
Schmidt, V. A. (2009). Putting the political back into political economy by bringing the state back in yet again. *World Politcs, 61*(3), 516–546.

Schmitter, P. (1979a). Modes of interest intermediation and models of societal change in Western Europe. In P. Schmitter & G. Lehmbruch (Eds.), *Trends towards corporatist intermediation*. London: Sage.
Schmitter, P. (1979b). Still the century of corporatism? In P. Schmitter & G. Lehmbruch (Eds.), *Trends toward corporatist intermediation*. London: Sage Publications.
Schmitter, P., & Lehmbruch, G. (Eds.). (1979). *Trends towards corporatist intermediation*. London: Sage.
Seawright, J., & Gerring, J. (2008). Case selection techniques in case study research: A menu of qualitative and quantitative options. *Political Research Quarterly, 61*(2), 294–308.
Shonfield, A. (1965). *Modern capitalism: The changing balance of public and private power*. London and New York: Oxford University Press.
Simmons, B. A. (1999). The internationalization of capital. In H. Kitschelt, P. Lange, G. Marks, & J. Stephens (Eds.), *Continuity and change in contemporary capitalism*. New York: Cambridge University Press.
Smith, A. (1991 [1776]). *The wealth of nations*. New York: Alfred A. Knopf.
Soskice, D. (1999). Divergent production regimes: Coordinated and uncoordinated market economies in the 1980s and 1990s. In H. Kitschelt, P. Lange, G. Marks, & J. D. Stephens (Eds.), *Continuity and change in contemporary captialism* (pp. 101–134). New York: Cambridge University Press.
Soskice, D. (2007a). Macroeconomics and varieties of capitalism. In B. Hancké, M. Rhodes, & M. Thatcher (Eds.), *Beyond varieties of capitalism: Conflict, contradictions, and complementarities in the European economy*. New York: Oxford University Press.
Soskice, D. (2007b). Macroeconomics and varieties of capitalism. In B. Hancké, M. Rhodes, & M. Thatcher (Eds.), *Beyond varieties of capitalim: Conflict, contradictions, and complementarities in the European economy*. New York: Oxford University Press.
Stephens, J., Huber, E., & Ray, L. (1999). The welfare state in hard times. In H. Kitschelt, P. Lange, G. Marks, & J. Stephens (Eds.), *Continuity and change in contemporary capitalism*. New York: Cambridge University Press.
Streeck, W. (2001). Introduction: Explorations into the origins of nonliberal capitalism in Germany and Japan. In W. Streeck & Y. Kozo (Eds.), *The origins of nonliberal capitalism in Germany and Japan*. Ithaca, NY: Cornell University Press.
Streeck, W., & Yamamura, K. (Eds.). (2001). *The origins of nonliberal capitalism: Germany and Japan in comparison*. Ithaca, NY: Cornell University Press.
Swank, D. (2001). Political institutions and welfare state restructuring: The impact of institutions on social policy change in developed democracies. In P. Pierson (Ed.), *The new politics of the welfare state*. New York: Oxford University Press.

Swank, D. (2002). *Global capital, political instiutions, and policy change in developed welfare states.* New York: Cambridge University Press.
Tarrow, S. (1995). Bridging the quantitative-qualitative divide in political science. *American Political Science Review, 89*(2), 454–481.
Thelen, K. (2001). Varieties of labor politics in the developed democracies. In P. A. Hall & D. Soskice (Eds.), *The varieties of capitalism: The institutional foundations of comparative advantage.* New York: Oxford University Press.
Toennies, F. (1961). Estates and classes (R. Bendix, Trans.). In R. Bendix & S. M. Lipset (Eds.), *Class, status and power: A reader in social stratification* (5th ed., pp. 49–63). New York: The Free Press.
Tsebelis, G. (1995). Decision making in political systems: Veto players in presidentialism, parliamentarism, multicameralism and multipartyism. *British Journal of Political Science, 25*(3), 289–325.
Van Kersbergen, K. (1999). Contemporary Christian Democracy and the demise of the politcs of mediation. In H. Kitschelt, P. Lange, G. Marks, & J. Stephens (Eds.), *Contintuity and change in contemporary capitalism.* Cambridge: Cambridge University Press.
Vatter, A. (2009). Lijphart expanded: Three dimensions of democracy in advanced OECD countries? *European Consortium for Political Research, 1*(1), 125–154.
Vitols, S. (2001a). The origins of bank-based and market-based systems: Germany, Japan, and the United States. In W. Streeck & K. Yamamura (Eds.), *The origins of nonoliberal capitalism: Germany and Japan in comparison.* Ithaca, NY: Cornell University Press.
Vitols, S. (2001b). Varieties of corporate governance: Comparing Germany and the UK. In P. A. Hall & D. Soskice (Eds.), *Varieties of capitalism: The institutional foundations of comparative advantage.* New York: Oxford University Press.
Vowles, J. (1995). The politics of electoral reform in New Zealand. *International Political Science Review, 15*, 95–115.
Vowles, J. (1998). A new post-MMP party system? In J. Vowles, P. Aimer, S. Banducci, & J. Karp (Eds.), *Voters' victory?: New Zealand's first election under proportional representation.* Auckland: Auckland University Press.
Vowles, J., Aimer, P., Banducci, S., & Karp, J. (1998a). Expectations of change. In J. Vowles, P. Aimer, S. Banducci, & J. Karp (Eds.), *Voters' victory?: New Zealand's first election under proportional representation* (pp. 1–27). Auckland: Auckland University Press.
Vowles, J., Aimer, P., Banducci, S., & Karp, J. (1998b). Voter rationality and the advent of MMP. In J. Vowles, P. Aimer, S. Banducci, & J. Karp (Eds.), *Voters' victory?: New Zealand's first election under proportional representation.* Auckland: Auckland University Press.

Vowles, J., Aimer, P., Banducci, S., & Karp, J. (Eds.). (1998c). *Voters' victory?: New Zealand's first election under proportional representation*. Auckland: Auckland University Press.

Wood, S. (2001). Business, government, and patterns of labor market policy in Britain and the Federal Republic of Germany. In P. Hall & D. Soskice (Eds.), *Varieties of capitalism*. New York: Oxford University Press.

Index

M.P. Arsenault, *The Effects of Political Institutions on Varieties of Capitalism*, DOI 10.1007/978-3-319-50892-4

Q

R

S

The manufacturer's authorised representative in the EU is Springer Nature Customer Service Centre GmbH, Europaplatz 3, 69115 Heidelberg, Germany. If you have any concerns regarding our products, please contact ProductSafety@springernature.com

Printed and bound by CPI Group (UK) Ltd, Croydon, CR0 4YY
30/09/2026
02225661-0004